22.99

*Living on the Edge
in Leonardo's Florence*

Map 1. Italy in 1494

Living on the Edge in Leonardo's Florence

Selected Essays

Gene Brucker

UNIVERSITY OF CALIFORNIA PRESS

Berkeley   Los Angeles   London

The publisher gratefully acknowledges the generous contribution
to this book provided by the Ahmanson Foundation Humanities
Endowment Fund of the University of California Press Associates.

University of California Press
Berkeley and Los Angeles, California

University of California Press, Ltd.
London, England

© 2005 by the Regents of the University of California

Library of Congress Cataloging-in-Publication Data

Brucker, Gene A.
    Living on the edge in Leonardo's Florence : selected
essays / Gene Brucker.
        p.   cm.
    Includes bibliographical references and index.
    ISBN 0-520-24134-7 (cloth : alk. paper)
    1. Florence (Italy)—History—To 1421.   2. Florence
(Italy)—History—1421–1737.   3. Italy—History—
1268–1492.   4. Renaissance—Italy—Florence.   I. Title.

DG737.55.B839   2005
945'.5105—dc22   2004017983

Manufactured in the United States of America
14   13   12   11   10   09   08   07   06   05
10   9   8   7   6   5   4   3   2   1

The paper used in this publication meets the minimum
requirements of ANSI/NISO Z39.48-1992 (R 1997)
(*Permanence of Paper*).

CONTENTS

MAPS

ACKNOWLEDGMENTS

Some time ago, James Clark, then director of the University of California Press, suggested that the Press might be interested in publishing a collection of my recent essays. I am grateful to Jim Clark, whom I have known since the 1950s, for supporting this enterprise. I also thank Mari Coates, Stephanie Fay, and Erin Marietta of UC Press, Sherrill Young of the staff of Berkeley's History Department, and Lisa Kaborycha, a graduate student in that department, for their invaluable assistance in preparing these essays for publication. Finally, I want to express my appreciation to the members of the Florentine Mafia and to my colleagues in Berkeley's History Department for their encouragement, their constructive criticism, and their camaraderie over the past half-century.

PERMISSIONS

"The Italian Renaissance" was published in *A Companion to the Worlds of the Renaissance*, ed. Guido Ruggiero (Oxford and Malden, MA, 2000), pp. 23–38. It is reprinted here by permission of Blackwell Publishing.

"Civic Traditions in Premodern Italy" was published in "Patterns of Social Capital: Stability and Change in Comparative Perspective" in *The Journal of Interdisciplinary History* 39 (1999): 357–77. It is reprinted here with the permission of the Massachusetts Institute of Technology and the Journal of Interdisciplinary History, Inc.

"From *Campanilismo* to Nationhood: Forging an Italian Identity" originally appeared in a symposium volume published by the Academia Sinica in Taipei, Taiwan (1994). It is reprinted with the permission of the director of the Institute of Modern History, Academia Sinica.

"The Horseshoe Nail: Structure and Contingency in Medieval and Renaissance Italy" was first published in *Renaissance Quarterly* 54 (2001): 1–9. It is reprinted here with the permission of the director of the Renaissance Society of America.

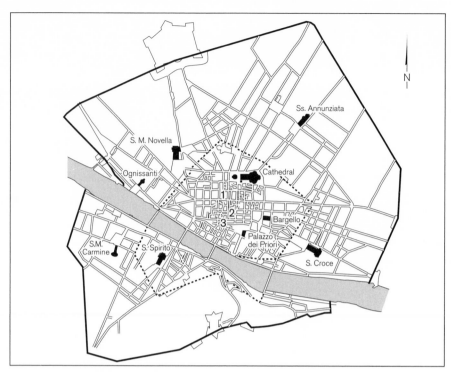

Map 2. The building of Renaissance Florence. Map showing city's walls, 1173–75 and 1284–1333; the central squares of (1) the Mercato Vecchio, (2) the grain market (Orsanmichele), and (3) the Mercato Nuovo; and major churches and public buildings

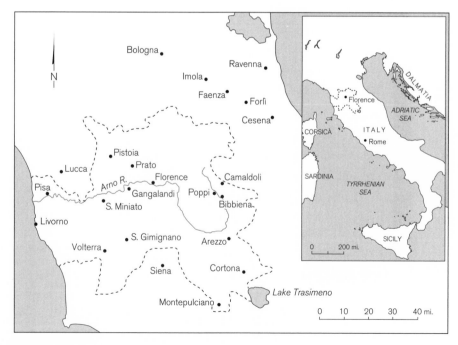

Map 3. Tuscany

Introduction

In a lecture on the history of Berkeley's History Department which I gave on the campus in February 1995, I said:

> Looking back over my own experience, I see the role of fortune looming very large and at some key moments decisively, in determining the course of my life. It was fortune that sent me to southern France during World War II and allowed me a glimpse of that Mediterranean world so vastly different from the Germanic agrarian society in which I was reared. It was fortune that inspired an enlightened federal government to enact the GI Bill and the Fulbright Act that enabled me to pursue my postgraduate studies in this country and abroad. And finally, fortune's greatest gift to me was the invitation to begin my academic career at Berkeley.[1]

This exercise in autobiography will expand and develop that theme, which could be formulated in these terms: "How did a boy raised on a prairie farm in Illinois in the depression years of the 1930s become a historian of Renaissance Florence?"

My interest in history was kindled at an early age. My older sister had taught me the rudiments of reading before I attended our one-room country school. I read avidly whatever newspaper or journal or book that I could find while growing up, though the availability of reading matter was very limited. The library at my school contained no more than fifty volumes, all of which I devoured. The titles that most attracted me were history books, particularly histories of our revolutionary and civil wars. Reading was a form of escape from the monotony of rural life. My first published work, an essay that I wrote as a freshman at the University of Illinois, was entitled "Hero Worship." I described my own images of heroic figures of the past, which included Washington and Lincoln, Grant and Napoleon, and a most inappropriate choice, a Confederate general of dubious talents but with a resplendent name: Pierre Gustave Toussaint Beauregard.[2] My allegiances in those early years were clearcut: the Americans and the French, our allies during the Revolution, were good; the British and the Germans were bad.

As a freshman in our local high school, I took a year-long course in Western history that included the early Near Eastern civilizations, the Greeks and Romans, the Middle Ages, and European history from the Renaissance to the present time. I found European history more fascinating than the American past. The high school library provided me with a richer diet of history and literature; I discovered Jane Austen, George Eliot, Charles Dickens, and Victor Hugo.

Fortune played no part in my parents' decision in the late 1930s to send me to the University of Illinois. My father had realized that I had no talent for farming, since I possessed no mechanical skills or aptitude. He knew that I would rather read books than work in the fields or tend livestock. No one in my father's family (eight siblings and their forty-two offspring) had been educated beyond high school. My mother had gone to a local normal school for her teaching credential, and she taught in a local rural school for two years before her marriage. Her younger brother was the first member of our family to go to the University of Illinois, where he studied agriculture and became a high school teacher. To the degree that I considered my future in those years, the career of secondary school teacher seemed attractive and achievable. I did give some thought to the law, but was discouraged by a lawyer whom my father had consulted, and who told us that there was no money to be made in that profession.

In the autumn of 1941, I began my studies at the University of Illinois, a radical turning point in my life. In my high school, four teachers had taught forty students; enrollment at the University of Illinois was fourteen thousand. Accustomed to life on a family farm with its daily and seasonal routines, I experienced for the first time an urban environment. I lived in a rooming house with fifteen other students, some of whom became close friends. My most memorable course was a survey of modern European history, taught by a Harvard PhD, Raymond Stearns, who became my mentor and friend and who was a profound influence on my professional life. As important as the courses I took was my exposure to the University library, with its million volumes. I was hired as a book shelver, which gave me immediate access to the library's vast riches.

I completed three semesters at the University before I was inducted into the army (March 1943). I spent the next three years in military service: twenty months of training in Alabama, Louisiana, and Illinois, and sixteen months in France and Japan. I was attached to a unit of army engineers responsible for operating a supply depot for that branch of the military. In France we were based in a camp outside Marseille; in Japan on a wharf in the port of Yokohama. En route to our base in southern France, we were billeted in Paris and its environs for three weeks, my first exposure to a European city. That brief encounter made an indelible impression; Paris remains one of my favorite cities. In our camp outside Marseille, I became acquainted with a Mediterranean world that has held me in its thrall ever since. Our depot was a veritable melting pot of the world's cultures. Local French girls worked there as secretaries and typists; Italian and German prisoners of war were manual laborers; Senegalese and Vietnamese units of the French colonial army served as guards.

I was demobilized in February 1946 and within a month had enrolled, together with several thousand other ex-GIs, at the University of Illinois. By taking summer courses and heavy course loads, I was able to graduate with a BA in history in June 1947. I then enrolled as a graduate student in the History Department, writing a master's thesis on the political career of a French astronomer, Jean-Sylvain Bailly, who was selected as the first mayor of revolutionary Paris (1789–91). Written under the supervision of Raymond Stearns, the thesis was published by the University of Illinois Press.[3] I had planned to remain at the University of Illinois in pursuit of a doctoral degree. My expectations for my professional future had risen to the point where I could visualize a career as a history teacher in some college or university in the Midwest. But at some moment in the autumn months of 1947, Raymond Stearns suggested that I apply for a Rhodes scholarship. That conversation dramatically changed my life.

I did not expect to win a Rhodes scholarship. I had no athletic skills or achievements, a basic requirement (so it was widely believed) for the award. Nor did I value my academic abilities very highly. I did not perform well in my initial interview with the state fellowship committee in Chicago. To my surprise, I was interviewed a second time and was selected as one of the state's three candidates for the final competition in Indianapolis. To my further surprise, I was chosen to be one of the Rhodes Scholars from the six midwestern states. With help from the two ex-Rhodes Scholars at the University of Illinois, I selected an Oxford college, Wadham, and decided not to read for a BA degree, with its heavy emphasis on British history, but for a research degree, a Bachelor of Letters (B.Litt).).

※ ※ ※

During my first term at Wadham College, Oxford, in the autumn of 1948, I was assigned a history tutor, F. W. Deakin, who was then assisting Winston Churchill in writing his history of World War II. Deakin assigned a cluster of books on medieval and early modern European history, focusing primarily on France. During one of our tutorials, I told him that I had become bored with French history. He then informed me that before the war, he had planned to write a thesis on Cesare Borgia under the supervision of Dr. Cecilia Ady. He suggested that I see her and discuss a possible topic in Italian Renaissance history. When I told him that I could not read Italian, he responded that since I could read

French, I would be able to master Italian in a few weeks. It took much longer. I did meet Dr. Ady, then retired but still giving lectures and supervising postgraduate students in Italian Renaissance studies. Though she must have found my lack of linguistic skills in Italian and Latin troubling, she was very supportive of this gauche colonial. She suggested that I write my B.Litt. thesis on the diplomatic career of Niccolò Machiavelli. I utilized the published correspondence of the Florentine secretary to write a thesis which deservedly remains unpublished. But its composition was a valuable apprenticeship, and an entrée into a field that would occupy my interest for the rest of my life.

While engaged in research on my B.Litt. thesis, I attended lectures by distinguished Oxford historians: A. J. P. Taylor, Christopher Hill, Isaiah Berlin, Richard Southern, E. F. Jacob, and E. L. Woodward, among other luminaries. They introduced me to the most recent scholarship in their fields, which contributed to the broadening of my intellectual horizons. I lived for one year in Wadham College, becoming acquainted with my fellow students and with the college faculty, led by the warden, C. M. Bowra. In my second year at Oxford, I lived in a flat in the city with my English wife and our young son. Through her family and their friends, I learned much about English society and its class structure, and those remarkable qualities that enabled the British people to survive the German assaults by air and sea in the early 1940s. My antipathy toward England as the oppressors of Americans during the Revolutionary War melted, and I became a staunch Anglophile and a strong supporter of the Labor government and its policies.

In the spring of 1950, I applied to Princeton University's History Department to pursue my graduate studies. I took courses with Joseph Strayer, E. H. Harbison, and Theodor Mommsen, whom I chose to supervise my dissertation. A refugee from Nazi Germany, Mommsen had done research in Italian archives and libraries in the late 1930s. As a research topic for my doctoral dissertation, he suggested that I study the political history of Florence in the mid-decades of the fourteenth century. In 1952, I was awarded a Fulbright Fellowship for research in Italy.

After a month in Perugia's Università per Stranieri, I settled in Florence with my family and began work on my topic in the state archives located in the Uffizi Palace. I have described elsewhere my early experiences in those archives: my initial difficulty in reading documents in Latin and Italian; the slow but steady improvement in my paleographical skills; and my realization that my study of Florentine politics in the mid-fourteenth century was an important subject.[4] I read through the records of communal legislation, the civic debates on policies, and judicial and financial records to understand the vicissitudes of Florentine politics in the aftermath of the devastations of the Black Death. In those months of intense research, I became an archival junkie, an addict. The most lucid description of this malady has been written by my Australian friend and colleague, F. W. Kent:

> Archival research . . . can be a delicious pleasure, at once cerebral and sensual. . . . There are only one or two human experiences, which will go nameless, that can be compared with the tactile pleasure of untying a bundle of documents which may not have been opened for centuries, of sniffing and handling the ancient paper or vellum within, that can be compared with the thrill, both intellectual and emotional, of seeing for the first time the hand of Machiavelli or Lorenzo de' Medici, or reading the half-formed script of a semi-literate woman whose letter begs some *gran maestro* for bread for her children. The sense of anticipation one feels when entering a new archive can be almost unbearable . . . Then there is the hunger, quite literally the hunger, you experience when on the trail of some vital lead, some new connection, and you know in the pit of your stomach that the register which you ordered for tomorrow morning may well hold information which clinches the matter.[5]

My experience in the Florentine archives had another critical dimension. I was introduced to an international community of scholars who worked alongside me in the archives and who gave me invaluable encouragement and support. I was befriended by older scholars: Felix Gilbert, Raymond de Roover, Nicolai Rubinstein, Delio Cantimori. I also met a cadre of younger historians with whom I exchanged information and ideas: Philip Jones and Louis Marks from England; Lauro Martines, Marvin Becker, David Herlihy, and Eric Cochrane from the United States: Elio Conti, Guido Pampaloni, and Roberto Abbondanza from Italy. A representative of a younger generation of *studiosi*, Anthony Molho, has well described this scholarly community:

> The Archivio di Stato in Florence, especially in its old location in the Uffizi, offered unparalleled collegiality and a sense of common enterprise among scholars—from great, world-renowned experts to neophytes—drawn from nearly every imaginable nationality. Many aspiring scholars such as myself, who first appeared on the doorstep of the Archives without technical expertise and historical learning, were taken in and nurtured by those senior to us. In the process, we gained a sense of what it means to belong to an intellectual community—a modern version of the *res publica litterarum*.[6]

My doctoral dissertation, "Political Conflict in the Florentine Commune, 1343–1378", was approved by Princeton University in 1954, and that year I joined Berkeley's History Department. I spent the next six years revising and enlarging my thesis, in particular, developing a socioeconomic context for the city's political experience. Entitled *Florentine Politics and Society, 1343–1378*, the revised manuscript was published by Princeton University Press in 1962. While that book was in press, I decided to write a sequel, a history of Florentine politics from the Ciompi Revolution of 1378 to 1434, the year that the Medici became the preeminent force in the republic. That book, fifteen years in the making, was published by Princeton in 1977: *The Civic World of Early Renaissance Florence*. With its publication, I had described the transformation of Florentine politics, from corporate to aristocratic, over a temporal arc of nearly a century.

While researching *Civic World*, I became involved in other projects pertaining to the history of Florence. A fellow student at Princeton in the early 1950s, Norman Cantor, invited me to write a synthetic history of Renaissance Florence for a series that he was editing for John Wiley. I chose to limit the focus of the book on the years from 1378 to 1450, and to treat those decades topically, not chronologically. I also sought to achieve a balance between generalization and specific illustrations, to utilize the evidence from the archival material that I had collected over the years. I collected documents from a wide range of sources: judicial records, tax reports, notarial protocols, private letters, and diaries. This material illuminated many aspects of this urban society, on such topics as relations between kinfolk, between spouses, between parents and children, between heads of households and their servants and slaves; the status of women, orphans, and bastards; disease and illnesses; literacy. I used some of these documents in seminars on Florence that I taught at Berkeley, and the positive response of students to this material persuaded me to organize these documents for publication: *The Society of Renaissance Florence: A Documentary Study.*[7]

In a lecture that I gave at the Harvard Center for Italian Renaissance Studies (Villa I Tatti) in the late 1970s, I argued that the least developed segment of Florentine Renaissance history was religion. For my next research project, I planned to fill that void. I began research on the Florentine church during a year's sabbatical leave in Florence in 1979–80. I made several excursions to Rome to work in the Vatican archives, and by the mid-1980s, had assembled a substantial corpus of material on my subject. In what I described as a "preliminary *sondage*," I published an article on the Florentine urban clergy in 1985; this was followed by articles on the city's monastic foundations, on ecclesiastical courts, on Savonarola, and on evidence concerning "religious sensibilities" that I had discovered in the records of the Holy Penitentiary in Rome. In recent decades, the religious history of the Tuscan church has attracted the attention of many scholars. Most notable are the published contributions of Roberto Bizzocchi, Samuel Cohn Jr., Ronald Weissman, James Banker, Daniel Lesnick, John Henderson, and Timothy Verdon, as well as the forthcoming work by David Peterson. So my ambitious plan to write a comprehensive history of the Florentine church in the fifteenth century had been rendered nugatory.

My archival research did provide the evidence and the inspiration for my last book: a microhistory entitled *Giovanni and Lusanna: Love and Marriage in Renaissance Florence.*[8] In the spring of 1980, I was reading through the protocols of a Florentine notary, Ser Filippo Mazzei, when I encountered some fragments of a judicial process in the court of Archbishop Antoninus concerning a dispute over a marriage. The plaintiff was the widow of a Florentine artisan, Lusanna, who claimed that she had contracted a legitimate second marriage with a businessman from a prominent Florentine family, Giovanni della Casa. Ser Filippo's record of this case comprised some three hundred pages of the testimony of thirty-one witnesses and the arguments of the lawyers and procurators involved in the dispute in the summer and autumn of 1455. I enjoyed the research and writing of this small book *(librucciolo)*. From the testimony of the witnesses, I was able to construct profiles of the main characters: the two lovers, Giovanni and Lusanna; their relatives and friends; the judges who rendered verdicts in this complex legal case. The judicial record also provided glimpses into this society and its mores. When Giovanni and Lusanna went on a summer holiday in the country, they were seen wandering through a meadow collecting salad greens for a meal. They joined their rustic neighbors in a feast celebrating the birth of a male child. And with Lusanna's brother and his wife, they went on a pilgrimage to the nearby monastery of Vallombrosa, the men on horseback, the women on foot.

The thirty-odd articles on fourteenth- and fifteenth-century Florence that I have published over the past half-century are all based on archival material. They cover a broad swath of Florentine experience, particularly its social dimensions.[9] While engaged in research on my doctoral dissertation and on its sequel, I made a practice of copying fragments from the sources that were not germane to politics, my primary focus, but threw light upon some murky dimensions of this milieu. I collected this material in a file that I labeled "miscellaneous." Over time, the evidence concerning particular themes or problems reached a critical mass that allowed me to develop an argument in an article. So, for example, reading through several thousand volumes of the city's criminal court records, I had collected information on a dozen sorcery cases that demonstrated the existence in Florence of practitioners and clients of the black arts. Scattered references to Florence's university—to its professors and students; to its curriculum and its finances—provided material for three articles on that beleaguered institution. In my article "Florentine Voices from the *Catasto*," I used material from the citizens' tax returns to describe their mental world: their perception of their lives and its vicissitudes. My "miscellaneous" file still bulges with undigested material: the testament of Bese Magalotti stipulating that his corpse remain in his house for twenty-four hours before burial; a case before Archbishop Antoninus concerning the mental state and behavior of the demented Filippa Covoni; a law passed in 1463 stipulated that physicians and surgeons who treated patients more than two times require their clients to confess their sins before a priest.[10]

My two books on Florentine politics from the 1340s to the 1430s describe a fundamental transformation from a corporate polity dominated by guild interests to a more elitist regime controlled by the city's prominent families. The glue that held this new system together was patronage. I first encountered this phenomenon in a collection of letters written by and to members of a mercantile family, the Del Bene, in the 1370s and 1380s. The private letters of upper-class Florentines revealed a vast network of patron-client bonds that, to a significant degree, had replaced older corporate ties and allegiances and severely limited any individualistic impulses that Jacob Burckhardt had mistakenly attributed to this society. Although most scholars have accepted the general outline of my interpretation of Florentine politics in these decades, they have revised and criticized some aspects of my analysis. Samuel Cohn has made a very important contribution to the historiography on Florentine state building in these years, in his analysis of peasant rebellions.[11] Riccardo Fubini has proposed a useful corrective to my interpretation of Florentine politics by stressing the arbitrariness and unconstitutionality of the institutional innovations developed by the Florentine ruling elite from the 1390s to the 1420s.[12] Dale Kent's *Rise of the Medici* has added new information and insights on factional conflict in the late 1420s and early 1430s.[13] John Najemy has argued that I have been too sympathetic to the aristocratic leadership that undermined the guild regime, relying too heavily on its propaganda as articulated in civic debates.[14] Richard Goldthwaite criticized my failure to discuss civic patronage of the arts: "This kind of political history might just as well have Poggibonsi as its subject for all its indifference to art."[15]

In his review of my *Giovanni and Lusanna*, Anthony Molho wrote: "What is striking about Brucker's book is its theoretical poverty."[16] This criticism I accept. My views on theory and its value for writing history were neatly articulated by Alisdair McIntyre in his review of Steven Lukes's biography of Emile Durkheim: "All the great social theories to date, including those of Marx, Weber, Durkheim and behavioral social science . . . are in fact false. They overextend categories appropriate only to a particular time and place; they offer us false predictions; they are deceived by the ideological structures of their own society; they formulate generalizations which they propose as laws where laws are inappropriate; they reify abstractions in misleading ways."[17] In my opinion, there are only two valid historical "laws": (1) everything pertaining to our species is in constant flux; and (2) accident and contingency play as important a role in history as does human design.

Among the various reasons that historians write essays and articles, David Cannadine has cited the desire "to avoid writing a book, to dabble but not delve too deeply, to revisit old friends and old haunts, to give as conference papers, to deliver as public lectures."[18] Some combination of these motives accounts for the essays in this volume. The initial version of "The Italian Renaissance" was delivered at a conference on that topic at Cameron University in Lawton, Oklahoma (1992); it was then revised for publication in Guido Ruggiero's edition of *A Companion to the Worlds of the Renaissance* (Oxford, 2002). "Civic Traditions in Premodern Italy" was written for a symposium (1997) sponsored by the *Journal of*

Interdisciplinary History entitled "Patterns of Social Capital." "From *Campanilismo* to Nationhood" was prepared for a conference on state building sponsored by the Academia Sinica in Taipei, Taiwan (1994). "The Horseshoe Nail" was delivered as the Bennett Lecture at the April 2000 meeting of the Renaissance Society of America in the Palazzo Vecchio in Florence. "*Fede* and *Fiducia*" was written for delivery at the Mid-Atlantic Renaissance and Reformation Seminar, held at Washington and Lee University, Lexington, Virginia, in April 2001. "Florence Redux" was presented at a symposium honoring William Bowsky at Stanford University (November 1998). An Italian translation of "The Florentine Cathedral Chaplains in the Fifteenth Century" was prepared for a conference in Florence (June 1997) celebrating the seven hundredth anniversary of the founding of the Florentine cathedral. "The Pope, the Pandolfini, and the *Parrochiani* of S. Martino a Gangalandi (1465)" was a contribution to a Festschrift dedicated to Eve Borsook. Two lectures, "Living on the Edge in Leonardo's Florence" and "Alessandra Strozzi," were written for delivery at meetings of the membership of the Museo Italoamericano in San Francisco.

CHAPTER ONE

The Italian Renaissance

THE BURCKHARDTIAN VISION

In the vast panorama of European historiography, one book stands out for its success in defining a major epoch. *The Civilization of the Renaissance in Italy* was published in 1860 by an obscure Swiss historian, Jacob Burckhardt. For years, the book attracted little attention from scholars and lay readers; not until the early 1900s did it achieve the reputation that it has sustained for a century. Rare is the book or article on any aspect of the Italian Renaissance that does not cite Burckhardt's "essay." The English translation continues to sell thousands of copies annually; it is required reading for many college courses on the subject. More powerfully and persuasively than any other historical work, Burckhardt's masterpiece has shaped our sense of our own past, our perception of how our culture has developed over the centuries from its classical and Christian origins to the present.[1]

The Italian Renaissance marked, for Burckhardt, the beginning of the modern world; and Renaissance Italians were, in his memorable phrase, "the first-born among the sons of modern Europe." Thus, the Renaissance was a sharp, decisive, dramatic break with the medieval age that preceded it. That radical transformation occurred (so Burckhardt argued) in the course of the fourteenth century, though the seeds of this revolution had been sown earlier, in the second half of the thirteenth century. The medieval world, against which Burckhardt juxtaposed the Renaissance, was characterized by an agrarian economy, by a society that was hierarchical and feudal, by a political system that was dominated by kings with sacral power, and above all, by a culture that was profoundly and pervasively Christian and other-worldly. By contrast, the world of the Italian Renaissance described by Burckhardt was characterized by an economy that was mercantile and capitalist, by a society that was urbanized and individualistic, and by a culture that had rejected its Christian heritage for the lure of classical antiquity. Two concepts were fundamental to Burckhardt's vision of the Renaissance: secularism and individualism. By secularism, he meant a society and a culture that was firmly anchored in this world, in the here and now, rather than in the medieval focus on life after death. In one of the most famous passages in his book, Burckhardt contrasted Renaissance individualism with the corporate and collective nature of the medieval mentality.

> In the Middle Ages both sides of human consciousness—that which was turned within as that which was turned without—lay dreaming or half aware beneath a common veil. The veil was woven of faith, illusion, and childish prepossession, through which the world and history were seen clad in strange hues. Man was conscious of himself only as a member of a race, people, party, family or corporation— only through some general category. In Italy this veil first melted into air; an *objective* treatment and consideration of the State and of all things of this world became possible. The subjective side at the same time asserted itself with corresponding emphasis; man became a spiritual individual and recognized himself as such.[2]

Burckhardt's view of the Renaissance, as a distinctive and revolutionary epoch in the history of Western civilization, became and has largely remained the authoritative interpretation: reflected in textbooks, in school and university curricula, in the media, and in the popular perception of the European past. Much has been written to explain the triumph of this historiographical scenario: the clarity and coherence of Burck-hardt's analysis; its dramatic features (sharp divisions, revolutionary change); and its broad and comprehensive vision. Burckhardt sought to integrate all aspects of human experience into his conceptual scheme: to explain cultural change in the context of political, social, and economic phenomena. This attempt to write "total history" was very congenial to the nineteenth century. Equally attractive to that age was Burckhardt's emphasis upon "national" character as a fundamental source for the cre-ation of a culture. "We must insist," Burckhardt wrote, "as one of the chief propositions of this book, that it was not the revival of antiquity alone, but its union with the genius of the Italian people, which achieved the conquest of the Western world."[3]

Every age creates its own image of the past to fit its particular needs and concerns. That Burckhardt's vision of the Renaissance, and more broadly his scheme of periodization, fitted neatly and comfortably into the values and concerns of late-nineteenth-century European culture can be clearly demonstrated. But it does not explain the remarkable per-sistence and durability of the Burckhardtian vision well into the twenti-eth century, with its series of convulsive revolutions—political, social, economic, and cultural—culminating in the traumatic events of recent years. Was Burckhardt a scholar of such brilliance, such phenomenal in-sight, such prescience, that he was able to create a historical perspective that was valid for all time? The answer to that question must be nega-tive. Burckhardt was a great historian—along with Ranke and Michelet, one of the greatest produced by the nineteenth century. But (and this is an obvious point) his understanding was limited by the relative paucity and narrowness of his sources, which were largely literary, and by the lack of a solid scholarly edifice that has since been constructed by the labor of thousands.

A major theme in Burckhardt's interpretation, Italy's radical break with its medieval past, would find little support among scholars today, who instead would stress historical continuity. Change there was, to be sure, but it occurred more slowly and gradually, and more selectively (in terms of regions and social groups) than Burckhardt suggested. The Swiss historian also emphasized the significance of Italian political developments in the late thirteenth and fourteenth centuries. Specifically, he described the emergence of a new type of political ruler, the *signore*, or despot, and the political structures crafted by those rulers ("the state as a work of art") as being a critical component in the formation of Italian Renaissance culture. Contemporary scholarship would place less emphasis on political influences and more on demographic, economic, and social patterns; for example, on the impact of the Black Death and on recurring epidemics of the plague; and on the emergence of new social elites and their systems of patronage.

Burckhardt's interpretation is also flawed, from our contemporary perspective, by its unarticulated premise (so basic to nineteenth-century historiography) that the only people who matter in history are kings and princes, popes and bishops, rich merchants, scholars and artists. His analysis largely ignored the common people (the *popolo*) in the cities and peasants *(contadini)* in the countryside. These poor and illiterate Italians appear only rarely in Burckhardt's account, as participants or witnesses to processions; or in urban rebellions. They are nameless and faceless figures who played no significant role in this world even though they constituted four-fifths of the population. Their rich culture, in its religious and secular dimensions, is only now being studied systematically, together with its links to elite or "high" culture. With respect to one very important group in this society, women, Burckhardt did have some opinions, but they were wrong. Generalizing from a few case studies of aristocratic women and from such books as Castiglione's *Courtier*, Burckhardt believed that Italian Renaissance women, at least upper-class women, had become emancipated. "We must keep before our minds," he wrote, "the fact that women stood on a footing of perfect equality with men."[4] The evidence contradicting that statement is conclusive and overwhelming; Italian women lived first under the total domination of their fathers or guardians, and then of their husbands.[5] Their condition was described pithily and poignantly by Nannina, the daughter of Lorenzo de' Medici, who wrote in a letter to her mother: "Whoever wishes to have control of his life should take care not to be born a woman."[6]

Burckhardt emphasized the secular, mundane concerns of Renaissance Italians, contrasting their preoccupation with the affairs of this world with the medieval preoccupation with the afterlife, with salvation and damnation. But the dichotomy that he formulated was much too sharp and rigid; it ignored the massive evidence of the secular concerns of medieval men: of feudalism, of chivalry, of courtly love; of money, markets, and trade; of war and conflict. And by stressing the paganism of the Italian Renaissance, Burckhardt ignored how deep and pervasive were Christian values, displayed in its art and literature, its rituals and its traditions. The men and women of Renaissance Italy were as pious as their medieval forebears and as deeply concerned about their fate after death. Their testaments, their funerary chapels, their bequests to charity, their participation in liturgical ceremonies and religious processions, all testified to the power and relevance of their Christian faith, which was a fundamental force in their lives.

The Burckhardtian concept of Renaissance individualism has been one of the most influential themes in his analysis. He believed that the unique historical conditions in thirteenth- and fourteenth-century Italy fostered the creation of a new type of man: free and independent, detached from the traditional social and psychological bonds of kinship and solidarity; above all, self-conscious, acutely aware of himself and his world, and capable of ordering and controlling his life. Burckhardt's concept thus has a social and a psychological dimension. The social argument is most easily refuted. Historians of Italian Renaissance society have demonstrated the power and the persistence of family ties and obligations throughout these centuries. They have also shown how Italians sought protection and support by integrating themselves into patronage networks. They were as dependent upon the favor and help of their patrons as any medieval knight or cleric. Whatever their social condition— peasant, laborer, artisan, merchant, scholar—they were not free.

Contradicting the vision of Renaissance man joyfully breaking the traditional bonds and exulting in his liberty is the picture of the Florentine who desperately sought new sources of security and identity to replace those which had disappeared. He forged bonds of friendship and obligation with protectors and benefactors, who would defend him against his enemies and also against the burgeoning power of the state. Nor was the powerful citizen, the patron, really free. He too was enmeshed in a network of obligations and commitments which limited and controlled his freedom of action. He could not release himself from these obligations without incurring loss of social prestige and political influence. The social freedom of the Renaissance man postulated by Burckhardt . . . is, in fifteenth-century Florence at least, a myth.[7]

Equally problematic is Burckhardt's claim for the psychological liberation of Renaissance men, their heightened self-awareness, and their potential for gaining honor and fame. It is possible to find Renaissance authors and texts that suggest this liberation from traditional bonds and constraints, and the emergence of a new type of "Renaissance man": Pico della Mirandola's *Oration on the Dignity of Man* is a prime example; or the career of the sculptor Benvenuto Cellini. But there is also much evidence to refute or to qualify this image: for example, Machiavelli's stress on the role of fortune in men's lives; and his depiction of men as "ungrateful, fickle, liars and deceivers, avoiders of danger, greedy for profit," who accept more easily the murder of their father than the loss of their property.[8]

THE CONTEXT

The Italian Renaissance did not represent so radical a break with the medieval past; change was more gradual and more spotty, the mix of tradition and innovation more complex than the Swiss historian had imagined. Traditional Christian values influenced every dimension of secular life. The social order remained hierarchical; the divisions between elites and masses, between rich and poor were as great in the fifteenth as in the thirteenth century. The economic system, based on the exploitation of the countryside and of foreign markets, did not change significantly from Dante's time to that of Lorenzo de' Medici. For the vast majority of rural Italians—poor, illiterate, marginalized—there was no Renaissance. This description of the French peasantry in the eighteenth century neatly fits their Italian counterparts three hundred years earlier: "Along rutted lanes, paths through cornfields, and sheep tracks in the mountains, we meet . . . a multitude of weather-beaten figures, a spectacle of broken teeth, gnarled hands, rags, clogs, coarse woolen stockings and homespun cloaks."[9]

Further, the Italian peninsula had not enjoyed a modicum of peace and stability since the fourth century A.D., and the Renaissance centuries were no exception to that pattern. Conflict was endemic, involving city-states, feudal lordships, the Hohenstaufen and Angevin monarchs in the south, the papacy, and invading forces from across the Alps. In the fourteenth century, bands of soldiers from wars in France and Germany filtered into Italy, pillaging, burning and killing peasants and townsmen, and extorting ransom from weak city-states. Contributing to the destruction and disorder caused by these marauders were the population losses from famines and recurring visitations of the plague. Between the Black Death of 1348 and the 1420s, Italy's population declined by one-third. In such crisis conditions, Italian regimes of every category were threatened by perils internal and external. These governments were built upon very shaky foundations. They lacked the patina of legitimacy enjoyed by the heads of sacralized monarchies in northern Europe, and they could never depend upon the solid allegiance of their subjects. The primary source of instability in the two hundred or so city-states that dotted the Lombard-Veneto plain and the hilly zones of Tuscany and Umbria were the noble clans, the urban and rural aristocracies, which sought to dominate these towns and their hinterlands.

Burckhardt's focus on Renaissance individualism had persuaded him that the most dynamic element in Italian politics and society in these centuries were the despots, the *signori*, who from the mid-1200s emerged as rulers of most communal regimes in northern and central Italy. He failed to see that the authority of these rulers was based on their families, and on the patronage networks which they had developed. Since the eleventh century, these clans had arisen from obscurity to establish their power in both city and countryside. These aristocratic families dominated Italian history throughout its medieval and Renaissance eras and beyond. Their names are ubiquitous in contemporary chronicles and histories: the Doria and Fieschi of Genoa; the Visconti and Della Torre of Milan; the Rossi of Parma; the Scaligeri of Verona; the Carrara of Padua; the Pepoli and Bentivoglio of Bologna. Even the history of a city with sturdy republican institutions and traditions like Florence was "in large measure the history of its principal families."[10]

The communal governments that emerged in the cities and towns of northern and central Italy did constitute a political order opposed to the hierarchical structures and the endemic violence and disorder so characteristic of feudal society. But these regimes, with their collective and egalitarian values, were systematically dismantled and overthrown by the aristocratic clans, who were supported by their networks of clients and dependents. Machiavelli pithily described the process: "Men do injury through either fear or hate . . . Such injury produces more fear; fear seeks for defense; for defense partisans are obtained; from partisans arise parties in states; from parties their ruin."[11] In *Romeo and Juliet*, Shakespeare captured the essence of these bitter factional squabbles, which no prince or commune could ever fully suppress or control. The lords of Verona, members of the Scaligeri family, did manage to achieve a tenuous control of their city and surrounding district for a century before succumbing to the superior power of Giangaleazzo Visconti, lord of Milan, in 1387. A small number of these princely dynasties (the Visconti and Sforza of Milan; the Este of Ferrara; the Gonzaga of Milan) did manage to govern their states for more than a few decades before being conquered by a more potent rival. Only Venice succeeded in creating a stable and durable polity which, though controlled by an oligarchic elite, did restrain factional violence and thwarted any effort by a single family or individual to dominate the city and its territory.[12]

The power and influence of these aristocratic families was based in part on their status and reputation and their penchant for violence, but also on their wealth. In the Lombard plain and in the mountainous zones of the Apennines, where feudal values and institutions persisted, their resources derived in substantial part from their landed estates, and from rents and leases of lay and ecclesiastical property. In the coastal cities (Genoa, Pisa, Venice) and inland towns like Asti, Piacenza, Florence, Lucca, and Siena, a larger portion of aristocratic wealth came from commerce, banking (including usurious loans), and industry. The quasi-monopoly of Italian merchants in the Mediterranean and northern European economies funneled vast sums into the coffers of these entrepreneurs. Florence's economy was one of the most dynamic and diversified of any Italian city. Its cloth industry provided a livelihood for some ten thousand inhabitants, of a total population in 1427 of thirty-five thousand. The most prosperous segment of the economy was banking and international commerce, from which derived the vast fortunes of families like the Medici, Pazzi, Pitti, and Rucellai. One-fourth of the city's wealth (calculated in 1427 to exceed 10 million florins) was owned by just one hundred households. Cosimo de' Medici was Florence's wealthiest citizen in the mid-decades of the fifteenth century. His fortune, estimated at 150,000 florins, was greater than that of most European monarchs.[13]

This extraordinary concentration of capital in the possession of Italy's urban elites was the essential material foundation for Renaissance culture. As the dominant political force in cities large and small, they subsidized municipal buildings which remain today as symbols of civic pride. They also funded and embellished cathedrals, monasteries, friaries, and convents in the towns and countryside. They built imposing family palaces and endowed burial chapels in parish churches and in monastic foundations. Their motives for these massive expenditures were a mélange of the spiritual and the secular. The wealthy fifteenth-century Florentine merchant Giovanni Rucellai wrote that his ambitious building program (which included a family palace, a burial chapel, and the facade of the Dominican Church of S. Maria Novella) was inspired by his desire to honor God, his city, and himself.[14] In 1471 Lorenzo de' Medici calculated that since 1434, his family had spent some 663,000 florins for charity, buildings, and taxes. "I do not regret this," he wrote, "for though many would consider it better to have a part of that sum in their purse, I consider that it gave great honor to our [his family's] state, and I think the money was well expended and I am well pleased."[15]

THE CULTURAL REVOLUTION

In the restricted world of these Italian urban elites, significant changes did indeed occur in these centuries: in their culture, in their educational system, in their palaces and churches, and in their lifestyle. During the fourteenth century, there emerged a small but dedicated group of intellectuals who studied intensively the surviving literature of classical antiquity, and who claimed that the culture of the ancient world was far superior to their own and worthy of emulation. These scholars, led by Petrarch (d. 1374), embarked upon an ambitious campaign to revive the study of the classics, to find copies of ancient writings that had been lost, and to enlarge the corpus of classical literature. Initially, that corpus was made up primarily of Latin authors, but later it included the writings of ancient Greek philosophers, scientists, and mathematicians, from both the classical and the Hellenistic eras. These scholars cultivated the discipline of rhetoric, the art of writing and speaking eloquently. They modeled their writing style upon the examples of the ancients. They tried to write moral treatises as Cicero had done, to write history as Livy had done, to write poetry as Vergil had done. As rhetoricians, they believed in the power of words to instruct, to educate, and to improve the quality of men's lives. Eventually they became known as "humanists" and their educational program was described as the *studia humanitatis*, or the humanities. They denigrated the disciplines that had been the foundation of medieval higher education: logic, natural philosophy, law, and theology. They sought to replace that curriculum, which they regarded as outmoded and irrelevant, with one based upon the writings of antiquity, which provided (so they argued) better training and guidance for living in this world.

As Erwin Panofsky has shown, this revival of interest and enthusiasm for the culture of the ancient world was not the first phenomenon of this kind; there had been earlier "renaissances" in the eighth and ninth and again in the twelfth century.[16] But this renaissance differed from its predecessors in several important ways. Unlike those earlier revivals, this one was largely if not exclusively created by laymen and not by members of the clergy. These men found in the writings of the ancients a cluster of themes and topics that seemed particularly meaningful and significant for their own lives; for example, discussions by ancient historians of the rise and decline of states; the formation and maintenance of a civil society. They also found in their reading of ancient texts guidance on moral and ethical issues that seemed more pertinent and relevant than the counsel proffered by priests and theologians. As they became more aware of the range and breadth of inquiry by the ancients—their views about the human condition, about fundamental ethical problems, about the nature of the physical universe—they became ever more convinced of the relevance of this knowledge to their own age. They accepted their Christian heritage and its message of salvation, while believing that classical antiquity was a legitimate source of human knowledge and wisdom.

Lauro Martines has described Italian humanism as a "program for the ruling classes," by which he meant that this cultural movement was congenial to Italian ruling elites, whether in republics, in signorial regimes, or in the papal curia.[17] These elites had only recently achieved power and status, and they employed humanists to justify and promote their rule and to glorify their achievements. And not only in Italy, but everywhere in Europe, new men were emerging to challenge the old elites, whether aristocratic or ecclesiastical. One can see this rising tide of new men at every social level and in every profession; in the Roman papacy, for example, where in the fifteenth century a cluster of new men from new families were elected to the Holy See, several of whom had humanist training.

The rise of humanism as a cultural movement was thus due in significant part to the perception of its relevance to contemporary concerns and to its special attraction to newly emerging elites. Also contributing to humanism's ultimate triumph was the effectiveness of its propaganda in promoting its agenda through the rhetorical skills of its adherents and (as we would say today) their mastery of the media. Humanists utilized the newly invented printing press to establish a fixed canon of classical texts and to make those texts more available to a wider audience at a much reduced cost. They also used the media to keep their opponents— the scholastic philosophers, the Aristoteleans, the theologians, and the lawyers—on the defensive, ridiculing their barbarous Latin style and their antiquated methodology. Anthony Grafton and Lisa Jardine have described the triumph of humanism and the establishment of Latin and Greek as the foundation of a new educational curriculum, which eventually displaced the old method of instruction, the so-called scholastic system, in European universities.[18] One can scarcely overemphasize the significance of this educational revolution. The classics dominated the structure and content of European (and American) middle and higher education for four hundred years. Relics of that educational structure survive today in German *gymnasia*, in Italian *licei classici*, and in the classical curricula at Eton and Harrow and Oxford and Cambridge. Not until the end of the nineteenth century were Latin and Greek abolished as required subjects in most American colleges and universities.

This educational revolution was the most significant consequence of the revival of antiquity in Renaissance Italy. It shaped the minds and values of generations of young Europeans, for it was widely adopted both by Catholic, and particularly Jesuit, educators and by most Protestant denominations: Lutheran, Calvinist, Anglican, to educate their clergy, and also the laity. The cult of antiquity was also the major force in another revolution: in the plastic arts, where again Italy was the arena for a fundamental transformation of style and esthetics. Art historians have traced the stages of that revolution, beginning around 1400 in Florence, with the innovations of Brunelleschi in architecture, Ghiberti and Donatello in sculpture, and Masaccio in painting. In fifteenth-century Italy, the combination of artistic talent, of wealthy patrons eager to hire that talent, and a new style based on antique models contributed to an explosion of creativity that still dazzles us and which has rarely been equaled and never surpassed in the history of Western civilization.

This classical style, based on mathematically defined proportions and emphasizing harmony and balance, spread from Italy across the Alps to every part of Europe, as far as Cracow and St. Petersburg; and across the ocean to America. Artists and their patrons accepted, as a fundamental truth, that this style, developed by the Greeks and adopted by the Romans, was the ideal esthetic form. Not until the nineteenth century did a few daring artists challenge that proposition and develop radically different styles in painting, sculpture, and architecture. The power, the tenacity, and the durability of classicism can be seen in the United States, where it became the model for the nation's capital in Washington, and for the buildings that were constructed there. The great majority of public buildings (state capitols, county courthouses, post offices, and libraries) erected in the nineteenth and early twentieth centuries were built with columns, arches, and pediments.

The Italian Renaissance was thus that strand in Italian and European culture that focused on recovering the literary and artistic heritage of antiquity. Its most powerful and most durable influences were in the realms of education and esthetics, where it established standards that survived for more than four hundred years. It did contribute to the promotion of secular concerns and values by making available a large body of classical writing devoted to men living in the world, to their political, social, economic, and moral problems. The Renaissance produced political thinkers like Machiavelli and historians like Guicciardini, whose secular orientation was strongly influenced by their reading of classical authors. The discovery of ancient scientific texts, either lost or known only in fragments, by Euclid, Archimedes, Galen, Pliny, and Ptolemy, contributed to the investigations and speculations that led ultimately to the revolutionary works of Copernicus, Vesalius, and Galileo. In yet another realm, that of religion, the influence of Renaissance humanism has been shown recently to be much greater than Burckhardt allowed. Scholars have pointed to the strong affinities between the Renaissance and the Reformation, both backward-looking movements: the one to antiquity, the other to the early centuries of the church. They have emphasized, too, the focus by reformers and humanists as the source of divine revelation in one case, and of human wisdom in the other. They have also noted the epistemological affinities between humanists and Protestant theologians, both of whom "distinguished between realms, between ultimate truths altogether inaccessible to man's intellect, and the knowledge that men needed to get along in this world, which turned out to be sufficient for his purposes."[19]

MATURITY AND DECLINE

Historians are in general agreement that the fifteenth century represented the mature phase, the apogee, of Italian Renaissance culture. After the crisis conditions of the late fourteenth century, the peninsula experienced a gradual recovery of its population and its economy, most notably in the decades after 1450. Italian politics became somewhat less chaotic, with the gradual formation of five powerful regional states: the republics of Venice and Florence, the signorial regime in Milan, the kingdom of Naples, and the Papal States. With varying degrees of success, each of these regimes developed larger and more intrusive bureaucracies, more exploitative fiscal systems, and more rational military structures. In 1454, these states formed a league which brought a limited measure of stability to Italian politics. The signatories agreed to seek peaceful resolutions to their disputes and to promote the idea of collective security. Pope Nicholas V (d. 1455) was the major advocate of the Italian League; he was motivated by the fear that "some Italian state . . . being desperate, might call the French or some other nation down into Italy and that the fire will spread so much that no one will be able to put it out."[20] The possibility of a foreign invasion, though often threatened, did not materialize until 1480 when a Turkish force temporarily occupied the city of Otranto on the Adriatic coast. In 1494, the French monarch, Charles VIII, led a large army across the Alps on his way to conquer the kingdom of Naples, thus initiating a process which led ultimately to the foreign domination of Italy.

Writing in the aftermath of the foreign invasions and "the calamities of Italy" which they had wrought, the Florentine historian Francesco Guicciardini (d. 1540) described the state of the peninsula in the late fifteenth century as a terrestrial paradise. Not since the fall of the Roman Empire a thousand years before had Italy enjoyed such peace and prosperity. Guicciardini pointed to the large number of "very noble and very beautiful cities" and their talented inhabitants, "skilled in every discipline and in all of the arts."[21] To support his argument, Guicciardini could have compiled a catalogue of his Florentine contemporaries who had achieved distinction in their disciplines and métiers. Among these intellectual giants were the humanists Cristoforo Landino and Angelo Poliziano; the philosophers Joannes Argyropulos and Marsilio Ficino; the natural scientist Paolo Toscanelli; the poets Luigi Pulci and Lorenzo de' Medici. Guicciardini himself was just beginning his career as lawyer, diplomat, and historian, as was his younger friend and compatriot, Niccolò Machiavelli. An earlier generation of renowned artists (the painters Masaccio, Uccello, Fra Angelico; the sculptors Donatello and Ghiberti; the architects Brunelleschi, Alberti, Michelozzo) had died, but their successors continued the grand Florentine tradition begun by Giotto and Arnolfo di Cambio. Sometime before his death in 1494, the father of Raphael of Urbino, Giovanni Santi, made a list of the most famous painters of the fifteenth century. Of the twenty-five Italian artists in his corpus, thirteen were from Florence, of whom six (Ghirlandaio, Antonio and Piero Pollaiuolo, Botticelli, Leonardo da Vinci, Filippino Lippi) were still alive.[22] Missing from the list was Michelangelo Buonarroti, who in 1494 was just beginning his illustrious career as painter, sculptor, and architect: the supreme artist of the Italian Renaissance.

While writing his biography of Michelangelo, the sixteenth-century artist Giorgio Vasari speculated about the remarkable concentration of artistic talent in Florence. "The Tuscan genius," he wrote, "has ever been raised high above all others, the men of that country displaying more zeal in study, and more constancy in labor, than any other people of Italy." In another passage, Vasari developed a sociological explanation for Florence's extraordinary achievement: "In that city men are driven on by three things: the first of these is disapproval, which many of them vent on many things and with much frequency, their genius never being content with mediocrity, but seeking what is good and beautiful . . . Secondly, industriousness in their daily lives, which means constantly drawing on their talent and judgment, and being shrewd and quick in their dealings, and knowing how to earn money . . . The third thing . . . is a quest for glory and honor, which is common to Florentines of all professions."[23] In recent historiography, there has developed a counter trend which has sought to minimize Florence's role and to promote the contributions of other cities: Venice, Milan, Rome, Ferrara, Mantua, Urbino.[24] But for many Renaissance scholars, the cultural achievement of Florence remains unsurpassed.

Leonardo da Vinci (d. 1519) has often been perceived as the epitome of the Italian Renaissance. "Athletics, music, drawing, painting, sculpture, architecture, town planning, perspective, optics, astronomy, aviation; hydraulic, nautical, military, structural and mechanical engineering; anatomy, biology, zoology, botany, geology, geography, mathematics— the list of his interests is seemingly endless."[25] His confidence in his talents, his genius, was displayed in a letter that he sent to the duke of Milan seeking employment: "I can carry out sculpture in marble, bronze or clay; and also I can paint whatever may be done as well as any other." He could build bridges, mortars and cannons; he could blow up fortresses; he could construct war chariots that would disperse any enemy force. His skepticism about theoretical knowledge divorced from observation and experiment set him apart from his contemporaries and identified him as a prophetic advocate of the modern scientific method. "It seems to me that all sciences are vain and full of error that have not been tested by experience . . . that do not pass through any of the five senses . . . Experience does not feed investigators on dreams, but always proceeds from accurately determined first principles . . . as can be seen in the elements of mathematics founded on numbers and measures called arithmetic and geometry." One passage from Leonardo's notebooks is an eloquent testimonial of the curiosity and excitement, and also the fear and anxiety, experienced by this intrepid explorer of the unknown:

> Unable to resist my eager desire and wanting to see the great profusion of the various and strange shapes made by nature, and having wandered some distance among the rocks, I came to the entrance of a great cavern, in front of which I stood for some time . . . Bending my back into an arch, I rested my left hand on my knee and held my right hand over my eyebrows; often bending first one way and then the other, to see whether I could discover anything inside; and this being impossible by the deep darkness within, and having remained there for some time, two contrary emotions arose in me, fear and desire; fear of the threatening darkness, and desire to see whether there were any marvelous things within the cave.[26]

Leonardo's professional career was profoundly affected by the invasions that transformed Italy into a permanent battleground for a half-century, from 1494 to 1559. When King Charles VIII and his army crossed the Alps, the Florentine artist was still employed by the king's ally, Lodovico Sforza. The French monarch did achieve his primary goal, the conquest of the kingdom of Naples, but was forced to retreat back across the Alps in the summer of 1495. In 1499, Charles's successor, Louis XII, launched an attack on Milan, occupying the duchy and imprisoning Lodovico Sforza. "The duke lost his state and his property," Leonardo commented, "and none of his works was completed for him." Having lost his patron, Leonardo traveled to Mantua, to Venice, and then to Florence in search of a stable environment. In 1502, he was hired as a military engineer by Cesare Borgia, son of Pope Alexander VI, who was then building a state in central Italy. When Cesare's state collapsed after his father's death in 1503, Leonardo returned to Florence but then moved back to Milan to serve the French rulers of the duchy. After the French were driven out of Milan by a Spanish army (1512), the peripatetic Leonardo traveled to Rome but received no support from Pope Julius II. He then returned to Milan and was invited by Louis XII to settle in France. He died in 1519 in a chateau in the Loire valley which the French monarch had given to him.

The depredations of these invading armies (French, Swiss, German, Spanish) and the Italian soldiery did enormous physical damage to the peninsula. In these "almost unremitting molestations of normal life," Francesco Guicciardini wrote in the 1530s, he "saw nothing but scenes of infinite slaughter, plunder and destruction of multitudes of towns and cities, attended with the licentiousness of soldiers no less destructive to friends than foes."[27] The single most devastating event in this orgy of destruction was the sack of Rome in 1527. This event was a graphic demonstration of Italy's weakness and the failure of its political and military leadership. Machiavelli's pessimistic judgment about Italy's prospects for recovering her independence was shown to be accurate: "As for the unity of the Italians, you make me laugh; first, because there will never be any unity . . . And even if the leaders were united, that would not be enough, both because there are no armies here worth a penny, and because the tails are not united with the heads, nor will this nation ever respond to any accident that might occur."[28]

In 1559, France and Spain signed a peace treaty which ended their sixty-year struggle for control of the Italian peninsula. Hapsburg Spain was the victor in this conflict, having established its direct governance of the Milanese duchy and the kingdom of Naples (including Sicily) and its hegemony over a cluster of satellite states: the Medici granduchy of Tuscany, Mantua, Ferrara, Genoa, Montferrat. Only the duchy of Savoy, the republic of Venice, and the Papal States survived as independent polities in this age of Spanish domination. During the last four decades of the sixteenth century, Italians experienced a rare interlude of peace and stability, during which the peninsula's population and economy revived, and the wartime damages to its infrastructure were repaired. The most remarkable example of this recovery was the city of Rome. Devastated by the ravages of imperial troops, its population reduced to fewer than ten thousand souls, Rome slowly recovered under the leadership of its popes, from Paul III (1534–49) to Sixtus V (1585–90). Churches, monasteries, and palaces were rebuilt, while new construction (St. Peter's, the Farnese and Massimo palaces, the Villa Lante) provided livelihood for architects, artists, and laborers. By the late sixteenth century, Rome's population had grown to one hundred thousand, and Sixtus V launched a massive campaign to restore the physical city: completing the dome of St. Peter's, building dozens of new roads and fountains, restoring and decorating the city's ecclesiastical buildings.

The two dominant powers in late sixteenth- and seventeenth-century Italy were the Spanish monarchy and the Roman papacy. Despite occasional disputes over their respective powers and jurisdictions, they forged an alliance to maintain their control over Italy's political and religious life. They were united in their commitment to repress political and religious dissent and to monitor and regulate the lives of their subjects. The Spanish monarchy and their satellite states established large, expensive, and intrusive bureaucracies to enforce the will of their rulers. The Roman papacy created its own institutions, the Inquisition and the Index, to defend religious orthodoxy and to repress heresy. The list of prohibited books grew incrementally each year; it included not only the writings of Protestant theologians, but the works of Dante, Boccaccio, Lorenzo Valla, Savonarola, Erasmus, and Machiavelli. Among the Roman Inquisition's most celebrated victims were the Florentine aristocrat Piero Carnesecchi and the Dominican friar Giordano Bruno (executed); the philosopher Tommaso Campanella (imprisoned for twenty-six years); and the scientist Galileo, condemned for his support of the Copernican theory and placed under house arrest. Interrogated about his depiction of the Last Supper, the Venetian painter Veronese was ordered (1573) "to improve and change his painting within a period of three months" or suffer penalties imposed by the inquisitors. Michelangelo was sharply criticized for painting nude human figures in his Last Judgment in the Sistine chapel. Pope Paul IV ordered the offending images to be covered by drapery.[29]

These episodes of repression and intolerance persuaded scholars like Francesco De Sanctis and Benedetto Croce that the unholy alliance between Spain and the papacy was responsible for the degeneration of Italian culture from the mid-sixteenth to the end of the seventeenth century. In Croce's view, Italy "was bereft of all political life and national sentiment, freedom of thought was extinguished, culture impoverished, literature became mannered and ponderous, the figurative arts and architecture became extravagant and grotesque."[30] But recent scholarship has modified this harsh judgment on the impact of the efforts by Spanish and papal authorities to impose orthodoxy on cultural activity. In certain disciplines (theology, philosophy, history, literature), the loss of vitality and creativity was significant. The quality of Italian historical writing declined dramatically from the level established by Renaissance authors of the caliber of Leonardo Bruni, Flavio Biondo, Machiavelli, and Guicciardini. With the exception of cosmology, the natural sciences were largely exempt from regulations by censors and inquisitors. Croce's denigration of the plastic arts ignores the achievements of painters and sculptors from Pontormo, Bronzino, Titian, Tintoretto, and Caravaggio in the sixteenth to Bernini, Borromini, and Pietro da Cortona in the seventeenth century. Throughout these years of "decadence" (Croce's term), migratory Italian scholars, poets, artists, and musicians were spreading the knowledge and techniques of their disciplines to every part of Christian Europe, from Ireland and Scandinavia to the Slavic world.[31]

Italian authorities, secular and ecclesiastical, were not unique in their efforts to regulate and discipline behavior and belief. This impulse was Europe-wide in scope: a response to the chaos and turbulence produced by incessant warfare and the religious controversies of the Reformation. The Renaissance freedom to explore, to innovate, to challenge traditional values and institutions, had caused intense anxiety among European elites and their leaders. They yearned for a more stable political and social order, for religious uniformity and for a culture that reinforced authority.[32] This pervasive mood was brilliantly captured by the English poet John Donne (d. 1631):

And new philosophy calls all in doubt,
The element of fire is quite put out;
The sun is lost, and th'earth, and no man's wit,
Can well direct him where to look for it.
And freely men confess that this world's spent,
When in the planets and the firmament,
They seek so many new . . .
Tis all in pieces, all coherence gone,
All just supply and all relation.[33]

This tension between the drive for freedom and innovation, for the breach of barriers and boundaries, and the contrary impulse for order and stability, would be a permanent feature of European culture in the long and tortuous transition to "modernity."

CHAPTER TWO

Civic Traditions in Premodern Italy

In the fifth chapter of *Making Democracy Work*, Robert Putnam argues that the origins of civic society in modern Italy can be traced back to the age of the communes (twelfth to fifteenth centuries) in its northern and central regions. The distinctive features of those republican regimes were a high degree of cooperation and collaboration among their members, an atmosphere of mutual trust essential for their survival and the achievement of common goals, and an egalitarian ethos based upon horizontal social bonds. The associative impulse that led to the establishment of the communes also inspired the creation of other civic organizations: tower societies; guilds, Guelf and Ghibelline "parties"; and confraternities. The contrast between the political and social structures of the feudal world, from which these associations emerged, was dramatic. In those parts of the peninsula that were not intensely urbanized—Piedmont and the Apennine region—or dominated by a strong, centralized monarchy—like the towns in the south—a social structure based upon vertical relationships survived intact.[1]

Putnam admits that the civic ethos of the communal world was weakened in the decades following the Black Death, and particularly after the foreign invasions and the hegemony established in the sixteenth century by Hapsburg Spain. Still, he insists that the values and ideals of the communal era survived into the modern age of the Risorgimento and unification: "In the North, norms of reciprocity and networks of civic engagement have been embodied in tower societies, guilds, mutual aid societies, cooperatives, unions and even soccer clubs and literary societies." "Mutual aid societies were built on the razed foundations of the old guilds, and cooperatives and mass political parties on the experience of mutual aid societies."[2]

The scenario developed by Putnam can stand some revisions, first and most fundamentally, his view on the civic culture of communal Italy. He presents too idealized a picture of that culture, with its communitarian and egalitarian components; his view neglects the darker side of that world—its factionalism, its violence and brutality, and its coercive and authoritarian dimensions. A second problem is Putnam's argument that the civic values of the communal age survived centuries of invasion, foreign domination, absolutist government, and a hierarchical social order—to be revived and rejuvenated in the twentieth century—as the key to Italy's modernization. For Putnam, that revival of a civil society in north and central Italy, and its absence in the south, is the primary explanation for the gulf still dividing the two Italies—the one civic, dynamic, progressive, and "modern" and the other "feudal," reactionary, backward, and depressed. To focus so exclusively on the "civic" theme in explaining the divergent paths of the two regions since unification is to simplify and distort a complex historical reality.

The character of the communal experience, and its role in Italy's historical evolution, has been one of the most controversial themes in recent historiography. The traditional interpretation, formulated initially by the chroniclers and historians of Italian towns and accepted by (among others) Jacob Burckhardt in his classic work, *The Civilization of the Renaissance in Italy* (New York, 1929), stressed the progressive, innovative, and "modern" qualities of that civic world. The institutions and values fostered by those urban governments were seen as the solvent that destroyed the old feudal system, with its hierarchical social structure, its land-based economy, and its fragmented political order. The towns were the dynamic engines that created a new capitalist economy; a social order based on wealth; a political system that stressed coopera- tion, equality, and freedom; and a culture that embodied secular rather than religious values.

Lane, the distinguished historian of Venice, articulated this vision: "My thesis here is that republicanism . . . is the most distinctive and significant aspect of these Italian city-states, that republicanism gave to the civilization of Italy its distinctive quality . . . and contributed mightily to its triumph later in modern nations and primarily in our own."[3]

Since World War II, however, this view of the communes and their historical significance has been challenged by scholars who have em- phasized the weaknesses, limitations, and failures of these urban re- gimes. Some critics have stressed their instability, their failure to over- come factional discord, and their tendency to rely upon powerful lords *(signori)* from feudal backgrounds to resolve their recurrent crises. By the end of the thirteenth century, independent communal regimes had been replaced by *signorie* in those regions of northern Italy where feudal nobilities were powerful. Communal regimes in Lombardy, the Veneto, and Emilia-Romagna were viewed as aberrant phenomena with brief life spans in a world that remained overwhelmingly feudal. Independent communes did survive longer in central Italy—Tuscany and Umbria— where rural nobilities were weaker, but these regions witnessed the gradual demise of these republics, which were either absorbed by their more powerful neighbors, like Florence, or, like Siena and Perugia, were taken over by local *signori*.[4]

Since World War II, an international cadre of scholars has studied the history of Florentine republicanism intensively, particularly its mature phase in the fifteenth century, and its demise in the sixteenth. Florence's past is too exceptional and idiosyncratic to serve as a model for the Ital- ian city-state experience, but no Italian city has left a richer documen- tary record, nor a more fully articulated civic ideology. In his treatise on Florence's constitution, written c. 1440, the civic humanist Bruni focused on the exercise of public power by the magistrates, and the limits imposed on their authority by the statutes. The executive bodies (the Signoria and its two advisory colleges) could initiate legislation, but their proposals had to be ratified by a two-thirds vote of the councils of the *popolo* and the commune. To prevent an excessive concentration of authority in the hands of a few, the tenure of all civic offices was brief (between two and six months), and eligibility for those positions was carefully regulated.[5]

Florence's constitution was a mixture of the aristocratic and the democratic. In Bruni's world, those citizens (magnates) "with too great a power of numbers and of force at their command" were excluded from the chief executive offices, while "mechanics and members of the lowest class" were not allowed any role in the state. "Thus, avoiding the extremes, the city look[ed] to the mean, or rather to the best and the wealthy but not over-powerful." That middling mass of politically active citizens comprised artisans and shopkeepers from the lower guilds and merchants, cloth manufacturers, bankers, and professionals (lawyers, notaries, physicians) from the greater guilds.[6]

Every year, more than a thousand citizens participated directly in the political process as members of the supreme executive and as officials who staffed the forty-odd commissions responsible for the administration of the dominion, the collection of taxes, and the enforcement of sumptuary laws. More than a thousand citizens assembled regularly each year as members of the legislative councils. They also participated in the administration of their guilds, as consuls and councillors. They attended meetings of their electoral districts *(gonfaloni)* and assemblies of their parish churches.

Thousands of Florentines also participated in the meetings and rituals of their confraternities and in the processions that commemorated civic and religious holidays. The anniversary (June 24) of John the Baptist, the city's patron saint, was celebrated by a procession that included the secular and religious authorities, representatives of the subject communities, and a large contingent of guildsmen. This annual ritual symbolized most dramatically the civic community and the bonds that united its members.[7]

The political agenda of this large and heterogeneous mass of middling Florentines, which constituted the *popolo*, was quite straightforward. These citizens wanted their traditional place and voice in the government, based upon their guild memberships. The essence of republicanism for these men was its corporate and collegiate quality, in which decisions were made and policies formulated by citizens chosen to represent the whole community. As John Najemy wrote, they believed in the principles "of consent and representation as the foundation of legitimate republican government, of officeholding as a public trust, of the supremacy of law, and of the delegated quality of all formal power." They felt that the common good *(ben commune)* was best served by the firm and equitable administration of justice, which would protect their persons and their property, regulate their business affairs, and adjudicate their private disputes. They also favored rigorous punishment for malfeasance.[8]

In the interest of a fiscal system that was fair, they supported the famous law of the *catasto* (1427), which allocated the tax burden according to the declared wealth of individual households. Appended to their tax returns were statements that articulated with clarity and eloquence their perception of an ideal civic polity. Giovanni Corbinelli informed the *catasto* officials that he prayed to God "to give [them] grace to do justice to each [taxpayer], and if [they did] so, [they would give] health to this city in perpetuity and . . . be the instrument to maintain this *popolo* in liberty forever." Giovanni Vettori wrote, "If you act according to your honor, you will maintain and strengthen this glorious city in triumph and virtue." A belt maker named Luca di Cino appended to his tax report, "I, Luca, have compiled this document with my own hand, and I believe that what I have declared is the whole truth. . . . So that the commune will have what it is owed, and you will have done your duty and [preserved] your honor, and we will be treated fairly, may Christ keep you in peace."[9]

The tenor of these statements reveals another dimension of the *popolo*'s agenda: the desire for strong, active, and even intrusive government. These citizens were convinced that their turbulent and violence-prone society required a heavy measure of discipline and regulation. This was not a community that trusted its members to live together in peace and harmony *(vivere civile)* without coercion. Florentines had no conception of a private realm immune from public scrutiny and intervention. No intimation is evident in either public or private records that the citizenry resented this close surveillance and regulation of their private lives.

By large majorities, they voted in favor of special magistracies to regulate (among other matters) their weddings and funerals, their clothing and jewelry, their relations with the Jewish community, and their sexual behavior. These officials hired informers to spy on their fellow citizens, and they established boxes *(tamburi)* into which secret denunciations could be deposited. Florentine statutory law gave broad powers to the Signoria and its colleges to elect certain officials, to cancel or alter judicial penalties, to issue safe conducts and grants of immunity from persecution, and to force individuals and corporate bodies to obey their decrees. These magistrates did not hesitate to intervene in private affairs—for example, to prohibit a mother described as "quarrelsome and prone to scandalous behavior" from living with her two nubile daughters.[10]

Two cases will illustrate the extent of this arbitrary executive authority. In April 1429, on the occasion of a tournament in honor of a visiting member of the Portuguese royal family, the Signoria issued an executive order that a penalty of 1,000 florins would be levied against five citizens unless they appeared with horses and armor to participate in the joust. Eleven years later, the Signoria threatened to impose a fine of 1,000 florins on Uguccione de' Ricci unless he could persuade his cousin, the archbishop of Pisa, to abandon a judicial process against an alleged usurer in his ecclesiastical court.[11]

Within this republican polity, that men from the city's most prominent wealthy lineages wielded more power and influence than did citizens of lesser rank was a perennial fact of political life, as valid for the fifteenth century as for that pristine age when Dante's ancestor, Cacciaguida, lived. These men of high social status *(ottomati)* viewed their political system from a somewhat different perspective than did the *popolo*. They, too, favored a strong, activist government, accepting the principle that the general welfare of the community took precedence over private interests. But they resented the political role of *popolo* in the regime, and after the Ciompi Revolution, they succeeded in limiting their access to civic office, and their influence on policy.

Even though the *ottomati* had gained a dominant role in the regime by the early fifteenth century, they were unable to control the bitter rivalries and factional quarrels that periodically threatened the stability of the regime. The primary source of these partisan conflicts was not political or ideological but personal and familial—the struggle among individuals and families for civic office, and the benefits and perquisites that accrued to those who held it. These conflicts intensified during times of crisis, particularly during the years of warfare (1391 to 1402, 1411 to 1414, and 1423 to 1431) that drained the city's wealth, sparked widespread unrest in Florence and throughout the dominion, and inspired bitter quarrels and recriminations within the leadership. An especially intense crisis in the early 1430s culminated in the emergence of one family, the Medici, which was able to create a party or faction composed of kinfolk, neighbors, friends, and clients that governed Florence for sixty years (1434 to 1494).[12]

The ability of the Medici to seize and maintain control of the republic was due not only to their political skills but also to the vast wealth that they could use to buy allegiance. They immobilized their rivals by exiling them and by excluding the rank-and-file from office, while restoring the political rights of old magnate families. They preserved many of the republican institutions inherited from the past, though they did replace the old legislative councils (in which the influence of the *popolo* was strong) by smaller and more tractable bodies of their adherents.

When the regime was threatened by internal discord and popular unrest, it created commissions *(balìe)* with extraordinary powers to reform the state. The Medici developed complex electoral strategies to ensure that their allies would control the major electoral offices, while excluding any current or potential rivals. They gradually dismantled the old judicial system administered by foreign (and supposedly impartial) judges, substituting magistracies staffed by citizens from the ranks of their partisans. Even though the statutes guaranteed the right "of citizens to be free to give counsel and to judge public affairs," the regime was prepared to silence its critics by accusing them of fomenting discord and engaging in treasonous activity. As had been true throughout the republic's history, the distinction between legitimate criticism and sedition was always a fine line.[13]

To the more equitable system of tax assessments embodied in the *catasto*, they favored the older method of *arbitrio*, by which tax commissions in each electoral district decided levies to be imposed on their neighbors. As the Medici long recognized, this was a powerful weapon for rewarding friends and punishing enemies.

The Medicean system of government reached its apogee under Lorenzo, who, following in his grandfather Cosimo's footsteps, built a polity that retained its formal republican facade while enabling its *maestro* to control the levers of power. Lorenzo's authority derived primarily from the elaborate network of patron-client relations that Cosimo had developed and that he and his father, Piero, had fostered and expanded. Lorenzo's network extended from the city throughout the dominion, even beyond Florentine territory to include the whole Italian peninsula.[14]

Lorenzo was the supreme patron of the Florentine state, and letters came to him from individuals, corporations, ecclesiastical foundations, and political authorities inside and outside the state's territorial boundaries. Petitioners appealed to Lorenzo for support and favor—for civic office, ecclesiastical benefices, tax exemptions, cancellation of criminal sentences, arranging marriages, and letters of recommendation. Lorenzo's influence was considered to be decisive in the operations of the Florentine government, and personal appeals for his help more useful than requests to the civic magistracies.

Writing to Lorenzo in 1478, Giovanni Capponi noted that Medicean support for his family was "the reason why . . . we have with assurance had recourse to you and to your ancestors, by whom graciously we have been exalted." In 1488, Piero Buondelmonti wrote to a close associate of Lorenzo "that everything proceeds from God by the virtue, merits and dignity of our God on earth, the magnificent Lorenzo, to whom I beg you to recommend me as his creature."[15]

Friends in high places were critical in this highly competitive and agonistic society. The wealthy merchant Giovanni Rucellai once wrote that he needed a large circle of *amici* to protect himself from his enemies. Alberti commented that "there is really nothing more difficult in the world than distinguishing true friends amid the obscurity of so many lies, the darkness of people's motives and the shadowy errors and vices that lie about us on all sides." Even close friends were capable of betrayal; discord within families over inheritances, marriages, and business transactions were common. Florence was a veritable cauldron of suspicion, mistrust, and envy, fueled by the struggle for wealth, status, and reputation, which in concrete terms signified the ability to obtain civic office and to arrange honorable marriages for daughters and lucrative careers for sons.[16]

In this "paradise inhabited by devils," the achievement of these objectives was an arduous enterprise. The attainment of high civic office could be thwarted by the machinations of one's enemies. A family's prosperity could be destroyed by business failures or confiscatory taxation. The competition for appropriate marriage partners led to the escalation of dowries and the inability of impoverished fathers from prominent lineages to contract "honorable" liaisons. The penalties exacted upon these losers included imprisonment for debt, withdrawal from the city to a marginal life in the *contado*, and unemployable sons and unmarriageable daughters.[17]

These unpalatable scenarios explain the desperate tone of the appeals to Lorenzo and other prominent figures in the regime—for instance, that of Bernardo di Nicola, who pleaded for a reduction of his tax bill, which would be "the cause of [his] coming again to life," and that of Bernardo Cambini, who, seeking to obtain a seat in the Signoria that his ancestors had occupied, "did not wish by comparison [with them] to appear 'a wooden man.'" Cambini added that his selection to the supreme executive "would be useful in enabling [him] to marry [his] daughters."[18]

In addition to manipulating the political system and promoting a citywide network of patron-client bonds, Lorenzo also developed a strategy to limit the autonomy of the city's corporate bodies and make them more responsive to the regime's agenda. Florence's major guilds—Lana, Calimala, and Cambio—had long since been taken over by Medici partisans, as had been the merchants' court *(mercanzia)*, which regulated commercial and financial affairs. Lorenzo's influence within the Florentine church was solidified by the appointment of Rinaldo Orsini, his brother-in-law, as archbishop. He intervened directly in the administration of San Lorenzo, his family's parish church, and in monastic and conventual foundations that had been subsidized by Medici largesse. The Medici also funded and governed the city's charitable foundations—hospitals, foundling homes, and hostels for plague victims.

Confraternities—approximately one hundred of them—constituted one of the most important segments of the city's associative life. These societies were an obvious target for Medicean penetration. Since their memberships comprised as much as one-fifth of the adult male population, they were potential sources of either support for or resistance to the regime. By joining these sodalities, Lorenzo was able to control their ritual and charitable activities and to exert a decisive influence on their internal administrations. After becoming a member of the confraternity of Sant' Agnese, for example, Lorenzo was recognized as its chief benefactor and patron. He also supervised the society's transformation from an egalitarian association of neighbors into a "more aristocratic organization, whose councils promoted Medicean political interests and whose rituals worshipped and magnified the aura surrounding the lineage."[19]

The Florentines never wholly accepted Medicean hegemony. Opposition to the regime came initially from those families whose members had been exiled, excluded from office, and penalized by the judicial and fiscal systems. But even the their close allies and associates came to resent the dominant and often domineering roles of first Cosimo and, later, Piero and Lorenzo. Playing subversive roles in the crises of 1458 and 1466, which threatened the regime's stability, they adopted republican slogans, calling for the restoration of "liberty," "freedom," and "good government" and the abolition of the Medici's self-aggrandizing electoral and fiscal strategies. Echoes of these sentiments are found in council debates throughout the 1450s and 1460s, testifying to the tenacious survival of republican ideology in the city.

No public criticism of Lorenzo and his authoritarian regime, however, was ever voiced; it would have invited "immediate imprisonment, exile or even death." Opposition took the form of conspiracies, which were inevitably crushed; of anonymous placards posted in the city squares; of negative gossip and rumors that circulated in public places; and of critical comments recorded in private diaries and account books. Although many of Lorenzo's detractors were motivated by a sense of personal mistreatment, they justified their opposition by appealing to the republican tradition, which (so they claimed) the Medici had destroyed. When Lorenzo died in 1492, the entire city participated in his funeral rites with expressions of grief and loss. Yet, according to one witness, many of these mourners "instead rejoiced, thinking that the republic would recover its liberty and they would escape from servitude."[20]

Two years after Lorenzo's death, a French invasion precipitated the expulsion of the Medici, and the city was given the opportunity to "recover its liberty." A makeshift republican regime restored most of the institutional structures that the Medici had dismantled. One significant innovation was the creation of the Great Council, whose members included all of the citizens whose fathers and/or grandfathers had qualified for the highest executive offices—the Signoria and its two colleges. The Great Council voted on all legislative proposals and selected the officials who filled the civic magistracies and those who governed the dominion. This "fundamental law of the republican period" shifted the balance of power from the elite back to the *popolo*. Given the large number of citizens newly integrated into the government, the reformers expected this revived commitment to the *vivere popolare* (republican government) to enable the regime to survive and prosper.[21]

The establishment of this republican polity could not have occurred at a more difficult time than in the wake of the French invasion. By maintaining its traditional alliance with the French monarchy, the republic incurred the enmity of those states and interests (Venice, Naples, and the papacy) that had fought to keep the French out. The arduous military effort to rescue the rebel city of Pisa drained hundreds of thousands of florins from the city's treasury and imposed heavy burdens upon the citizenry. These fiscal problems were compounded by a series of poor harvests that threatened the urban poor with starvation, and by the disruption of trade routes that resulted in unemployment among the workers in the cloth industry.

These crises exacerbated the deep and pervasive divisions within the government. A hard core of Medici supporters sought to weaken the new regime and to prepare for the Medici's resumption of power. Furthermore, the conflict that had resulted from Savonarola's brief and tumultuous career as a religious leader with a political agenda still persisted after his execution in 1498. But the issue that ultimately doomed the republic concerned the balance of power between the elite and the *popolo*. Members of the old and prominent lineages attempted to monopolize the major offices and to formulate civic policy by curtailing the authority of the Great Council, with its guild constituency, and enacting institutional reforms that would give them a greater voice in fiscal matters and foreign policy. The *popolo* strongly resisted these efforts, consistently voting against proposals to levy taxes for military operations. During this period, the regime was periodically threatened by Medicean conspiracies, rebellions in the dominion, and military incursions by foreign troops. Instead of uniting the citizenry in defense of the regime, these perils intensified the factional quarrels and divisions.[22]

The republican regime that governed Florence from 1494 to 1512 was the city's most "democratic" polity since the late fourteenth century. Some three thousand citizens—one-fourth of the adult male population—belonged to the Great Council. Not since the 1460s had Florentines been so free to express their opinions in council deliberations. But this unaccustomed freedom to discuss the *res publica* did not result in coherent and constructive policies, but, rather, in lengthy and inconclusive debates that revealed the deep fissures within the city and the regime's inability to respond effectively to crises.

The civic mood throughout these years was one of pervasive anxiety: "We are in such a state that our demise appears to be imminent . . . To live in this manner is the height of insanity . . . It is not necessary to describe the dangers and disorders that confront the city; they are so great that one can speak of chaos." Speakers repeatedly criticized every facet of government—the fisc, the administration of justice, the selection of officials, and the conduct of military affairs and foreign policy. They also speculated about the sources of "disorder" and the failure of the citizenry to unite in defense of the liberty that their ancestors "had acquired with so much bloodshed." One popular explanation was that private interest had become more important than the general welfare. An ominous sign of civic alienation was the frequent absence of a quorum at sessions of the Great Council, leading to the postponement of legislative action and a halt to the selection of magistrates.[23]

Civic debates exposed all of the systematic weaknesses of republican government throughout the communal era. From city to city, the scenario varied only in the details: beleaguered regimes plagued by internal divisions, weak and indecisive leadership, the erosion of civic institutions and values, and the transfer of power from the community to an individual or a family. In Florence, this process was more prolonged than else-where; republican ideals there were stronger and more deeply rooted in the urban culture. The Medici were finally successful in regaining control of the state, with the assistance of their two popes, Leo X (1513–21) and Clement VII (1523–34). The transformation was solidified with the selection of Cosimo de' Medici as Duke of Florence in 1537, establishing a dynasty that ruled the city and its territory for two centuries.

The Florentine elite accepted the Medicean *principato* in exchange for the recognition of its privileged position in government and in society. Francesco Guicciardini, a historian and a prominent figure among the *ottomati*, preferred that the regime be controlled by the city's leading families, but he accepted a high office under the Medici that brought him *onore e utile*, honor and profit.

The educational process by which upper-class Florentines were converted from citizens to courtiers was described by Alamanni, a Medici partisan, in 1516:

> Florentines are not accustomed to be deferential to anyone except their magistrates and then only with some pressure and effort. They felt that it was beneath their dignity to doff their hats, and this ancient practice became embedded in their customs. . . . The older generation will never abandon this habit, but being wise, these men will not revolt *(non fanno mai novità)*. But the younger generation is more flexible, more malleable, and the prince can win their support and loyalty by inviting them to join his court, and by granting them offices and benefits.[24]

The construction of an authoritarian government and a hierarchical social order, begun by the Medici in the fifteenth century, was completed in the sixteenth. The *popolo* were too weakened and demoralized by successive crises (plagues, famines, the depredations of military forces, heavy taxation, and conspiracies) to challenge their exclusion from the polity. Under the Medici, the *popolani* (citizenry) had become accustomed to a political and social order based on patronage and clientage, which offered them more support than did their civic institutions and their guilds. After the expulsion of the Medici in 1494, a merchant named Piero Vaglienti expressed the view of many citizens of middling rank: "Now one does not know to whom to turn for help. . . . With a prince *[signore]* there is only one [leader], but now in Florence there are a hundred, and some pull you in one direction, and others in another."[25]

Within the ranks of the *popolo*, too, were hundreds, perhaps thousands, who had benefited from Medicean favors and welcomed their return to power. In the dominion, the peasantry, which comprised some 70 percent of the total population, were largely indifferent; they could not distinguish between rulers and exploiters, whether republican or Medicean. For the residents in the subject towns, who were governed by officials sent from Florence, the words "liberty" and "freedom," so often articulated in council deliberations, had little meaning.[26]

The demise of the republic at the hands of Medici rule did not signal a revolutionary change in the lives of the Florentine populace. It brought no abatement to the plagues, famines, and marauding armies that afflicted every urban community in Italy at the time. Nonetheless, the establishment of the *principato* produced a degree of political stability that the city had not experienced for decades. Medici princes continued the tradition of a strong and intrusive government. The implementation of its policy was the task of the granducal bureaucracy, the upper echelons of which were recruited from the city's elite families. To bolster their status and reinforce the principle of hierarchy, members of these lineages also received titles of nobility when they enrolled in the exclusive knightly order of S. Stefano. The Medici also utilized the city's traditional rites and ceremonies, both secular and religious, to enhance their reputation and curry favor with the populace.[27]

The Medici grand dukes gradually eradicated all traces of the *vivere popolare* and civil society. Although Cosimo I once asserted that he was bound "by the laws, the order and the magistrates of our city," in reality he was the sole fount of power. "Our advice is our will," he once wrote to a councillor, "and we consider as adversaries all those who oppose it." The historian Varchi told his readers not to marvel "that [he spoke] only of Cosimo, and never of the state or magistracies, since . . . Cosimo alone govern[ed] everything, and nothing [was] said or done, however great or small, concerning which he [did not say] either 'yes' or 'no.'" Early in his rule, Cosimo had published a decree that prohibited "any kind of assembly, congregation or conventicle," since such gatherings were viewed as potential sources of dissent and conspiracy.[28]

Under the Medici grand dukes, guilds lost their autonomy and became state agencies for the regulation of commerce, industry, the retail trades, and the crafts. The confraternities were also radically transformed: "In contrast to traditional confraternities of republican Florence, sixteenth-century confraternities reveal major departures in ideology, ritual and social organization, introducing principles of hierarchy into confraternal membership, localizing new confraternities in parishes, bringing city-wide confraternities under the control of the duke, stressing a new ethic of obedience, and replacing older rituals that emphasized community, equality and the suspension of social differentiation and hierarchy with ritual celebrations of status, honor and rank." For example, when a group of Florentine intellectuals spontaneously formed a cultural society in the early 1540s, Cosimo first disbanded and then reconstituted the association as the Academia Florentina, its membership and its constitution strictly controlled by the prince.[29]

The establishment of the Medici *principato* brought Florence and its territory into the larger Italian world dominated by autocratic rulers and landed nobles, in which, as Machiavelli asserted, "no republics nor any *vivere politico* had ever existed, since those men are totally hostile to civic life." Members of Florence's leading families adapted easily to this milieu, changing their mode of dress to conform to courtly fashion and intermarrying with noble lineages from other Italian provinces. Some acquired fiefs in Tuscany and elsewhere; those with military training found employment in the armies of Italian and foreign princes. The church provided career opportunities for the younger sons of these families, and convents became a convenient depository for their unmarried sisters.[30]

The Medici recruited substantial numbers of aristocrats into their bureaucracy; the economic benefits of state service were an important source of revenue for these noble houses. The *ottomati*, whose ancestors had once proudly governed their free city and its territory, had become loyal subjects and servants of their prince, competing with their rivals for his favor and largesse.[31]

Certain distinctive features of post-invasion Italy were inherited from city-state republics. The concept of individual rights and liberties, and of a private realm immune from state intervention, had never been a part of the communal legacy. Nor did it emerge, either in theory or practice, during this age of autocratic government. The impulse toward scrutiny, surveillance, and control was no less present in republican than in despotic regimes, or, for that matter, than in the feudal governments of Piedmont and Sicily. This intrusive and invasive mentality was manifest in the flood of legislation emanating from these governments, and in the publication of edicts *(bandi)*, the repetition of which testified to their limited efficacy.[32]

The responsibility for enforcing this thicket of legislation was entrusted to a large, expensive, and burdensome bureaucracy, which was trained to execute the ruler's will and to regard his subjects with suspicion and condescension. For example, to implement Cosimo I's prohibition against the export of grain from the duchy, the Medici government employed a veritable army of "functionaries, agents, rectors, notaries, police officials, spies and informers." These officials inspected all goods in transit at the borders; they examined the account books and the storage facilities of grain merchants; and they invaded the cottages of villagers and peasants to search for hidden food supplies. Their methods were as arbitrary and ruthless as those of the tax officials who collected the gabelles and the levies that subsidized the regime's administrative and military structures.[33]

These tactics, employed by every regime from Sicily to Piedmont to enforce obedience and raise revenue, created a pernicious legacy for the future—a pervasive and deeply rooted distrust of, and hostility toward, the state, its institutions, its operations, and its personnel. Subjects did not perceive the state as a protector and defender but as an exploiter and predator. It is as true today as it was in the seventeenth and eighteenth centuries that "by and large, the state bureaucracy has oppressed rather than served the Italian citizen . . . Far from exercising over time a pedagogic role in Italian society, the state has rather itself been shaped by those patron-client and kinship relations which are so deeply rooted in Mediterranean culture." From the highest to the lowest level of the bureaucracy, officials were commonly viewed as arrogant, inefficient, and corrupt.[34]

An Austrian diplomat in the 1730s sent this report on the Tuscan bureaucracy back to his master in Vienna: "Theft is everywhere in the military and civil administration, in the finances; there is no tribunal, no receivership where the prince is not deceived and the people oppressed . . . [The officials] all *eat*, to use the local term, they eat off everything, off the vilest things, off the most miserable people." Since the state was not a reliable source of protection and justice, the majority of Italians instead depended upon kinship ties and the support of powerful patrons. As Gerard Delille has noted, the truly poor in early modern society "are not those who have nothing whatsoever, but those who are outside any network of solidarity."[35]

The post-Tridentine Catholic church supported the efforts of secular rulers to discipline and control their recalcitrant subjects. The church's ideology was, in most respects, identical to that of Italy's princes, and it defended the principle of hierarchical organization, which it exemplified, as it applied to Italy's "society of orders." While insisting upon its own autonomy, and its immunity from secular control, the church advocated the doctrine of submission to both lay and ecclesiastical authority, developing strategies to instruct the laity in doctrinal matters and to persuade laymen to perform their Christian obligations.[36]

Priests were required to keep records of their parishioners' vital statistics (births, marriages, and deaths) and to threaten those who violated the church's rules with excommunication. More effectively than in the past, the parish clergy established tighter controls over marriage, sexual behavior, and social life and brought the confraternities under their surveillance. The clergy also tried to weaken kinship ties in their communities, but with only limited success.[37]

Behind all of these strategies were the revitalized coercive powers of the Roman church: excommunication, the Index, and the Inquisition. The Medici grand dukes were more receptive to the operation of these mechanisms than were most other Italian rulers. Civic life in the Tuscan duchy was vitiated by Cosimo's subservience to the Roman papacy: "The persecutions of the Inquisition . . . against any citizen suspected of heresy, the vigilance of the clergy in scrutinizing the behavior and thoughts of Tuscans . . . created a climate of heavy, bigoted conformism."[38]

The most potent and influential legacy received by postrevolutionary Italy was not a civic tradition inherited from the communal era but the structures and patterns developed during the "age of absolutism"—authoritarian government, both secular and religious, and a hierarchical social order in which patron-client networks flourished, in both the north and the south. Only a few urban communities—Venice, Genoa, Lucca, and San Marino—retained some degree of political autonomy. The primary objective of urban elites in those cities was the preservation of their privileged status. In towns governed by princes or viceroys, elites (both secular and ecclesiastical) were able to minimize their tax burdens and maintain their property and influence in the countryside.[39]

No associations of any kind could be established without the approval of secular and religious authorities. Unlike the European states across the Alps, those in Italy effectively stifled religious dissent in their territories, with the sole exception of the Waldensian community in Piedmont. The absence of any serious challenge to religious orthodoxy was, and long remained, a significant deterrent to the revival of civic values and traditions. The popularity of Italy's most celebrated novel— Alessandro Manzoni's *I promessi sposi* (Milan, 1827)—was due primarily to the familiarity of nineteenth- and even twentieth-century Italians with its depiction of seventeenth-century Lombardy as overwhelmingly "feudal," with its lawless and arrogant nobles and their *bravi* (hired thugs), its dependent and deferential lower orders, its autocratic but fundamentally weak government, and its religious culture of submission and obedience.[40]

※ ※ ※

If the definition of "civil society" includes as a central feature "a complex tissue of voluntary associations which occupy a public space and have a public voice," then it is difficult to find evidence for this phenomenon in prerevolutionary Italy. The academies and fledgling masonic lodges that were formed in the eighteenth century did not have a political agenda, nor any significant influence on princes and their administrators. Italy's elites were united only in their determination to preserve their traditional privileges.[41]

Not until the revolutionary era, which witnessed the radical overhaul of Italy's political and socioeconomic structures, were conditions ripe for the first tentative efforts to establish a civil society. This process was painfully slow and halting in a country whose citizens viewed the state as "a hostile presence . . . not merely in terms of the identification of the state with the landowner, the tax-collector, and the *carabiniere*, but because of the paucity of intermediary strata attached to the values of the state." Even though the associations established before and after unification helped to contribute to this fledgling form of civil society, the assumption of "any simple correlation among voluntary associations, civil society and liberal democracy" is hardly warranted. As Mary Nolan recently suggested, scholars "should pay less attention to quantifying civil society and more to understanding the qualitatively different meanings of associational life in different contexts. Societies can be, and since the nineteenth century have been, bourgeois without necessarily being liberal."[42]

CHAPTER THREE

From *Campanilismo* to Nationhood

Forging an Italian Identity

"Nations are strange, capricious historical formations. Out of the myriads of tribes and peoples mentioned in chronicles, only a few have survived into the modern world, with its urban culture, its mass education and its diversified social structure. Most have fallen victims to larger or more determined peoples, and seen their languages wither, their costumes reduced to museum exhibits, their folklore cherished only by antiquarians and ethnographers."[1] This quotation, from a recent review of a book on European nationalism, stresses the problematic nature of this process, which involved as many failures as successes, and which was in no sense inevitable or preordained. Italy's route to nationhood was as tortured and as vicissitudinous as that of any European state. Her experience throws light on the massive obstacles that impeded the formation of a national identity, and on the vagaries of the historical path by which it was ultimately achieved.

My account of this complex tale begins, somewhat arbitrarily, in the year 1494, when a French army crossed the Alps and inaugurated a new era in Italian history: the peninsula's domination by foreign powers. Twenty years after that invasion, an obscure Florentine named Niccolò Machiavelli wrote *The Prince*, one of the most influential works of political theory in the history of the West. In the final chapter of *The Prince*,

Machiavelli made his impassioned appeal for Italians to unite under the leadership of a Medici prince, to expel the barbarians from their home-land. After two decades of foreign occupation, he wrote, "Italy remains without life and awaits the man who can heal her wounds and put an end to the plundering . . . and who can cure her of those sores which have been festering for so long. Look how she prays to God to send someone to redeem her from these barbaric cruelties." Italians were eager, Machi-avelli insisted, to join in a crusade of liberation; all that was required was a forceful and determined leader to galvanize their energies: "I cannot express with what love he will be received in those provinces that have suffered through these foreign floods; with what thirst for revenge, with what obstinate loyalty, with what compassion, with what tears! What doors will be closed to him? Which people will deny him obedience? What jealousy could oppose him? What Italian would deny him hom-age? This barbarian domination stinks in the nostrils of us all!"[2]

Only a handful of Machiavelli's friends read his appeal in manuscript at the time that it was written. *The Prince* was not published until 1532, seven years after Machiavelli's death. By that time, the yoke of foreign domination, that of Spain, was firmly established in the peninsula, and Machiavelli's argument would have seemed utopian and unrealistic to contemporaries. Scholars have not been able to agree on the meaning and significance of Machiavelli's "exhortation to liberate Italy from the barbarians." Some have argued that this chapter of *The Prince* reflected his true sentiments, and that he was an early and eloquent exponent of the idea of a united Italy. This view was widespread among nineteenth-century Italians who supported the Risorgimento. Others, however, have questioned the authenticity of Machiavelli's appeal, noting the striking difference between the idealism of that final chapter and the cold and realistic analysis of contemporary politics that pervades the rest of the work. The idea of Italy as a distinctive community set apart from and superior to the rest of Europe by virtue of its Roman inheritance and its revival of classical culture was a common theme in fifteenth-century humanist writing. But no one before Machiavelli had suggested that the concept of an Italian nation should be the basis of a concrete program of political action, a movement of liberation.[3]

Those sixteenth-century Italians who, like Machiavelli, could dream of a united Italy, strong enough to defend itself against foreign aggression, did have some concrete foundations for their vision. They could look back to their Roman past, and to the military valor and political will of those ancient ancestors who had created, first, a unified Italian state and then a vast empire centered on the Mediterranean Sea. They could emphasize the role of the Latin language and of the Roman Catholic church as two fundamental sources of their culture and of Western Christendom. They could also point to the gradual emergence of the Italian vernacular, and specifically its Tuscan variety, as forming a cultural matrix that bound together the various regions of the peninsula. Roman law was another cohesive element; its theoretical principles and its methods governed relations in both the secular and ecclesiastical spheres. By contrast to transalpine Europe, still largely rural and "feudal" in its political, social, and economic structures, Italy (or, more accurately, its northern and central regions) was dominated by its cities and by urban life.

But counterbalancing these elements of cohesiveness were even stronger forces that promoted division and fragmentation.[4] The peninsula's geography, and particularly the rough terrain of the Apennine mountains, made land communication difficult and fostered regional differences. But the most powerful force contributing to Italian disunity was its own history. Not since the collapse of the Roman Empire in the West had the peninsula been unified under one political authority. For a thousand years, Italy had been divided among a cluster of states of varying size, strength, and durability. The major powers competing for control of the peninsula in the medieval centuries were the German emperors, the heirs of Charlemagne; the Roman papacy; and the dynasties that governed the southern regions: Naples and Sicily. For nearly three centuries, German emperors and Roman popes fought each other for control of the peninsula. With their allies, the north Italian communes, the popes did manage to thwart the imperial challenge. These urban polities, formed in the political vacuum created by imperial weakness, became the dominant form of government in northern Italy from the late eleventh to the fourteenth century. These communes were the political expression of their urban populations: dynamic, vibrant, aggressive. Their internal histories were filled with conflict, between rival families, factions, and ideologies. Their institutional structures were in constant flux, changing according to shifting economic and social pressures. But despite this history of incessant conflict and turmoil, these communes did foster powerful sentiments of loyalty to the native city. That spirit of *campanilismo* was expressed most eloquently by Dante in a statement which the poet attributed to a Sienese noblewoman, Pia de' Tolomei: "Siena mi fe" (Siena made me). In another passage of the *Divine Comedy*, Dante visualizes an encounter between his companion, the Roman poet Vergil, a native of the town of Mantua in northern Italy, and the musician Sordello, his contemporary. "O Mantovano," Sordello cries; "O Mantovano, io son Sordello della tua terra. E l'un l'altro abbracciava" (O Mantuan, I am Sordello, from your city. And the two embraced each other).[5]

These intense feelings of identification with the town of one's origin were universal in those regions of Italy where communes flourished. They were as powerful as the bonds of blood and lineage, and of religion. They are reflected in the urban chronicles and in communal legislation, which describe the glorious achievements of these towns, and the determination of their inhabitants to be greater than any of their rivals. They are echoed, too, in the writings of exiles like Dante whose yearning to return to their beloved homeland was counterbalanced by their anger over their perceived maltreatment at the hands of their enemies. The willingness of the citizenry to spend large sums of their money on civic monuments—like Siena's *palazzo communale* and Florence's cathedral—was yet another testimonial to their patriotism. Citizens paid taxes to subsidize the wars which these towns were constantly waging against their enemies, and they also participated personally in these conflicts. And when, as happened frequently in the fourteenth and fifteenth centuries, their towns were conquered and occupied by their larger and more powerful neighbors, they did not cease to dream of the time when they would regain their liberty. Pisa was conquered by Florence in 1406, but ninety years later, seizing the opportunity provided by the French invasion, the Pisans rebelled and fought a valiant but ultimately unsuccessful war against their Florentine overlords. The reconquest of Pisa in 1509 was, incidentally, the high point of Machiavelli's career as an official of the Florentine republic.

Machiavelli's efforts to create a native army that (he hoped) might someday replace Florence's reliance upon mercenary troops did reveal some major problems in forging a polity larger than the city-state. The republican regime established in 1494 after the expulsion of the Medici was one of the most "popular" governments in Florentine history, with membership in the Great Council exceeding three thousand. But several thousand Florentines—artisans and laborers—were still excluded from the government, as were tens of thousands more who lived in the Florentine dominion. These disenfranchised groups did not feel such strong allegiance to the republic as did those citizens wielding power and influence. Florentine statesmen were acutely aware of the limited and tenuous nature of that love of *patria* which (so they had been taught) was so important in the history of the Roman republic. The legislation creating the Florentine militia stipulated that the soldiers would not be recruited from within the city, nor from the towns in the dominion. To put arms in the hands of cloth workers or residents of Prato or Pistoia would risk rebellion. Among the difficulties facing Machiavelli in his efforts to organize and train this militia was a refusal of residents of the village of Campana (near Pontasieve, east of Florence) to serve alongside the men of the neighboring village of Petrognano, whom they detested.[6]

The Tuscan peasants who responded so grudgingly to Machiavelli's efforts to transform them into loyal and disciplined soldiers willing to fight (if not die) for Florence can be taken as an example of that 80 percent of the peninsula's population that lived precariously from its labors on the land. The vast majority of these *contadini* lived in conditions of extreme poverty and insecurity, exploited by their landlords, money-lenders, and the state. They received little protection or help from the institutional structures (rural communes, parishes) to which they belonged. Their identification with and allegiance to those structures of authority were tepid in the best of times, and in periods of crisis, they tended to dissolve. The Italian peasantry played an essentially passive role in the wars spawned by the invasions. As always, they bore the brunt of the ravages by armies foreign and domestic; as always, their primary goal was survival. Just prior to the French invasion of 1494, Lombard peasants who were subjects of the duke of Milan refused to pay their taxes, asserting that "the king of France is coming and he will exempt us from all levies."[7] They were prepared to give their allegiance to any prince, foreign or domestic, who would lighten their burdens and provide some measure of security.

In their reaction to the crisis of the invasions, the rulers of Italian states were no more responsive to any consideration of "national" interest than were the peasants whom they governed and exploited. Concerned primarily with preserving their power, they regularly formed alliances or agreements with foreign powers, including the Turks, to achieve their particular objectives. Lodovico Sforza, the ruler of Milan, began this strategy when he first invited the French king, Charles VIII, to cross the Alps and occupy the territory of his enemy, the king of Naples. That invasion did, momentarily, shock the Italian political establishment into taking united action. In 1495, an alliance was forged by Milan, Venice, the papacy, and the Neapolitan king to oppose the French, and a major battle was fought between the retreating French army and the Italian forces at Fornovo in Lombardy. Though inconclusive, that military confrontation demonstrated that Italians could defend themselves against foreign invaders if they were united. But that coalition soon dissolved, and Italian states reverted to their earlier strategy of using foreign powers to promote their interests. The Florentine republic had steadfastly refused to join the Italian League, preferring instead to maintain their alliance with the French monarch, who had promised to help them recover Pisa. Niccolò Machiavelli was a member of the Florentine mission to France in the summer of 1500, urging the French king, Louis XII, to cross the Alps to conquer the Milanese state and to provide reinforcements for the Florentine effort to recover Pisa.

The great Florentine historian Francesco Guicciardini wrote the most coherent account of the foreign invasions, and of the primary responsibility of the rulers of Italian states for the calamities visited upon the inhabitants of the peninsula: "the cruelest accidents, endless murders, sackings and destruction of many cities and towns, military licentiousness . . . religion violated and holy things trampled underfoot."[8] He condemned those princes for their ambition and greed, for their lack of vision and their failures of leadership. Italy had become the battleground of European powers: the French, the Swiss, the Spaniards, the Germans. Of the major Italian states, only two—Venice and the papacy—were successful in maintaining some degree of autonomy and independence. The Venetian republic survived the attack (1509) of a major coalition of powers, Italian and foreign, organized by Pope Julius II. They were able to regain most of their lost territory on the *terrafirma*, and a substantial part of their maritime empire. Contributing to their preservation as an independent state were the civic spirit of their inhabitants, both nobles and commoners, their diplomatic success in dividing their opponents, and their perceived role as bulwark against the Turkish threat. The ability of the Roman papacy to preserve a territorial base in central Italy was a more significant development, with momentous consequences for the future of the peninsula.

Renaissance popes had long played an active role in Italian politics, forging alliances and participating in military enterprises. Their goals were remarkably consistent: to exercise effective control over papal territory and to resist any effort by other Italian states to dominate the peninsula. The foreign invasions widened the scope of papal diplomacy, without altering these objectives. The Borgia pope, Alexander VI, negotiated an agreement with King Louis XII of France to obtain that monarch's support for his son Cesare's efforts to build a territorial base in central Italy. Pope Julius II was a dynamic and aggressive prince, determined to impose his rule on the Papal States and to expel the "barbarians" from Italy. Both Guicciardini and his friend Machiavelli were amazed by the success of Julius's enterprises, which seemed to defy reason and logic. Guicciardini wrote that Julius "was a prince of inestimable spirit and resolution, but impetuous and given to boundless schemes, and if these traits did not hurl him to his ruin, he was sustained more by the feeling of reverence felt toward the Church, the disagreement among princes and the condition of the times, than by moderation and prudence."[9] In Machiavelli's judgment, "Julius achieved with his impetuosity what no other pontiff would ever have achieved with the greatness of human wisdom."[10] Though he admired the dynamism of the pope's political style, which he thought worthy of emulation, his judgment on the papacy's role in Italian politics was profoundly negative. "We Italians owe this first debt to the Church and to priests," he wrote in *The Discourses*. "We have become irreligious and wicked; but we owe them an even greater debt still, which is the second reason for our ruin, that the Church has kept, and still keeps this land of ours divided." While the papacy was never strong enough to dominate Italy, it was able to prevent its control by any other power; "and from this has come so much disunity and so much weakness that she has continued to be at the mercy . . . of anyone who might attack her."[11]

By the time Guicciardini wrote the last books of his *History of Italy* in the late 1530s, he had become reconciled to the reality of the peninsula's domination by the Spanish monarchy, which directly governed the duchy of Milan and the kingdom of Naples and exercised its hegemony over a cluster of satellite states: the Medici Grand Duchy of Tuscany, Mantua, Ferrara, Genoa, Montferrat. After the treaty of Cateau-Cambrésis (1559), the French monarchy, weakened by internal divisions, ceased to challenge Spain's preeminent role in the peninsula. So for two centuries, Italians lived in a world controlled by Spanish arms and by the counter-Reformation papacy. They learned the bitter lesson that they no longer controlled their destiny; their fate and fortunes were decided in foreign capitals: in Madrid, Paris, Vienna. The wars that periodically ravaged parts of the peninsula were not launched by Italian princes, who did not dare to challenge Spain, but by foreign powers. The Venetian republic and the Papal States did survive as quasi-independent governments, but the other Italian principalities were simply pawns in the European power struggles: their boundaries, their dynasties, their existence dependent upon outside forces. The instability of these states inhibited the development of regional loyalties to their princes. The great majority of Italians continued to bestow their primary loyalties on their native city, town, or village.

Italian cultural life continued to exhibit vitality in certain areas (the arts, music, natural science), but the European hegemony enjoyed by her humanists and her artists during the Renaissance gradually waned. The repressive atmosphere of censorship and control imposed by secular and religious authorities inhibited the free exploration and expression of ideas that were deemed subversive or heretical. Italian historiography in these centuries reflects the cultural milieu quite accurately. No historian of Guicciardini's skill or vision can be found among the hundreds, indeed thousands, of pedantic antiquarians who wrote laudatory accounts of their city's past, or (in the case of some clerical writers) treatises justifying papal authority.[12] In this repressive and sterile climate, the notion of a free and independent Italy found little soil for nourishment. The landed nobility, urban elites, and the upper ranges of the ecclesiastical hierarchy concentrated their energies on preserving their privileges. Their perspective was intensely parochial, focused upon their rural estates, their place in the court or in the local bureaucracy. They accepted so completely the status quo, from which they derived significant benefits, that they did not consider the possibility of transforming the political or social order, and certainly not any notion of a free and independent Italy. Indeed, the idea of Italy as a cultural unity found little resonance in this profoundly conservative society. Some progress was made in the development of a common literary language, based on the Tuscan dialect, notably the publication in the early seventeenth century of an Italian dictionary by the Accademia della Crusca. But this highly formalized Italian language was spoken and understood only by a small minority of the country's elite. The vast majority of the inhabitants of the peninsula and the islands spoke either their local dialect or a foreign language: French in Piedmont, Spanish in Naples and Sicily, and German in the Adige region.[13]

In the last years of the seventeenth century, Italy had reached the lowest point in a downward trajectory that had begun in 1494. Reports from foreign visitors were filled with descriptions of the miserable living conditions of the peasantry in every region of the peninsula. In a Europe whose rural population was nowhere prosperous, the extreme destitution of the Italian peasantry was striking to northern visitors. Living conditions in the cities were somewhat better, though observers commented on the large number of beggars and on the decline in the commercial and industrial activities that had sustained these communities during the Renaissance.[14] Foreign scholars like the poet Milton and the distinguished medievalist Mabillon were eagerly welcomed by members of the learned societies that had been established in the major cities and by officials of the Roman curia. Their letters and reports described the low level of intellectual activity in these societies and the widespread ignorance of the works of transalpine philosophers and scholars: Descartes, Leibnitz, Newton. They tended to attribute the decline in the quality and productivity of Italian intellectual activity to the repressive atmosphere of the Roman Inquisition and the Index. If occasionally they commented on what they perceived to be flaws in the Italian character, their remarks were not as negative and condemnatory as those of Italians themselves. Serving in Spain as an official of the Bourbon monarch Phillip V, Cardinal Alberoni wrote (1717): "The king, my master, cannot rely at all on the Italians, who have become so debased by their indolence and cowardice . . . so miserable and slothful is that nation that it deserves to be treated as slaves."[15]

How Italy (or some groups in Italian society) emerged from this torpor is a complex story with many threads and dimensions. Among the peninsula's educated classes, there gradually developed a sense of dissatisfaction with their inferior condition, by comparison with the rest of Europe. The revived interest in Italy's medieval and Renaissance past was promoted by Lodovico Muratori, who published a massive collection of historical sources, the *Rerum Italicarum Scriptores*, which reminded Italians of the glorious achievements of their ancestors. Rather than lamenting Italy's decline and blaming her sorry condition on the nefarious influence of the Spaniards and the papacy, a small but growing number of intellectuals began to think about the possibilities of change.[16] The problems and difficulties facing these early reformers were truly formidable. They included an economy based largely on subsistence agriculture with very little commercial or industrial activity; a rigid and hierarchic social structure dominated by deeply entrenched privileged groups; an authoritarian but inefficient political order based on a cluster of small, weak states whose ruling elites were exclusively concerned with preserving their power and privileges. The Roman papacy was perhaps the most formidable obstacle to any reform movement in early modern Italy. The territories under their control, stretching from the Adriatic to the Tyrrhenian Sea, were demonstrably the worst governed regions in the peninsula. And from Rome, the popes directed the repressive institutions of the Inquisition and the Index, which effectively censored all intellectual activity. Through their control over the ecclesiastical hierarchy, they exercised a powerful influence over such matters as education, mores, and social behavior.[17]

Acutely aware of the massive obstacles confronting them, the Italian reformers opted for a strategy of cautious and incremental reform. Like their counterparts elsewhere in Europe, they believed that change could only come through the existing political system. They concentrated their efforts on winning converts to their cause among princes and their bureaucrats. They concentrated their efforts on making their governments more efficient, and on limiting the privileges of the nobility and the clergy. The church's wealth and privileges were major targets of the reformers, who sought to expropriate some ecclesiastical property and to eliminate the church's tax exemptions. The reformers also attacked the Inquisition's repressive control over intellectual life and the Jesuit order for its support of papal authority and its dominant role in education. In those states where reform movements were most successful, the church's authority and privileges were significantly reduced. But the Italian nobility was a tougher adversary, and this privileged group was generally successful in protecting its interests. The labors of the reformers did achieve some positive results, most notably in Lombardy and Tuscany, in improving regional economies and in developing more efficient administrative structures. But their achievements seem quite paltry in the context of the massive problems confronting Italian society in the eighteenth century. And none of these reformers developed a national vision or perspective; there was (one historian has written) "a total acceptance of the political fragmentation of Italy."[18]

The French Revolution was a decisive event in the formation of an Italian national consciousness. A large majority of Italian elites were naturally frightened by the specter of a revolutionary movement fueled by national sentiment, and the ideals of *"liberté, egalité, fraternité."* They were shocked by the demolition of the ancien régime, by the dethronement and execution of the king, and by the excesses of the Terror. But they were no more capable than their French counterparts of controlling the revolutionary movement; their role in the tumultuous events of these years was essentially passive. Italy's history after 1796 was dominated by invading French armies and their generals and, after 1799, by Napoleon's efforts to create and sustain a continental empire. The political map of Italy was continually restructured to satisfy French imperial interests, just as her resources were exploited to support French armies.

In this Italian society (or, more accurately, in this cluster of parochial societies), which was largely hostile or indifferent to the French Revolution, there was a small but active minority promoting the ideals and goals of the revolution. Its members included intellectuals—writers, journalists, professors, jurists—and a sprinkling of nobles, merchants, and clerics, many of whom had been influenced by the Enlightenment. These men called themselves "patriots," but their enemies labeled them Jacobins and denounced them as dangerous radicals whose goals were the destruction of order, property, and religion. They did favor the policies advocated by the French Jacobins in the 1790s, and specifically, the creation of a unified Italian republic. But they were never strong enough to exert any significant influence in the French satellite states established in the late 1790s. After Napoleon came to power in 1799, they were marginalized by an emperor who based his Italian policy on the support of the conservative propertied classes and on a politically fragmented peninsula. Excluded from power and influence, many patriots joined secret societies and engaged in clandestine activity against these puppet regimes. They succeeded in keeping alive the dream of a united republican Italy that would restore their nation to its proper place in Europe.

The difficulties confronting these "patriots" as they sought to promote their vision of a united Italy were truly formidable. The privileged classes from which they came were largely hostile to their political objectives, fearing the loss of their status and privileges. Business and professional groups, which had strongly supported revolutionary groups in France and her transalpine neighbors, were small in numbers and tepid in their commitment to a united Italy. While some expressed "a preference for a different order of affairs, extremely vaguely conceived," they were unable to understand (in the views of one observer) "what is a nation, what is the price for independence."[19] Recruits for the national cause were found among the youth of Italian cities, but as one French official noted, they were a volatile and unstable force. "One must be extremely mistrustful of the petulance and dash of the youth of Italy, excited and carried away by the ideas borrowed from our revolution, who want to stir things up, without any clear and balanced ideas about what sort of thing they want to set up."[20] In spite of their vision of a united Italy, their programs and strategies were frequently weakened by parochial interests, by *campanilismo*. One quality lacking in these young nationalists was discipline, which in other European societies (but not in

Italy except for Piedmont) had been provided by military training and service. A young soldier in the Napoleonic army wrote in 1804: "I believe that military training must be the main aim of every good Italian . . . The principal task must be to learn warfare, which is the sole profession that can make us free. We are still too young to think of liberty. Let us think of being soldiers, and when we have a hundred thousand bayonets, then we can talk."[21]

With the defeat and exile of Napoleon after Waterloo (1815), the French control of Italy was replaced by that of Austria, whose leader, Metternich, was committed to the destruction of the revolutionary legacy and the restoration of the old European order. At the Congress of Vienna, Italy was divided into fragments roughly comparable to its political geography before the revolution. Lombardy and Venetia were incorporated into the Austrian empire; the Papal States were restored to Rome, and prerevolutionary dynasties were again established in Tuscany and the Neapolitan kingdom. The key concepts that governed this restoration were "absolutism" and "legitimacy." Stendhal neatly captured the spirit of this reactionary age in his novel *The Charterhouse of Parma*. The hero, Fabrizio, is suspected of being sympathetic to the ideals of the French Revolution. To exonerate himself, he "went to mass every day; he chose as his confessor a man devoted to the monarchy . . . He was not to consort with anyone who had the reputation of being clever, and when occasion offered, he was to speak of rebellion with horror; he was never to be seen in a cafe . . . He was to express dislike of reading in general, and he was never to peruse any works printed later than 1720 . . . and lastly, he must not fail to pay open court to some pretty woman in the district, which would prove that he had none of the gloomy and discontented spirit of the conspirator. For the rest he must be simple—no wit, no brilliancy, no swift repartee."[22]

These efforts by Metternich and his conservative allies to dismantle the revolutionary legacy were doomed to failure, though they did manage to keep Italy divided and malgoverned for several decades. But the revolutionary ideals of freedom and equality, and the nationalist impulse, could not be expunged from the minds and hearts of a growing number of Italians. These patriots joined secret societies dedicated to the goal of a free and united Italy; some participated in conspiracies and uprisings that broke out sporadically in Naples and Sicily in 1820, in Piedmont in 1821, in central Italy in 1831, in Genoa in 1834. These rebellions were fueled not only by the ideology of the French Revolution, but also by deteriorating economic and social conditions, a consequence of transformations in the European economy. But none of these rebellions were able to attract widespread support beyond their place of origin, or in large segments of the society. They were suppressed by the military and police forces of the Austrian government and the satellite regimes.

Among the welter of programs formulated in these post-Napoleonic years to achieve national unity, two basic patterns can be identified. Giuseppe Mazzini was the primary architect of the more radical plan for unification. He believed that Italians must achieve their independence through their own efforts, without any foreign assistance. They could not rely upon French support and guidance; they had to liberate themselves. Freedom and unification were to be won through revolutionary activity, by means of organized uprisings that would spread through the length and breadth of the peninsula. To implement his program, Mazzini forged a network of clandestine supporters in major Italian cities, encouraging them to prepare for the moment when the old order would collapse in the struggle for national liberation. He was a staunch republican, but unlike many of his colleagues, he did develop a social agenda. For Mazzini, political goals were paramount, and he deplored class conflict as impeding the movement toward a free and independent Italy. The revolution that he envisaged was to be organized and led by a cadre of young, idealistic patriots recruited from the elite. He saw no active role for Italy's poverty-stricken, illiterate peasantry, which comprised 80 percent of the peninsula's population.[23] The methods advocated by Mazzini and his supporters—revolutionary action as the catalyst for unification—were discredited after a series of unsuccessful rebellions.

The political program of the "moderates" was more pragmatic and less sharply focused than that of the Mazzini republicans. Eschewing violence, they placed their faith in gradual change, promoting parliamentary government and education as basic prerequisites for a free and united Italy. Some moderates, particularly in Piedmont, were monarchists, and looked to the Savoy dynasty as the potential savior of Italy. Elsewhere in the peninsula, voices were raised in support of a federal alliance of regional states. Vincenzo Gioberti advocated such a coalition under the titular leadership of the Roman papacy. Carlo Cattaneo, who has been described as "the most serious, penetrating and versatile intellectual of the Risorgimento,"[24] was a strong supporter of a federation of regional and republican governments, which he considered more realistic and viable than Mazzini's vision of a unified and centralized Italy.

The year 1848 was a significant milestone in the historical process that culminated in the creation of an Italian nation-state. The uprising in Sicily in January 1848 was the first major upheaval in that year of European revolutions; the virus of rebellion then spread to Naples, to Rome and the Papal States, to Tuscany, to Lombardy and Venetia. Not until the spring of 1849 were the last embers of rebellion finally smothered in Venice and Rome. The scope and intensity of these revolts revealed the degree of penetration of nationalist propaganda, not only among urban elites but also among craftsmen and laborers in the cities. Italian patriots fought and died in the streets of rebellious towns and in battles against Austrian armies. The nationalist movement now had its heroes, like Garibaldi and Daniele Manin, and also its martyrs. But these events also revealed the deep fissures in Italian society: the strength of parochial sentiment and of class antagonisms. Divisions between cautious and pragmatic "moderates" and radicals who promoted violence weakened the revolutionary movements everywhere in the peninsula and contributed to their eventual repression. The specter of social revolution frightened many of the moderates who (as in Milan) stayed home in their palaces instead of participating in the formation of provisional governments. The rift between the nationalist movement and the

Roman papacy widened during these revolutionary months. Pope Pius IX was forced to flee Rome (November 1848) and when he returned, bolstered by a French military force, he became a tenacious opponent of the supporters of unification and of liberalism. The Italian peasantry was generally indifferent to the idea of national unity. Their participation in the 1848 uprisings was limited; it was focused upon local targets of their anger (landlords, tax collectors, police) and fueled by local enmities and vendettas.[25]

After the failure of the 1848 revolutions, the initiative of the nationalist movement shifted decisively from the republicans, led by Mazzini, to the moderates, led by Cavour. Mazzini's contributions to the nationalist cause were significant; he continued to propagandize his view effectively through his publications and his network of clandestine societies. Cavour, as prime minister of the Piedmontese monarchy, developed a strategy that eventually led to unification. By establishing the foundations for parliamentary government in Piedmont, he created a political system that appealed to liberal sentiment throughout the peninsula. He also promoted social and economic reforms that made Piedmont the most prosperous region in Italy. Cavour's political model was the English monarchy; he had no sympathy for Mazzini's republicanism. He believed that Italy could best achieve her independence under the leadership of the Savoy monarchy. Nor did he share Mazzini's conviction that Italians could achieve their liberation without outside support. Napoleon III was Cavour's chosen agent to force Austria out of Italy. In 1859, he conspired with the French ruler to provoke the Austrian government into a war, which led to the liberation of Lombardy (but not Venetia) and its incorporation into the Piedmontese state.

The events of 1859 were the result of shrewd calculation and planning, whereas those of 1860, the decisive moment of Italian unification, were wholly unforeseen and unpredictable. From his base in Turin, Cavour could only watch the unfolding scenario, unable to control or influence events. The "wild card" was Giuseppe Garibaldi, whose invasion of Sicily with his army of one thousand volunteers led to the collapse of the Bourbon monarchy. Cavour was able to regain the initiative from Garibaldi by sending Piedmontese troops to occupy the Papal States (except Rome, protected by its French garrison). He then organized plebescites in Sicily and on the mainland, all of whom supported the incorporation of these territories into the Piedmontese monarchy. Symbolizing the triumph of unification was the famous meeting (October 1860) between Garibaldi and King Vittorio Emmanuele. The final chapters in this history of Italian unification occurred during the next decade when the Italian government, taking advantage of the military defeats of Austria by Prussia in 1866, and of France by Prussia in 1871, occupied the province of Venetia and the city of Rome.

So the unification of Italy was finally achieved, but the price was heavy and the costs were to weigh upon this fledgling state and its inhabitants for many decades. At that historic moment when Garibaldi and King Vittorio Emmanuele met and embraced, peasant revolts against the new regime were breaking out everywhere in the old Bourbon kingdom of the two Sicilies. The monarchy was able to suppress these uprisings, but its policy of repression alienated not only the peasantry but also the elites. The chasm between the Piedmontese and the Sicilians was dramatically illustrated by Giuseppe di Lampedusa in his novel *The Leopard.* The hero of the novel, the Sicilian prince Don Fabrizio Salina, was being courted by a young Piedmontese official, Chevalley, who offered the prince a post as senator in the new, unified monarchy. "You will represent Sicily . . . You will make us hear the voice of this lovely country which is only now coming into sight of the modern world." Don Fabrizio refuses the offer, explaining to Chevalley that "since your Garibaldi set foot at Marsala, too many things have been done without our being consulted for you to be able now to ask a member of the old governing class to help develop things and carry them through . . . In Sicily, it doesn't matter whether things are done well or done badly; the sin which we Sicilians never forgive is simply that of 'doing' at all . . . Sleep, my dear Chevalley, sleep, that is what Sicilians want, and they will always hate anyone who tries to wake them, even in order to bring them the most wonderful gifts, and I must say . . . that I have strong doubts whether this new kingdom will have many gifts for us in its luggage." Undiscouraged by this rejection,

Chevalley thought: "This state of things won't last; our lively new modern administration will change it all." Don Fabrizio's perspective was very different: "All this shouldn't last but it will, always . . . a century, two centuries . . . and after that it will be different but worse."[26] History has surely validated Don Fabrizio's pessimistic judgment.

This chasm between north and south remains one of the fundamental "lacerations"[27] in modern Italian history, as intractable now as it was a century ago. Another significant division within Italian society is that between city and countryside, and the centuries-old exploitation of the peasantry by the city dwellers, including absentee landlords. The policies of the Piedmontese monarchy aggravated the tensions between town and country, especially its support of the propertied classes and its system of taxation, which fell most heavily upon the rural population. Their reaction to this systematic policy of exploitation was well described by the novelist Ippolito Nievo: "The illiterate inhabitants of the countryside hate us, the literate residents of the towns . . . They do not trust us because they see us invested with the power of the *padroni*, exercising arbitrary control over their lives. They do not believe us because they have been accustomed to hear us accusing them of malice and avarice, which they know to be false and unjust. They respond with indifference to our appeals because we have for so long ignored theirs . . . That hatred, that mistrust, that division of interest has become so deeply ingrained because we have systematically maltreated them, ridiculed them and ignored them."[28] The state (wrote one knowledgeable authority) "was a hostile presence, particularly for the peasantry, not merely in terms of the identification of the state with the landowner, the tax-collector and the *carabiniere*, but because of the paucity of intermediary strata attached to the values of the state and in continuous contact with the people."[29]

Regional differences and class antagonisms were problems facing every European nation-state in the nineteenth century, even the oldest and most solidly entrenched. But the Italian monarchy was bequeathed a unique source of discord: the Roman papacy. The Risorgimento publicist Giuseppe Ferrari deplored the fact that Italians had inherited "this original curse of being born in the land of pope and emperor, of Christ and Caesar."[30] Pope Leo IX refused to recognize the legitimacy of the unified Italian state after its military forces had occupied the Papal States in 1860. When a contingent of Italian troops breached the walls at Porta Pia and occupied Rome itself in 1870, the pontiff isolated himself in the Vatican and declared that he was a prisoner of an illegitimate state. He refused to enter into diplomatic relations with the monarchy, and he warned pious Catholics against any participation in national politics. Though Pius IX's intransigent policy was modified by his successors, this breach between church and state remains a major source of conflict in contemporary Italy. The concordat negotiated in 1929 between Mussolini and Pope Pius XI did not fully resolve these tensions, which remain very much alive today.

Hindsight permits us to identify the problems that have plagued the establishment and sustenance of the Italian nation-state since its foundation. These include those historical forces that continue to impede the process of unification: *campanilismo;* class conflict, divisions between town and country; and tensions between secular and ecclesiastical structures and mentalities. Some pattern of federalism would clearly have been preferable to the highly centralized administrative structure, borrowed from Napoleonic France, that was imposed upon the country. It now seems obvious that the exclusive focus on political, diplomatic, and military issues by the architects of unification was a mistake, since this policy ignored the critical social and economic problems that seriously weakened the new state. The monarchy's inability to promote the creation of a genuine civil society is, in retrospect, its most glaring failure.[31] When, at some distant time in the future, the inhabitants of Lombardy and Sicily feel that they are brothers, that they belong to the same community, then the terminus of that long and tortuous route, first charted by Machiavelli, will have been reached.

CHAPTER FOUR

"The Horseshoe Nail"

Structure and Contingency in
Medieval and Renaissance Italy

The reference in the title of this chapter to "the horseshoe nail" is from a poem by George Herbert:

> For want of a nail the shoe is lost
> For want of a shoe the horse is lost
> For want of a horse the rider is lost
> For want of a rider the battle is lost
> For want of a battle the kingdom is lost
> And all for the loss of a horseshoe nail.[1]

This passage emphasizes the crucial importance of contingency in human history: the view that chance and accident play as important a role as does structure. Those lines were published in 1640, at a moment in British history when contingency played a decisive role in the course of events on that island. One can cite the policy decisions of King Charles I, beginning with his determination to engage in battle with his Scottish subjects, which led to the outbreak of the civil war and, ultimately, to his military defeat, to his execution, and to the eventual establishment of a parliamentary form of government. Had Charles made different choices, an absolutist regime similar to those in France and Spain might well have been established in the British Isles.[2]

This scenario is an example of "virtual history" or "counterfactual history," which has achieved a certain vogue in current historiography. The particular appeal of this approach is its challenge to forms of historical determinism, whether of the providential variety (God's hand in human history) or the scientific brand (the Marxist version). Practitioners of virtual history have been predominantly British and American, who have traditionally given more weight to accident and contingency than have their continental colleagues, who have been more attracted to grand theories of historical development. Virtual history has found no place in Italian historiography, for a variety of reasons. Some Italian scholars would argue that it is difficult enough to understand what actually occurred in their complex past; looking at alternate scenarios merely complicates the task. "The usual initial challenge to any kind of counterfactual theory," one historian has written, "has been the common-sense one that this is not the way things actually turned out, and therefore that speculation is pointless about how they might have turned out."[3] Like their continental brethren, Italians have long been attracted to forms of determinist history, whether of the providential kind practiced by some Catholic historians or, more commonly, the model of Marxism or the *Annales* school, with its denial of human agency, its deprecation of the significance of "events" ("surface disturbances, crests of foam that the tides of history carry on their strong backs," so Fernand Braudel has written),[4] and its emphasis upon structure and the *longue durée*. Benedetto Croce was as hostile to counterfactual history as any Marxist or Annaliste: "When judgment is brought to bear upon a fact," he wrote, "the fact is taken as it is and not as it otherwise might have been . . . Historical necessity has to be affirmed and continually reaffirmed in order to exclude from history the 'conditional', which has no rightful place there."[5]

Although our discipline has a mandate to chart and explain change, we historians are much more comfortable with stability and continuity, and with the structures that promote those qualities. Every society possesses these normative systems, which establish parameters, limits, constraints, and which act to impede change. For example, French history has been neatly encapsulated by Tony Judt, who stresses "the sheer ancientness and unbroken continuity of France and the French state . . . and the corresponding longevity of the habit of exercising authority and control from the center." "This is not merely a matter of political power," Judt adds, "the propensity of French rulers of all ideological persuasions to aggregate to themselves the maximum of sovereignty . . . The urge to classify, to regulate everything, from trade and language to theater and food, is what links the public sphere of France with cultural and pedagogical practices."[6] In no other European society does the past weigh so heavily as it has done, and continues to do, in Italy. The British historian J. M. Roberts has argued that the most fundamental quality of Italian history is its conservatism: "the sheer weight of the past, the inertia of custom and culture, the sloth and stagnation imposed by decaying but still formidable structures."[7]

A major difficulty confronting the historian seeking to explore the role of contingency in Italian history is the elusiveness of the subject. Pre-unification Italy, Edward Muir has written, "only existed . . . as a peninsula and a dream, a dream that has been given more credit as an idea than it deserves, an idea far more ephemeral than the persistence of local and regional identities."[8] The political fragmentation of the peninsula was the result of a series of invasions, by land across the Alps, and by sea from maritime invaders: Byzantine, Saracen, Norman, Angevin. With the possible exception of the Balkans, no European region is so diverse, with respect to geography and climate, political systems, economic and social organization, language and culture. The climate varies from Alpine glaciers to semitropical Sicily; the geography, from mountain uplands over 1,000 meters to flat, marshy, fever-ridden plains. The rough, uneven terrain was an impediment to communication, the network of Roman roads notwithstanding, and contributed to the peninsula's fragmentation. In the northern and central regions, the rise of towns and their political creations, the communes, created a mosaic of autonomous units, some two hundred by the early thirteenth century, within which intense particularist sentiments developed. Each community possessed its own distinctive pattern of political and social organization, its local saints and its dialects. In this chaotic and fragmented world, how can one identify significant events whose outcome would resonate beyond the castle, the hamlet, or the town?

Though the idea of Italy as a distinct community with a common heritage and culture was embraced in these centuries by only a handful of intellectuals—the poets Dante and Petrarch, the historians Biondo and Guicciardini—there were bonds both material and emotional that linked together the peninsula's inhabitants and, to a degree, counterbalanced its fragmented structure. Although the Latin language had been replaced by a cluster of regional dialects, it remained the standard mode of discourse of university education and of the professions: law, medicine, theology, and "humane letters." The principles of Roman law governed the administration of justice in every Italian court, whether secular or ecclesiastical. The Roman papacy's power and influence in Italy was based on its wealth, its administrative structure, its regulation of religious practices and beliefs, and of the social behavior of the laity. From the thirteenth century onward, mendicant friars spread out to every corner of the peninsula and the adjacent islands, establishing their convents and preaching their message. Italian towns, most of which traced their origins to Roman times, still retained the physical features of those ancient sites. A native of Florence or Milan or Naples could travel to any other Italian city and feel immediately at home in that urban milieu: its buildings, its streets, its churches, its social and political structures, its economic activity, its culture. The merchants who inhabited these towns formed a vast economic network, which embraced not only Italy but the entire Mediterranean basin. They were the most widely traveled and the most cosmopolitan segment of Italian society. Joining them on roads and on ships were pilgrims traveling to shrines and sanctuaries, soldiers seeking employment, and migratory workers who, like the merchants, became aware of belonging to a community larger than their native town or village.

Before beginning the search for contingent circumstances and events that influenced the course of Italian history in these centuries, I want to consider the decisive role of a few major figures in Italy's religious and cultural life. How, for example, would the peninsula's religious experience have been different if Francis of Assisi had died of pneumonia after stripping off his clothes and giving them to his father? Can one imagine how Italian culture would have developed if Dante had been seized and executed after his death sentence by vengeful Florentine Guelfs in 1302? What if Petrarch had succumbed to the plague in Avignon in 1348, instead of his beloved Laura? Then consider how the history of Renaissance art might have been very different if Giotto, or Masaccio, or Donatello, or Brunelleschi, or Leonardo da Vinci, or Michelangelo had died before reaching their teens, which was indeed the fate of 40 percent of Italian children born in these years.

The Roman papacy is the only Italian institution that provides a focus for the peninsula's history in these centuries. The papacy's fortunes had a direct and immediate impact upon every region; and its vicissitudinous history can serve as a barometer for developments from the Alps to the shores of Sicily. Medieval popes were as preoccupied by concerns for their security as they were about expanding their authority over the Catholic church and clergy, and over lay society. The patrimony of St. Peter, that swath of territory stretching from the Adriatic coast southward to the Roman Campagna, was a key element in their defensive strategy; another was the establishment of a feudal bond with the Norman kingdom of the two Sicilies. To guarantee the security and independence which they required to establish their claims to religious authority, and to defend themselves against the powerful Roman noble clans, the popes regularly turned to ultramontane rulers: first the Carolingians, then the German dynasties, and finally the French Angevins. These incursions by foreign princes and their armies were profoundly destructive, and they did not always benefit the papacy. By the thirteenth century, popes were no longer chosen by German emperors, as they had been in the eleventh century, nor were any occupants of the see of St.

Peter murdered or imprisoned, as they had been in the tenth century. Though the papal link to Rome as the site of the tombs of the apostles Peter and Paul was a crucial ingredient of their authority, medieval popes spent as much time outside of the Eternal City as within its walls. The papacy was always vulnerable to being captured and controlled by a local Italian dynasty or by a foreign power, as indeed happened during the Babylonian captivity in Avignon. The survival of the Roman papacy as an independent and autonomous institution was a fortuitous and unpredictable development; it was not preordained.[9]

In the middle decades of the thirteenth century, the Hohenstaufen emperor Frederick II sought to achieve what his predecessors over three centuries had failed to do: to gain permanent control over the Italian peninsula and its adjacent islands. Through a dynastic marriage between his father, Emperor Henry VI, and Constance, the heiress to the Norman kingdom of Sicily, Frederick possessed a solid territorial base to pursue his goal. At Palermo he established his esoteric, multicultural court and there built the bureaucratic and military structure that so impressed Jacob Burckhardt. Against his implacable enemy, the Roman papacy, Frederick could muster, in Lombardy, German troops together with his Italian Ghibelline allies; and on the southern flank of the Papal States, his Moslem mercenaries. Much of the Papal States was intermittently occupied by imperial forces. But in 1244, Pope Innocent IV escaped from Frederick's clutches and took refuge in Lyon in France, from which he launched a fierce ideological campaign against the emperor. And though Frederick's armies did win several battles against their Guelf enemies, the imperial cause lost the war. To maintain the support of his Ghibelline allies, the emperor was forced to make concessions, to alienate regalian rights. His empire was too unwieldy, its administrative structure too primitive, and its material resources too limited. The triumph of the papacy and its Guelf allies was, fundamentally, the victory of wealthy, urbanized, communal Italy (Lombardy, Tuscany, Emilia-Romagna, Umbria) over a feudal, rural, impoverished, and exploited south. Frederick II was an intelligent, charismatic ruler, but his ambition was greater than his resources, and his grand vision of a German-Italian empire was a fantasy with no serious prospect of realization. His kingdom, Philip Jones has written, "was obsolescent, with nothing left, except momentarily in a few places, of administration, revenue or allegiance."[10] Though Frederick's heirs, his sons Conrad and Manfred and his grandson Conradin, continued to fight for the Ghibelline cause after his death, they all failed, leaving their supporters, like Dante Alighieri, to dream of what might have been.

Frederick II was a European prince on the scale of a Charlemagne or a Napoleon: the ruler of an empire that stretched from the North Sea and the Baltic to Sicily and the kingdom of Jerusalem. For two centuries after his death, Italy was not seriously threatened by a foreign power, though its geography—the porous Alps and its thousand-mile coastline—rendered it extremely vulnerable to attack. A series of German princes—Henry VII, Louis of Bavaria, Charles IV, Sigismund, Frederick III—periodically crossed the Alps to be crowned emperor or to collect ransom from their Italian subjects, still legally under their overlordship. But the resources of these princes were too skimpy to threaten the municipal regimes, whether republics or *signorie*, that dominated the Lombard plain and the hilly terrain of the Romagna, Tuscany, and Umbria. These survived as vibrant and dynamic communities in an atmosphere of incessant conflict: rival factions, Montagues and Capulets in every town, and constant warfare between them. Politics in this environment was intensely parochial, focusing on quarrels between neighbors over boundaries, commercial disputes, the depredations of exiles and outlaws. Rarely were these city-states involved in relations, diplomatic or military, with regimes outside their own environment. The horizons of these townsmen, David Abulafia has written, "did not extend beyond the next range of hills."[11]

The Roman papacy had engineered the destruction of the Hohenstaufen dynasty by employing its spiritual weapons—excommunication, interdict, and the deposition of Frederick II—and by relying upon the resources of a temporal prince, Charles of Anjou, to whom Pope Innocent IV gave the kingdom of Naples. These successes seemed to justify the exalted claim for papal supremacy that found its most extreme formulation in Pope Boniface VIII's bull, *Unam Sanctam.* But there was a wide chasm between papal rhetoric and reality. The popes could not rely upon the continuous support of their Angevin allies, nor of their feudal vassals: the kings of England, Scotland, and Aragon. In Rome itself, they were often hostage to the whims of a fickle populace and to the power struggles among Roman families. Much of papal history in the fourteenth and fifteenth centuries can be understood as a series of desperate efforts by the popes to find security in a very dangerous environment. An article of faith among these princes of the church was the belief that the papacy's independence required a territorial base in central Italy.

The transfer of the papacy from Rome to Avignon was an historical accident, unplanned and unpremeditated, an improvisation that over time created a stable ecclesiastical structure, with its grandiose palace, its opulent court, and its efficient bureaucracy. There had been a precedent for a pope to leave Italy for the greater security of France; Pope Innocent IV had made the journey to escape from Frederick II in 1244. The humiliating maltreatment of Pope Boniface VIII by French agents and their Colonna allies was a warning to any pontiff that his exalted status was no guarantee of security in Rome or anywhere in the Papal States. Selected as a compromise candidate by a divided college of cardinals, the French pope, Clement V, chose to remain in France instead of venturing into the Italian maelstrom. There, for seventy years, a series of popes presided over a court that became, in effect, an appendage of the French crown. Over 80 percent of the cardinals appointed in those years were French, as was the curial bureaucracy. That a French-controlled papacy did not become a permanent reality was due partly to the efforts by Avignonese popes to escape from the tutelage of their monarchs, and partly to the weakened condition of the French crown in its long struggle with English invaders. Even as they built their great palace as their headquarters in Avignon, the popes continued their efforts to regain control of papal territory in central Italy, the cost of which ate up the lion's share of their revenue. They remained captive to the notion that the papacy required a secure territorial base in Italy. Pope Urban V and his successor, Gregory XI, resisted the pressure of the French monarch Charles V to journey south to Italy, believing that their presence in Rome was a necessary precondition for the recovery of the Papal States.

King Charles V of France is usually credited with primary responsibility for the beginning of the Great Schism. His resentment over the election of an Italian pope, Urban VI, in 1378, which signified the permanent relocation of the papacy to Rome, prompted the defiance of thirteen cardinals who elected a rival pope, the Frenchman Clement VII. The Schism was the most prolonged and most serious crisis of the papacy, and its resolution, after four decades, in the election of a single pope, Martin V, was as fortuitous as its origins. The scandal of the Schism inspired a broad range of efforts at a resolution, but these were all resisted by the intransigent claimants to the Holy See, their cardinals and their entourages. In this bitter and prolonged struggle, the Roman papacy could claim a majority of European states in their camp, but their Avignonese rivals enjoyed a more efficient administrative structure, already in place, and much larger revenues. Not for centuries had papal authority been so weak and discredited as in the four decades that spanned the Schism. To gain support for their cause, popes were prepared to surrender substantial portions of their territorial state. So, in 1379, the Avignonese pope, Clement VII, offered to create the principality of Adria out of papal lands for the French prince Louis of Anjou. And in 1408, the Roman pontiff, Gregory XII, sold the entire papal dominion to King Ladislaus of Naples for 20,000 florins.[12]

The selection of a pope by the Council of Constance in 1418 was yet another fortuitous event, a radical breach with tradition with profound consequences for Italian and European history. No pontiff had ever been chosen by an ecumenical council. But if the method was revolutionary, the choice was very conventional: Oddo Colonna, Pope Martin V, a representative of the Roman nobility that for centuries had been deeply involved in papal politics. That choice defined the character of the papacy for the next four centuries; it became essentially an Italian institution. Had the council chosen an ultramontane pope instead of an Italian, he might have accepted the theory that an ecumenical council was the supreme authority of the church, superior to popes. Another possible scenario might have been the council's failure to select a pope, which could have strengthened the trend toward the formation of national churches, already developing in France and England. Though still quite rare, some voices were advocating a system of multiple popes. A Florentine statesman, Gino Capponi, wrote in 1420 that "a divided church benefits our commune and our liberty." Several decades later, Lorenzo de' Medici asserted that "there were definite advantages in having three and even four popes." A spokesman for the University of Paris in the early fifteenth century argued that "little does it matter how many popes there are, two or three or ten or a dozen; each kingdom might as well have its own."[13] Had the fifteenth century witnessed the precocious formation of national churches, based on the Gallican model, the authority of the Roman papacy would have been dramatically diminished. The popes might still have been recognized as the spiritual head of the Catholic church, with the specific responsibility for protecting the tombs of the apostles Peter and Paul. But they would no longer have exercised any control over ecclesiastical benefices, nor would they have had access to church revenues across the Alps. A decentralized church, a constellation of national and regional churches, might seem implausible, but I would argue that this example of counterfactual history has much to recommend it. The European state, Brian Tierney has written, was the product of a cluster of "contingent circumstances," "a series of discontinuous idiosyncratic episodes."[14] I suggest that these characteristics apply equally to papal history in these years.

The history of the papacy after the Schism can indeed be described as "a series of discontinuous idiosyncratic episodes." In 1419, Pope Martin V was staying in Florence on his way to Rome when he heard boys in the street chanting "Papa Martino non vale un quattrino" (Pope Martin is not worth a penny).[15] And indeed that pontiff enjoyed very little material support—financial, military, diplomatic—for restoring the authority and prestige of his office. The strategy that he developed, and which was followed by his successors, was an ad hoc construction, pieced together in response to immediate problems and contingencies. Martin's first priority was the recovery of the Papal States, a daunting task which occupied most of his energy and resources. To blunt the challenge of conciliarism to papal authority, he negotiated concordats with ultramontane princes, giving them greater control over ecclesiastical appointments and revenue. During his and later pontificates, the papal bureaucracy was thoroughly italicized, as was, to a lesser degree, the college of cardinals. This process effectively guaranteed that future popes would be Italian, thus eliminating the possibility of locating the papacy outside of Rome. The conclave that elected Eugenius IV in 1431 consisted of six Italians and six ultramontane cardinals; participating in the election of Alexander VI in 1492 were twenty-three cardinals, all but one Italian.[16] This pattern would continue until the late twentieth century.

After conciliarism, the most serious threat to the papacy in these decades was its domination by a secular power. In the last years of the Schism, King Ladislaus of Naples occupied Rome, and his forces controlled most of papal territory. He died prematurely in 1414 at the age of thirty-four, but had he lived, he might have been able to integrate the Neapolitan kingdom with the Papal States and thus controlled the southern half of the peninsula, including Rome. A similar project was hatched in 1435 by King Alfonso of Aragon (eventually the ruler of the Neapolitan kingdom) and the lord of Milan, Filippo Maria Visconti. These princes contracted an alliance that contemplated the partition of the Papal States between them.[17] In the 1470s, officials of the French monarchy and the Holy Roman Emperor, Frederick III, discussed the possibility of moving the papacy back across the Alps, the Holy See to be shared in turn between the French and the Germans.[18] At the end of the fifteenth century, the prospect of a dynasty gaining control of the papacy and its territory rose again during the pontificate of the Borgia pope, Alexander VI. His son Cesare's audacious campaign to wrest control of papal lands from their *signori* (witnessed and described by Machiavelli) would have laid the foundation for a territorial state controlled by the Borgia, and thus put them in a position to manipulate papal elections. Had Cesare not been seriously ill when Alexander died in the summer of 1503, he could have been able (so Machiavelli believed) to select his father's successor to the Holy See.[19] The Medici pope Leo X developed a similar strategy by integrating the administration and finances of papal territory with the Florentine state. Responding in 1517 to an alleged plot organized by a group of dissident cardinals, the pope executed the ringleader and created thirty-one new cardinals in a single day.[20] But though Leo created the conditions for the election of his cousin Giullio as Pope Clement VII, the Medici strategy foundered in the crisis conditions following the French invasion. Even if an Italian dynasty had managed to gain control of papal territory and of the papacy itself, it is doubtful whether that state of affairs would have survived the post-invasion crisis. A more likely scenario would have been the absorption of the Papal States and control of the papacy by either the Hapsburg or the Valois dynasty.

The Roman papacy played an increasingly significant role in Italian politics after the end of the Schism, as it gradually recovered its ecclesiastical and temporal authority. By mid-century, it had become one of the five major regional states in the peninsula: a consortium that included the republics of Venice and Florence , the duchy of Milan, and the kingdom of Naples. Pope Nicholas V had been instrumental in negotiating the peace of Lodi in 1454, which ended thirty years of almost continuous warfare, and in organizing the Italian League, which obligated its members to seek peaceful solutions to their disputes. By promoting the idea of collective security, Nicholas sought to bring a measure of peace and stability to a war-ravaged peninsula. He was also motivated by the fear that (as one diplomat reported) "some Italian state . . . being desperate, might call the French or some other nation down into Italy and that the fire will spread so much that no one will be able to put it out." Nicholas was a realist who, in a conversation with Florentine ambassadors in 1454, remarked that "no peace could be forever, because the things of this world were not stable." But he did hope that peace would endure as long as Italian rulers behaved (in his words) "like two animals that after attacking and hurting each other, must just stare each other down without further action."[21] But the popes who succeeded this astute and prescient pontiff, notably Sixtus IV, Innocent VIII, and Alexander VI, were less interested in maintaining peace in the peninsula and more concerned with promoting the aggrandizement of their families. Their willingness to engage in warfare with their rivals contributed to the unstable conditions and the pervasive atmosphere of suspicion and distrust that characterized Italian politics on the eve of the French invasion of 1494.[22]

The diplomatic correspondence of late-fifteenth-century Italy provides convincing evidence of the peninsula's vulnerability to invasion by foreign powers. The five regional states had abandoned any pretense of being committed to collective security, as each pursued its own narrow interest in alliances forged to maintain a tenuous balance of power. The bankruptcy of the system was demonstrated by a series of diplomatic and military crises, beginning with the Pazzi war of 1478–80, which was ignited by the rivalry between Florence and Pope Sixtus IV over their respective zones of influence in the Romagna. In the summer of 1480, a Turkish army embarked in Apulia and for a year occupied the town of Otranto before withdrawing. Italy was saved from the prospect of a permanent Turkish base in the peninsula, not by her own efforts, which were paltry, but by a succession crisis caused by the death of Sultan Mohammed II. No lesson from this invasion was learned by the Venetian government, which launched an attack on Ferrara in the spring of 1482. That war involved all of the major Italian states until peace was restored in the summer of 1484. A few months later, another fire broke out in the kingdom of Naples, where a group of barons who had rebelled against their Aragonese ruler, King Ferrante and his son Alfonso, were supported by Pope Innocent VIII. As in the case of the Ferrara war, this uprising involved all of the major Italian states except Venice, and in addition, King Ferdinand of Aragon, and the king of Hungary, Matthew Corvinus. So a major lesson from the barons' revolt was how quickly an Italian crisis could become a European problem.

With the sole exception of Lorenzo de' Medici, Italy's rulers in the 1490s were not distinguished for their political skills. They were certainly not men of the caliber of an earlier generation: Pope Nicholas V, Cosimo de' Medici, Francesco Sforza. Except for the Venetian republic, their regimes were built upon very shaky foundations. As Burckhardt observed long ago, they lacked the patina of legitimacy enjoyed by the heads of sacralized monarchies, and they could never depend upon the allegiance of their subjects. As had been true for centuries, the primary source of this instability was the urban and rural elites, whose penchant for violence and disorder has been well described recently by Trevor Dean and David Chambers.[23] While these elites could be controlled or placated by "a judicious mixture of patronage, threats and, if necessary, force,"[24] they could also become rebellious, secure in the knowledge that even after failure, they could survive comfortably in exile. These regimes faced three distinct challenges in the late Quattrocento: from the Ottoman Turks on their eastern flank; from the Aragonese-Castilian state on the west; and from a revived and aggressive French monarchy on the north. By their conquests of the north African littoral and their sustained pressure on the Venetian maritime empire, the Turks constituted a very real threat to Italian security. The two Christian powers, France and Spain, had been sporadically involved in Italian politics since the thirteenth century. The intensification of their focus on the peninsula in the late fifteenth century was the result of a series of dynastic accidents affecting the major European powers.

Princely government in Christian Europe was dynastic; territory and authority passed from generation to generation via inheritance. The success of a ruling dynasty depended upon the production and survival of legitimate (preferably male) heirs, as the Capetian experience demonstrated. Dynastic events (marriages, births, deaths) far beyond Italy's borders were to have a profound impact upon her fortunes. The French monarchy had barely survived a series of disasters in the fifteenth century: the English occupation, which coincided with the reign of an insane monarch, Charles VI; the threat from a powerful Burgundian state on its eastern flank; revolts by groups of dissident barons in the 1460s and again in the 1480s; and a weak and unstable regency following the death of King Louis XI in 1483. Louis's successor, the young and ambitious monarch Charles VIII, was able to launch his campaign to conquer the kingdom of Naples as a result of two fortuitous events. First, the death in battle in 1477 of Charles the Bold, duke of Burgundy, resulted in the dismemberment of the Burgundian state and the removal of a potent rival to the French crown. Had the duke negotiated with, instead of challenging, a Swiss army, he might have preserved his Lotharingian state as an autonomous buffer zone between France and Germany. "The Swiss were only peasants (a Milanese diplomat commented), and if they were all killed that would be no satisfaction to the Burgundian nobles who might fall in the war. If the Duke got possession of all Switzerland without a struggle, his income would not be 5000 ducats the greater."[25] The Burgundian dukes had been as deeply involved, diplomatically and militarily, with northern Italian states (Savoy, Montferrat, Milan, Genoa) as the French monarchs, which raises the question of the feasibility of a French invasion of the peninsula in the 1490s. The second event that facilitated that enterprise was the extinction of the house of Anjou-Provence, whose head, King René, died in 1480 and whose heir died without legitimate issue in the following year.[26] Had the Angevin dynasty survived to pursue its rights to its Italian possessions, neither Charles VIII nor his successors would have had any legitimate claim to the kingdom of Naples or the kingdom of Jerusalem.

The emergence of Aragon-Castile as a major European power, and a serious threat to Italian independence, was even more problematic than the French connection. "For much of the fifteenth century," an authority on late medieval Spain has written, "it appeared highly improbable that the Spanish kingdoms . . . would shortly rank amongst the leading powers of Western Europe."[27] Both kingdoms suffered from endemic civil conflict, motivated largely by the efforts of powerful aristocracies to gain power at the expense of the crowns of Aragon and Castile. Princess Isabella's claim to the Castilian throne was dubious; her brother, King Henry IV, had a daughter, Juana, whom he recognized as his legitimate heir. Isabella's marriage to Ferdinand of Aragon (which under church law was illegal on account of consanguinity) was a desperate effort to gain support for her usurpation of the Castilian throne. Her rival, Juana, married the king of Portugal, which suggests an alternate scenario for the Iberian peninsula: a Castile-Portuguese alliance developing an overseas empire in Asia and the Americas, juxtaposed with an Aragonese state focusing on Sicily, Sardinia, and southern Italy. But Isabella survived the challenges from her rivals, and she and Ferdinand created a viable integrated government of their two realms. They negotiated marriages of their children with royal dynasties in Portugal, England, and the Netherlands, thus laying the foundations for the empire ruled by their grandson, the Emperor Charles V. But that vast inheritance was the product of a series of dynastic accidents: the early death of their only male child, Juan, in 1497; the death of their son-in-law, Philip of Burgundy in 1506; and the failure of Ferdinand to produce an heir to the Aragonese throne from his second marriage to the French princess Germaine de Foix.[28] Rarely, if ever, have dynastic accidents played so critical a role in European history.

For Italy, the consequences of these dynastic gyrations was the formation, on her northern and western frontiers, of two powerful and aggressive regimes, whose rulers were eager to engage in military enterprises. In France, the pressures to invade Italy had been steadily building in the late 1480s and early 1490s, as the monarchy expanded its territory, its revenues, and its military force. Having inherited the long-standing Angevin claim to the Neapolitan kingdom, Charles VIII was pressured by his advisers, his nobles, and influential exiles to mount an expedition into Italy. The specific invitation to cross the Alps by the duke of Milan, Lodovico Sforza, was only the last in a lengthy list of such appeals: the Venetian republic during the Ferrara war (1484); Pope Innocent VIII during the Barons' War (1486) and again in 1489.[29] Still, there was strong opposition in the French court to the Italian enterprise. "One is always struck when studying late fifteenth-century politics," Michael Mallett has observed, "by the difficulties in generating action. On both sides of the Alps there seemed to be an increasing conflict between 'men of action' and a sort of lethargic consensus . . . Vested interests, factional rivalries, personal jealousies, other preoccupations . . . slow communications, lack of cash, all militated against action. Discussion, rhetoric, bargaining, temporization, prevailed."[30] But in this particular case, the "men of action" carried the day, as they were to do again and again in subsequent years. There were few European rulers in these decades who favored peace over war.[31]

Commenting on the initial French invasion of 1494, Pope Alexander VI allegedly remarked that the invaders had conquered Italy "with a piece of chalk," a reference to the French practice of identifying the houses where their soldiers were to be quartered.[32] The real significance of Charles VIII's descent lay, not in the military superiority of the invaders, but in the failure of the Italian states to organize effective resistance to the French. Limiting the capacity of these rulers for collective action were the attitudes, the *mentalités*, formed by past experience and practice: the pervasive atmosphere of mistrust and fear of their rivals; the sacrifice of the general welfare for self-interest. Machiavelli's searing indictment of Italian princes in his *Arte della Guerra* is worth quoting in this context. These men, he wrote, "thought it sufficient to write handsome letters, or to compose clever responses at their writing desks, to show wit and wisdom in conversation and repartee, to know how to weave a web of deceit, to decorate themselves with jewels and gold . . . to govern their subjects in a haughty and avaricious manner, to fester in inactivity, to dispense their military preferments as favors, to despise anyone who showed the slightest merit, and to wish that their words be considered the sayings of oracles."[33]

The sole exception to this pattern of indulgent self-interest was the formation, in the spring of 1495, of the Holy League, a coalition of the major Italian powers, except Florence, dedicated to the expulsion of the French from the peninsula. This alliance created a formidable military force to challenge the French army retreating from Naples. The battle at Fornovo in Lombardy was a bloody affair, with both sides suffering heavy casualties. King Charles VIII barely escaped capture by Italian troops, and some historians have argued that had the king been seized or killed in the battle, "the course of Italian and European history would probably have been very different."[34] That scenario is not supported by the evidence. Lost battles, for example, by the Spaniards at Ravenna in 1512, or imprisoned kings, for example, Francis I at Pavia in 1525, did not deter the losers or the captives from pursuing their objectives. The captain of the Italian army at Fornovo, Francesco Gonzaga, claimed that the battle had resulted in the restoration of Italian liberty, a judgment that was somewhat premature.[35]

By the second decade of the sixteenth century, it was already clear to perceptive observers that Italy's fate would be determined by foreign powers; the only issue still to be decided was the identity of her future master. For Machiavelli, writing to his friend Francesco Vettori in the summer of 1513, the contenders for that role were the Spaniards, the French, and the Swiss. In response to a query from his friend, he sent this bitter observation: "As for the unity of the other Italians, you make me laugh; first, because there will never be any unity to any good purpose. And even if the leaders were united, that would not be enough, both because there are no armies here worth a nickel . . . , and because the tails are not united with the heads, nor will this nation ever respond to any accident that might occur."[36] Though in the last chapter of *The Prince* he did express the hope that a leader might emerge, like Moses, to lead Italians out of their subjugation, his deeply pessimistic view of their condition ("poor, ambitious and cowardly")[37] was corroborated by events. The competition for the domination of Italy was still not resolved when Machiavelli died in the spring of 1527. It was left to his close friend, Francesco Guicciardini, to write Italy's epitaph.

Of all the chapters in the dreary history of the invasions, and its record of Italian disunity and ineptitude, the most dramatic and most poignant was the sack of Rome in 1527. That traumatic event was the result of a series of accidents: of miscalculations by Pope Clement VII, beginning with his formation of a league against Emperor Charles V, the League of Cognac, and ending with his failure to provide an adequate defense of Rome. The imperial army, an undisciplined band of twenty thousand German, Spanish, and Italian mercenaries, unpaid and poorly supplied with provisions and arms, meandered aimlessly down the peninsula in the spring of 1527. This force could have been bought off by the papacy, or its march southward impeded by the papal-Venetian army commanded by the duke of Urbino. But these decisions were not taken, and by early May, this ragtag army had marched to the gates of Rome. The invaders broke through the makeshift fortifications, attacked and occupied the Vatican and the Trastevere quarter, and then crossed the bridges to ravage the districts on the east bank of the Tiber. It was estimated that, in the early days of the sack, ten thousand Romans were killed, and another ten thousand fled into the countryside, where they were harassed by the local peasantry. The pope and members of the curia took refuge in Castel San Angelo, where throughout the summer and autumn of 1527 they witnessed the carnage wrought by the imperial troops. In a frantic attempt to end the devastation, Clement VII signed a peace treaty in June, which ceded to the emperor large swatches of papal territory: Ostia, Civitavecchia, Modena, Parma, and Piacenza, a grant which he later repudiated. The failure of Italian princes and military leaders to rescue the pope and stop the devastation does suggest a willingness, even a desire, to retaliate against an institution and a city which they both adored and detested. Guicciardini reflected this attitude when he wrote that "no one loathes the ambition, the avarice and the sensuality of the clergy more than I," and if it had not been for the material benefits he gained from papal service, he would "have loved Martin Luther as much as myself."[38] After news of the sack of Rome reached Valladolid, where Charles V was then in residence, one of his counselors wrote that "we expect that Your Majesty will give us accurate instructions so that we may know how you intend governing Rome henceforward, and whether some form of Apostolic chair is to remain or not . . . I will not conceal from Your Majesty the view of some of your servants that the Holy See should not be utterly and entirely abolished."[39] Then serving as a papal official in the Romagna, Guicciardini wrote to the pope that "it is to be believed that he [Charles V] will want to take away the temporal and to reduce the popes to the condition in which they were when their election and all their power depended on the emperors."[40]

In early December 1527, Pope Clement VII managed to escape in disguise from Castel San Angelo, and like so many of his medieval predecessors, he sought refuge in the fortified towns of Viterbo and Orvieto in the Papal States. The remnants of the imperial army finally abandoned Rome in February 1528 and six months later, in October, the pope returned to the ravaged city, its population reduced to one-third (some thirty thousand souls) of its numbers before the sack. The recovery of Rome and of the papacy was the achievement of a series of sixteenth-century popes who were united in their commitment to an independent papal state and to a rejuvenated Catholic church under the curia's control. Fifty years after the death of Clement VII in 1534, the papal throne was occupied by Pope Sixtus V, whose five-year reign (1585–90) represented the culmination of this process of reconstruction. Rome's population had grown to one hundred thousand, and Sixtus launched a massive campaign to restore the city: completing the dome of St. Peter's, building dozens of new roads, and employing architects and artists to restore and decorate the city's churches. Rome's recovery was designed to reflect the revival of the Catholic church under papal guidance. That revival contributed to the significant recovery of territories previously lost to Protestantism, so that between the 1590s and the 1650s, the Catholic proportion of Europe's population grew from one-half to four-fifths.[41] And the restoration of a papal state under Rome's direct control was a defining feature of the early modern history of Italy, a deeply entrenched structure that would survive for three centuries before it was finally dismantled.

During these turbulent centuries, from Frederick II's failed effort to create a Ghibelline empire to the sack of Rome, there is no single event, no battle (Benevento, Tagliacozzo, Fornovo, Agnadello, Ravenna, Pavia) whose different outcome would have altered significantly the course of Italian history. I have suggested that the history of the Roman papacy is replete with fortuitous moments (in 1305, 1378, 1418, 1527) that could have changed the fortunes of that institution and of Italy. I have described the accidents of births, marriages, deaths, and inheritances that created the context for the series of foreign invasions that culminated in Italy's domination by Hapsburg Spain. I do believe that Italy was destined to lose its independence in the sixteenth century, if not to one, then to another, conqueror. The spirit of particularism and of pervasive distrust, so deeply rooted in the *mentalité* of this society, doomed any sustained effort to unite against a foreign invader. While attempting to recruit a militia from the rural inhabitants of the Florentine dominion in 1506, Machiavelli encountered this attitude. "Two causes have contributed to give me the greatest trouble in this matter," he wrote, "the one is the inveterate habit of disobedience of these people, and the other is the enmity existing between the people of Petrognano and those of Campana."[42] The villagers of Campana refused to serve alongside recruits from Petrognano, whom they detested. It was this mentality, as characteristic of poor peasants as of great nobles, that persuaded Machiavelli that "the tails are not united with the heads, nor will this nation ever respond to any accident that might occur."

CHAPTER FIVE

Fede and *Fiducia*

The Problem of Trust in Italian History, 1300–1500

In a well-known passage of his chronicle, the Florentine merchant and civic official Matteo Villani wrote: "In providing for the needs of the republic, faith *(fede)* is more useful than anything else."[1] Villani was referring specifically to Florence's large municipal debt, which, in 1345, had been consolidated into a funded debt, or *monte*, with regular payments of interest to the debt's shareholders. Villani believed that Florentines were willing to subsidize the commune through forced loans because they trusted the government's promise to repay its obligations. This notion of the crucial importance of honoring civic commitments was not limited to the fisc, but extended to every aspect of public and private activity: from the commune's diplomatic relations with other states to the regulation of private contracts between Florentines, and between Florentines and foreigners. No theme was more commonly articulated in civic debates than the commune's commitment to honor its treaties with other states, as well as its contracts with *condottieri*. Establishing the merchants' court *(mercanzia)* in 1308, with jurisdiction over all business contracts involving Florentine merchants, the commune recognized the need to regulate this primary source of the city's prosperity. Civic scrutiny and regulation applied to business contracts and private pacts: peace agreements between feuding families; marriage contracts and dowry settlements; last wills and testaments. All were the subject of communal legislation and efforts to enforce obligations among the inhabitants of this fractious and fragmented community.

In burgeoning Italian towns all the new forms of economic, social, and political organization that developed from the tenth century onward were based on the cooperation and mutual trust of their members. The focal points, the marketplace and the civic piazza, where the earliest mercantile and communal institutions were forged, existed symbiotically for both were created and operated by the urban elites of these cities. In a recent book review, Alan Ryan described an ideal society as one "where the citizenry trust each other; where they are inclined to keep their bargains; where they are not inclined to cheat strangers; or to give and take bribes; and where they encourage good citizenship in one another by unofficial means."[2] In such a utopian society every promise would be kept, every contract honored; and there would be no need to impose sanctions on individuals who failed to fulfill their obligations. In the contentious and agonistic urban societies of medieval and Renaissance Italy, trust was a commodity in short supply.[3] This chapter considers the problem of *fede* and *fiducia* in Italian urban society from the fourteenth to the end of the fifteenth century. I examine *fede* in an economic context—the development of mercantile structures and practices—and then in politics, both internal and external. To reduce this subject to more manageable proportions, I exclude any treatment of trust in private relationships: between family members, between neighbors, between patrons and clients. Still, the terrain that I propose to cover is vast enough. My analysis, though necessarily sketchy and summarial, will nonetheless, I hope, be informative and provocative. I shall identify the mechanisms developed by Italian city-states to promote trust among their citizens and with other Italian states. I will identify the areas of civic experience where *fede* was generally sustained, and where it was not. Much of my evidence comes from Florentine sources, with which I am most familiar, but I also utilize material from other societies, particularly Venice and Genoa.

In Italian civic life during the medieval era trust first became a critical, decisive element in the creation and maintenance of economic relationships. Buying, selling, and exchanging commodities requires some trust among the participants, and we can assume (even without concrete evidence) that the Italian markets that survived throughout the Dark Ages were based upon some degree of *fiducia*. The miracle of the Italian commercial revolution, succinctly described by Philip Jones as the construction of "a cosmopolitan system unprecedented in range, wealth and technical sophistication,"[4] was based upon three foundations: the ability of the Italian mercantile class to amass large amounts of capital; their willingness to take risks in investing that capital; and their skill in creating mechanisms to minimize those risks. That this system worked can be seen most clearly in twelfth-century Genoese notarial records. These protocols reveal that Genoese of every social category—feudal nobles, non-noble rentiers and merchants, artisans, petty shopkeepers, widows, sailors—invested heavily in sea voyages, confident that their partners or associates were men of *fiducia* who would honor their obligations. The notarial documents spelled out these obligations precisely, often stipulating that the borrower who violated the terms of the contract pay twice the amount of the investment. The investor could present such a document to a merchants' court as tangible evidence in a suit to obtain redress. In addition, the major Italian cities engaged in international trade developed other mechanisms for settling disputes (including reprisals) and protecting the interests of their merchants throughout the Mediterranean, including Byzantine and Moslem areas. Steven Epstein has commented on the effectiveness of this system in promoting Genoa's economic growth: "Family ties seem to have been a natural basis for some trust, but circumstances all required people to repose some trust outside the kinship network. Kin made contracts and used notaries to redact them. Friends also trusted each other's word yet in the main the written word guaranteed as much as possible in a world filled with risk, nosy people, faithless partners and ill winds."[5]

Undergirded by *fiducia*—the belief that contracts would be honored and penalties enforced against violators—this economic system remained in place for the next four centuries. The risks which Epstein identified (faithless partners, ill winds) remained, and there were other dangers as well: political upheavals and the disruptions caused by biological disasters like the plague. In his magisterial synthesis, Philip Jones has sketched the evolution of Italian business organization and techniques, all designed to protect the interests of the entrepreneurial class: "It was in response largely to commercial needs . . . that legal business was liberalized, notarial . . . transactions validated and freed from the restrictions of civil, canon and customary law. Legal practice and learning devised new, flexible forms of contract, warranty, insurance and clandestine usury. The commercial classes profited from legal innovations: their professional and trade associations, guilds and business companies, secured legal personality; collective liability for debt among kinsmen was extended . . . and the penalties and proceedings for bankruptcy were harshly and ignominiously sharpened."[6] The communal regimes that had gained control of most Italian cities, and the mercantile interests increasingly influential in them, promoted these developments. Philip Jones has emphasized the wide-ranging powers of these urban regimes, which promulgated "a mass of laws and regulations in manners and morals, in practice if not theory more interventionist and totalitarian than the pretensions of ancient city-republics."[7]

I focus here on Florence in the fourteenth and fifteenth centuries to examine the degree to which the entrepreneurial class promoted and sustained *fiducia* and detected and penalized violations. The authority of the *mercanzia*, the Florentine institution most directly involved in the settlement of mercantile disputes, was stipulated in a 1394 constitution to include everything from disputes between Florentine merchants and foreigners, to bankruptcies, to internal problems within companies, to insurance, to money and credit.[8] Until the mid-fifteenth century, the court was held in high repute. In about 1400, the merchant Gregorio Dati wrote that "before this court came all of the great issues and disputes from all over the world, and quarrels over events on land and sea, on bankrupt companies, on reprisals; all of these disputes decided by fair and impartial judges."[9] A cursory examination of these court records (still largely unexplored) indicates the vast range of the *mercanzia*'s jurisdiction. Bankruptcy cases were brought before the court, as creditors petitioned the judges to force bankrupts to repay their obligations. These debtors, pressured by their creditors and facing possible imprisonment, also had to endure the opprobrium of a society that regarded business failure as a moral offense. In describing the bankruptcy of a company operated by her cousins, Lodovico and Gianfrancesco Strozzi, Alessandra Strozzi noted that their insolvency had resulted in a loss of honor, and she wrote in 1465 of her fear that the blemish on the entire Strozzi lineage "could last forever."[10] Alessandra may have been thinking of the Florentine practice of painting images of fugitive debtors on the walls of the palace of the *podestá*, which (so Poggio Bracciolini asserted) "is to us a form of ignominy similar to eternal damnation."[11]

The stern penalties facing Florentine entrepreneurs who defaulted on their debts did not reduce the number and magnitude of business failures, described in detail in the records of the *mercanzia* and in *catasto* reports. The tax declaration by Florentine merchant Jacopo di Filippo da Ruota in 1427 contained the names of dozens of debtors (several identified as dead and bankrupt) in Tuscany and also in Apulia where, according to da Ruota, "we have many bad debts from consignments of cloth, from which we do not expect to receive a penny."[12] Niccolò Machiavelli's father, Messer Bernardo, described in his diary the efforts to recover a small debt owed him by a butcher, Romolo Cecchi.[13] The butcher had repeatedly promised to repay Messer Bernardo 6 *lire, sopra mia fede,* and just as repeatedly failed to do so. Finally, after several days, Messer Bernardo and a friend, Carlo Bartoli, went to Cecchi's shop, where Bartoli, as arbiter, established terms for repayment agreeable to both disputants. Messer Bernardo's diary is filled with descriptions of petty transactions in which he was involved. He recorded that he had loaned a feather bed to a cousin, Battista Machiavelli. "And to bear witness to this loan," he wrote, "I have made this record in Battista's presence." Below this entry by Messer Bernardo was this codicil: "I, Battista di Buoninsegna Machiavelli, acknowledge my agreement to what was written above, and on my honor I subscribe to it this day in my own hand."[14] All this for the return of a feather mattress!

Recently scholars have suggested that after Cosimo de' Medici's death in 1464, his grandson Lorenzo manipulated the *mercanzia's* personnel and procedures to favor his friends and clients. In the 1520s, Francesco Guicciardini recorded a widely held opinion that the *mercanzia*, which "in the past had a great reputation in every part of the world," could no longer claim that distinction.[15]

As the reputation for probity of this guardian of economic *fiducia* had declined, so too (it was claimed) had the ethical standards of the citizenry. Their ability to hide their assets from tax collectors has been well documented. Raymond de Roover has demonstrated that Cosimo de' Medici falsified his *catasto* report of 1457; he "who should have set the example of civic spirit was the first to conceal that wealth for the purpose of diminishing his tax burden."[16] Still, the Medici were acutely aware of the danger to the Florentine economy if fraudulent practices were tolerated. Thomas Kuehn has documented the efforts of the Medici regime to reduce fraud by requiring the registration of emancipations that limited collective liability and by obligating bankrupts to bring their books to the Signoria for inspection. "It is well known," a 1477 law stated, "that more than ever before, men flee from fulfilling their obligations to their creditors and think little of shame."[17] Florentine legislators wrestled with the problem of fraud, though their efforts, Kuehn has argued, were largely ineffective. It would be difficult to prove that Florentine businessmen in the late fifteenth century were more given to engaging in fraud than their ancestors a century earlier. But the evidence does suggest that more were troubled by the problem, which inspired discussions by Franco Sacchetti, Leon Battista Alberti, Giovanni Rucellai, and Giovanni Morelli as well as a cadre of Florentine lawyers.[18]

We now shift our focus from Florence to Venice and its vibrant economy. On the wall of the church of S. Giacomo di Rialto was carved this inscription: "Round about this church may the law merchant be equitable, the weights just, and may no fraudulent contract be negotiated."[19] The Venetian government played an active role in supervising mercantile and banking activity, the major source of the city's wealth and power. The regulation of the market was divided among several commissions until 1524, when a new magistracy, the *proveditori sopra banchi*, was given responsibility for regulating every aspect of the market. Venice was the major European center for trading in precious metals, and the authorities required moneychangers to post bond. Yet despite a regulatory system as tight and comprehensive as any in Europe, Venetian bankruptcies were a common occurrence in Venice. According to Tommaso Contarini, writing in 1584, "in the 1200 years during which this republic exists by the grace of God, one finds that 103 private banks were created of which 96 failed . . . and seven alone succeeded."[20] Reinhold Mueller's survey of the Venetian money market from the thirteenth to the end of the fifteenth century describes the periodic failures of banks and their replacement by new firms able to attract investments from a broad spectrum of Venetian society. The prospect for profit was always a powerful incentive, but these lenders also had faith that their government could protect their economic interests. The government did not stigmatize bankrupts as morally delinquent but sought to recover their assets for distribution to their creditors. Those who fled Venice to avoid their obligations, however, "were excluded from the public and economic life of the city."[21]

By the middle of the sixteenth century, Genoa had surpassed its rivals—Florence, Venice, Milan—to become the major entrepreneurial center of Italy and indeed of Europe. Fernand Braudel described the century from 1557 to 1650 as "the age of the Genoese," when the city's bankers dominated Europe's financial markets and provided most of the capital for the Hapsburg monarchs.[22] Richard Goldthwaite reminds us that "Genoa had the earliest documented banks in Europe, complete with deposit accounts, interbank transfer, overdraft and fictitious exchange."[23] The city's government, one of the weakest municipal regimes in all of Italy, contributed little to these achievements. The Casa di San

Giorgio, the association of the commune's creditors, effectively controlled the Genoese state finances from the early fifteenth century. With the establishment of the Hapsburg hegemony in Italy as a consequence of the foreign invasions, Genoese merchant bankers achieved a preeminent role in the economy and the finances of the kingdom of Naples. Much of the capital that Genoese financiers invested in Hapsburg lands in Europe and in the overseas colonies was drawn locally from prominent noble families like the Doria, the Spinola, and the Fieschi, as well as shopkeepers, sailors, fishermen, clerics, and widows.[24] The Genoese entrepreneurs also attracted capital from other Italian cities, whose residents placed their *fede* in the ability of these astute and knowledgeable bankers to protect and augment their investments. The periodic bankruptcies of the Hapsburg monarchs in the late sixteenth and early seventeenth centuries only momentarily disrupted this flow of capital into Genoese coffers. "Through Genoa," so Braudel has argued persuasively, "the Mediterranean long held the key to the control of the world's wealth."[25]

In the marketplace, where obligations were most commonly honored, their breach was most harshly penalized. "The great symbolic power of the marketplace," Edward Muir has observed, "came from the fact that there men learned to trust one another and to represent their mutual confidence in the little rituals of striking a deal, such as the kiss . . . or standing for drinks in a tavern."[26] The moral taint attached to individuals who violated their trust was a powerful deterrent to businessmen of every rank and condition, from wealthy bankers to retail merchants and artisans, whose fortunes depended on their reputation for probity in their business affairs. The recent study by Richard Marshall of retail merchants and artisans in fourteenth-century Prato has revealed the key importance of credit in that society, far more widespread than previous scholarship had suggested.[27] Not all debts were repaid, as Florence's *catasto* records demonstrate. But creditors had long memories and often would pursue their debtors in the courts for decades to obtain their due. In 1465, Alessandra Strozzi complained that a pork butcher from the Mugello village of Borgo San Lorenzo harassed her to collect a small debt incurred by her husband thirty years earlier.[28] Bankrupt artisans and shopkeepers were expelled from their guilds and threatened with loss of their livelihood. Business failure brought dishonor to upper-class delinquents and their kin, excluding them from civic office and from respectable marriage for their children. Among the rituals of humiliation civic authorities in Florence devised were the display of bankrupts' portraits on the walls of public buildings alongside those of criminals and, in the Veneto, "the bankrupt's striking his naked buttocks three times on the 'stone of infamy' . . . while pronouncing the words of total surrender: '*Cedo bonis*'" (I give up my property).[29]

Economic relationships in medieval and Renaissance Italy were characterized by a high degree of trust, bolstered by institutions such as merchants' courts and by the sustained efforts of governments to protect the markets on which their revenue and consequently their authority so heavily depended.[30] To move from that milieu to politics is to enter a more problematic and unstable environment. The burgeoning cities of north and central Italy during the eleventh and twelfth centuries plunge us into a turbulent milieu of familial and factional conflict, of Montagues and Capulets, with their armed clienteles and their penchant for violence. Though the documentation on the origins of the Italian communes is scanty, it is received wisdom that the urban residents formed associations to defend themselves against overmighty families and factions. The oath taken by this first generation of communards who joined these urban societies was the glue designed to hold them together, to guarantee their members' commitment to collective action in defense of their interests. The oath, so well analyzed recently by Paolo Prodi, became the defining symbol of membership, not only of the commune, but also of the cluster of associations (tower societies; Guelf and Ghibelline parties; *alberghi;* confraternities) that sprouted in every city.[31]

Of the more than two hundred Italian communes that emerged in these centuries, only a handful survived as independent entities: the great majority "dissolved into distrust and violence or were absorbed by their powerful neighbors." Machiavelli described succinctly the process by which these communes foundered: "Men do injury either through fear or hate . . . Such injury produces more fear; fear seeks for defense; for defense partisans are obtained; from partisans rise factions in states; from factions, their ruin."[32] Of the three cities that I have used as examples (Florence, Venice, Genoa), the Adriatic republic was by far the most successful in creating a stable polity and in fostering a climate of civic trust in its political institutions. If Venice scores very high on a scale of one to ten, Florence might receive a five, while Genoa would rank at the bottom: "a city with such a frail civic identity," as Edward Muir has noted, "that its long history of aristocratic violence produced chronic political instability."[33]

From its origins in the twelfth century to its demise in the early sixteenth, Florence's communal government was based upon the sworn oaths of its citizens to obey the statutes and the civic authorities who administered the laws. The members of the commune's supreme executive, the Signoria, took this oath in a very public ceremony, initially on the *ringhiera*, the platform in front of the Palazzo Vecchio, and then in the 1380s, in the loggia adjacent to the palace. When foreign judges (the *podestà*, the captain of the *popolo*, the executor of the Ordinances of Justice) assumed office, they likewise took an oath to observe the communal statutes. Every Florentine who matriculated into one of the twenty-one guilds (and thus became eligible for civic office) took an oath to abide by guild regulations, and in the case of some guilds, also swore to obey communal laws and authorities.[34] But the power of the oath to command support for and obedience to the commune became weaker over time, in a process that Paolo Prodi has called "the desacralization of the oath." In January 1429, a proposal submitted to a council meeting invited citizens to swear an oath on the Bible "to abandon all hatreds, to divest ourselves completely of partisanship and loyalty to factions. To consider only the welfare and honor and greatness of the Republic."[35] Some seven hundred citizens took this oath, but two years later, a prominent statesman and party leader, Rinaldo degli Albizzi, had to admit that partisan conflict was as intense as ever.[36] The oligarchic regime that governed Florence from 1382 to 1434 was the target of numerous conspiracies organized to overthrow it by violence. In the first two years of its existence, more than a dozen plots that involved armed attacks on the city itself were discovered and defused, and judicial records list some thirty plots to promote rebellions in the territory.[37]

The sources of these conspiracies, the most extreme manifestations of pervasive discontent within the city and throughout its dominion, were analyzed at length in the *consulte e pratiche*, the debates which charted the temper of the citizenry from the late fourteenth century to the early sixteenth century. Participants in these civic debates were attuned to the complaints and criticisms of their constituents, as they struggled to find solutions to their problems. Inequitable tax assessments were most frequently cited as a cause of civic malaise; other causes include perceived flaws in the "distribution of honors" (the methods of choosing civic officeholders) and the administration of justice, and the propensity of citizens to favor their private interest over the welfare of the city. Particularly in times of crisis (a military threat, a famine, a shortage of revenue), these denunciations of the regime and its leadership were harsh, often brutally so. For example, in July 1456, the lawyer Girolamo Machiavelli stated that "nothing is healthy in our *rei publica*. Everything is in decline; our fortresses are unmanned, our subject cities neglected; our obligations are not honored."[38] As early as the 1390s, a Florentine chronicler had noted that the commune had violated its *fede* by reducing the rate of interest it paid on the shares of its funded debt. Throughout the fifteenth century, similar complaints were voiced in the *pratiche* about the commune's failure to honor its fiscal obligations.[39] The skepticism of bondholders about the commune's trustworthiness reduced the price of these *monte* shares, which fell to as low as 20 percent of their nominal value. In 1469, Marco Parenti wrote to his brother-in-law Filippo Strozzi that "*monte* shares are worth only 24%, and we still have not received the interest payments that are owed to us."[40]

Reading through the reports of these council meetings and the chorus of complaints and laments about the government's policies and practices, one wonders how this republican regime could possibly have survived for more than two hundred years. Fortune certainly played a role in its survival: the fortuitous death of Charles of Calabria and Castruccio Castracani in 1328, of Giangaleazzo Visconti in 1402, of King Ladislaus of Naples in 1414. Civic humanists—Coluccio Salutati, Leonardo Bruni, Poggio Bracciolini, Carlo Marsuppini—might argue that their writings and speeches stimulated the patriotic fervor of the Florentines, persuading them to make sacrifices for their liberty. I am inclined to give greater weight to David Peterson's argument that the regime used "religious ritual and other public manifestations of religious sentiment to construct public consensus and to legitimize their power."[41] Though Florence never managed to resolve some of the thorniest problems that bedeviled its leadership, most notably the fisc and its military strategy, it did create a more efficient and more rational administrative structure, particularly in the governance of its Tuscan dominion. But the most important factors in its survival as an independent republic were the durable civic traditions and institutions to which citizens gave their support. Most Florentines gave their allegiance, their trust, to their republican institutions, even when they had serious reservations about the men who filled civic offices and formulated policy. This mentality was reflected in a statement Giovanni Vettori attached to his tax return in 1427, addressing the officials responsible for administering the newly created *catasto:* "If you do your work properly and honorably, then you will sustain this glorious city in triumph and well-being, and you and your sons will enjoy perpetual fame and reputation, and so I pray God and the glorious Virgin Mary!"[42]

During the crisis years of the early 1430s, a Florentine citizen, Giovanni Baroncelli, suggested that there were two ways to bring peace and unity to the city: "first, love; and if that fails, then fear."[43] Throughout the republic's history, Florentines oscillated between them. The Venetian government, by contrast, invariably opted for the stick instead of the carrot. Venetian authorities enjoyed a well-deserved reputation for rigor and ruthlessness in responding to internal crises or any challenges to its regime. So well protected by its lagoons and its navy, the city was rarely threatened by hostile forces, internal or external. The stability and longevity of the Venetian republic were essential elements of the "myth of Venice," a self-image the republic's citizens carefully constructed and promoted. The foundation of Venice's stable regime was the cluster of about two hundred "noble" families whose male members formed an exclusive governing class. The benefits of this monopoly of power and privilege were sufficient to guarantee the *fede* of the vast majority of the Venetian nobility. In the five hundred years of this oligarchic regime, the authorities discovered only two significant conspiracies, a number that the Florentine republic could expect in any given year. This ruling class was remarkably homogeneous. Nearly all of its members engaged in mercantile activity, with none of the unruly feudal elements that were so disruptive of communal regimes on the mainland. According to Elisabeth Crouzet-Pavan's compelling argument, the Venetian nobility was unified because "the imperatives dictated by conquering the lagoon for habitation through reclamation projects and protecting the city from the destructiveness of water [which] necessitated social concord and collective cooperation."[44] Edward Muir has demonstrated the significant role of religious ritual in promoting allegiance to and legitimization of this oligarchic regime. "The most characteristic feature of the Venetian civic ideal," he wrote, "became unanimity, the convergence of a multitude of wants and aspirations into a single will."[45] Recent research has shown that this regime was not so virtuous or honest, or so free of corruption, as the myth has suggested. Still, despite its flaws, this "most serene republic" survived longer than any of its rivals until Napoleon suppressed it in 1797.

In the early sixteenth century, a coalition of European and Italian princes, under the leadership of Pope Julius II, formed an alliance to overthrow the Venetian republic and parcel out its territory among themselves. A Venetian army was defeated at Agnadello in the summer of 1509, and her mainland territory occupied by the forces of this so-called Holy League. The urban elites of Venice's subject towns—Verona, Vicenza, Padua, Treviso—joined in this assault on Venetian rule. But the peasants, artisans, and boatmen from the *terrafirma* resisted the foreign invaders, proclaiming their allegiance to their Venetian masters with loud cries of "Marco! Marco!" Machiavelli, no friend of Venice, witnessed this remarkable manifestation of loyalty while on a diplomatic mission to the north. These peasants, he wrote, "have become more obstinate and enraged against the enemies of the Venetians than the Jews were against the Romans, and every day one of them who has been captured gets killed for refusing to deny the Venetian name." It will be impossible (he concluded) "for these princes to hold onto these lands as long as these peasants are alive."[46] Machiavelli was prescient. Within a few years, Venice had recovered all of her mainland empire and in 1530 negotiated a settlement with the papacy and the Holy Roman Emperor, Charles V, which enabled her ruling elite to preserve their independence and their political system for another two hundred years.

Among the major Italian cities, Genoa stands out as a case study in political instability. The contrast between the city's economy—dynamic, buoyant, efficient—and its politics is dramatic. After the Black Death, the Genoese commune was weakened by bitter factional conflicts, between rival noble clans and between a mercantile urban elite and a powerful feudal aristocracy which controlled most of the city's hinterland and its coastal zones. The commune was never strong enough to discipline and subdue this unruly noble class, with its feudal enclaves, its mountain castles, and its penchant for involving itself in civic affairs. Genoa's urban geography provides the most striking evidence of civic weakness and aristocratic power. The commune did not stake out its own public space, like Venice's piazza San Marco and Florence's piazza della Signoria, no buildings or monuments that could serve as a locus of civic identity. The Genoese, to the degree that they gave their allegiance and their *fede* to any institution, gave it not to the commune but to a kin group or to one of the artificial families, the *alberghi*, that dominated the city's neighborhoods. In their frequency, the rebellions and coups d'état of Genoa rivaled those of Florence, with over thirty violent episodes and changes of regime in the fifteenth century.[47] There can be no doubt that the economic resources of Genoa could have made it a regional power, had the citizenry resolved its factional rivalries. But the commune had allowed the Casa di San Giorgio to take over its finances, and the city and its territory were occupied in the early fifteenth century by a French nobleman, Marshal Boucicaut; then by the lords of Milan in the 1420s, the 1450s and the late 1480s. In 1487, a disgruntled Genoese ambassador referred to his fellow citizens as eunuchs who were tired of being sold at auction and who wanted to get out from under the yoke of clerics.[48] The Genoese *popolo* made one final convulsive effort to gain control of their city in 1507, but this popular rebellion was quashed by the nobility, which effectively maintained its power and privileges for the next two hundred years.

The political experience of Genoese was perhaps atypical in the degree of instability, in the failure of that society to resolve its tensions, and in the lack of trust in its institutions and personnel. One notable manifestation of the Genoese failure to develop a civic ethos, an atmosphere of trust, was the exodus of exiles who left the city with every change of regime. Most exiles congregated in nearby towns, awaiting the opportunity to return home by either force or invitation. A Sienese diplomat described a cluster of exiles in Rome: "They flock together like starlings, and they are discontented, and they have spread many rumors, as those who have been turned out do."[49] Florentine exiles in the fifteenth century were scattered throughout the peninsula. When the Medici returned to power in 1434, they sent over one hundred of their political rivals into exile, only a handful of whom ever returned to their native city.[50] The Florentine government also implemented a policy of exiling large numbers of the citizens of subject towns, such as Arezzo and Pisa. In 1432, a civic magistracy wrote to its subordinate in Pisa: "We have written so many times to the captain (of the Florentine fortress in Pisa) that the best means of securing Pisa is to empty it of Pisans."[51] Fifty years passed before the regime began to realize that its exile policy had contributed significantly to the decline of the Pisan (and thus its own) economy. Christine Shaw, in her study of the exile phenomenon in fifteenth-century Italy, has amassed some startling statistics: "of the 627 citizens [of Siena] who took the oath imposed on all members of the Council of the People at a ceremony of reconciliation in November 1482, 225 (36 percent) were exiled at least once between 1480 and 1500."[52]

The vast majority of Italian exiles in these decades (and they numbered in the thousands) were penalized not for any violation of laws, but simply for belonging to a discredited faction or for being perceived as a threat to their city's regime. Only the Venetian republic felt secure enough to exile only those citizens who had committed crimes against the state. The notion of a legitimate opposition was wholly alien to Italian governments, where any form of dissent was viewed as potentially treasonous. But this resort to exile as a defense against rebellion may have weakened rather than strengthened these regimes. Exile disrupted families and depleted fortunes and promoted distrust among its victims. In 1487, Lorenzo de' Medici, whose grandfather and father, Cosimo and Piero, had exiled hundreds of Florentine citizens, counseled the Sienese to abandon the strategy: "[They] should not create any exiles if they can help it, and if they feel they can live in peace and quiet without having them; or at least let them be few, and necessary for peace and quiet, because it is exiles that ruin cities and keep those within always in doubt."[53] The exile experience often transformed political opponents into rebels. As Lucien Pye has noted in describing a comparable context in twentieth-century Asia: "Since these societies recognize no legitimate display of political opposition, they make it difficult for dissidents to disagree without becoming disagreeable."[54] The surveillance of exiles could be costly, and the loss of manpower and capital depleted the resources of these states. Florence, for example, could certainly have used the financial resources and the entrepreneurial skills of the Strozzi and Guadagni, whose exiled members made large fortunes in Lyon and became integrated into the upper echelons of French society.

In the fourteenth century, the diplomatic correspondence of city-states in north and central Italy was primarily concerned with security. Florence constant communicated with its counterparts in Tuscany, Umbria, and the Romagna, and more rarely, with Lombard regimes to negotiate alliances to provide mutual assistance against aggressors. These leagues often had an ideological dimension, Guelf or Ghibelline, that bound their members together. During the formal ceremonies that symbolized the formation of a league, representatives of the participants swore an oath that their governments would abide by the terms of the alliance. But violators of these pacts (and they were numerous) suffered no penalties beyond a loss of honor and reputation; they were regarded (in the words of a Florentine diplomat) "as the most shameless men who ever lived."[55] From a Florentine perspective, the despots who had taken over control of many Italian communes were particularly untrustworthy. The lord of Milan, Bernabò Visconti, was described as a traitor and a violator of his oath "who cared nothing for the agreements that he had made with us."[56] "Who can justify," the Florentine chronicler Matteo Villani lamented, "the seductions, the tricks, the betrayals, that despots commit in their lust for power, ignoring honor, charity and even family ties?"[57] But communal regimes were not blameless in maintaining their *fede* with their allies. The communes of Perugia and Siena were accused, in 1354, of violating the terms of their pact with Florence, by bribing instead of fighting the mercenary company led by Fra Moriale. "This is the *fede*," Matteo Villani observed bitterly, "that, so often in the past, the commune has made with its neighbors who, finding it to their advantage, have broken their promises."[58] Florence's Tuscan neighbors—Siena, Lucca, Pisa—accused the Arno city of duplicity, specifically, in making secret agreements with mercenary bands to ravage their territories. This unflattering portrait of Florentines was painted by a Lucchese citizen in 1388: "They are as sly as foxes. . . . They are cunning in everything they do, and their mischief knows no bounds. I urge you to take good care, for the wicked Judas, full of evil and simony, never sleeps."[59]

No phenomenon contributed more to the climate of mistrust and suspicion than the mercenary companies which, like a swarm of locusts, ravaged the Italian peninsula throughout the fourteenth century. These bands were formed by foreign soldiers—German, Hungarian, French, English—and also by Italian recruits. Though these companies were never able to conquer and pillage walled towns, they did enormous damage to the unprotected rural areas—looting, burning, killing—and thus to the local economies of the cities. From the 1340s to the end of the century, the commune of Siena spent nearly 300,000 florins in bribes to these companies, whose members frequently violated their promises not to pillage Sienese territory. With mercenary companies, the Florentine *novellista* Franco Sacchetti wrote, "there is neither love nor faith."[60] How could one expect a foreign soldier like the German Werner von Urslingen to keep faith when he described himself as "an enemy of God, pity and mercy"? Still, the beleaguered communes sought to fortify their treaties with these bands by requiring their leaders to swear an oath to abide by their commitments. Representing the Florentine commune in negotiations with the Italian company of San Giorgio in 1379, the chronicler Marchionne Stefani drew up a formal treaty which thirty-nine corporals swore an oath to uphold, attaching their seals as a guarantee of their promise. All to no avail, for the company soon violated the pact by ravaging Florentine territory. Stefani appeared to believe that Italian mercenaries were more likely than foreigners to honor their obligations, and he noted that the breach of *fede* by the San Giorgio company was the first such transgression by an Italian mercenary band.[61]

By the end of the fourteenth century, the companies had ceased to be a serious threat to Italian regimes, as they transformed themselves into soldiers for hire under the leadership of *condottieri*. Michael Mallett has described the pervasive atmosphere of distrust that characterized relations between these military captains and their employers. Italian governments, he wrote, "wanted quick and inexpensive victories; the *condottieri* wanted to make their living and save their skins," goals that were mutually incompatible.[62] Rulers had only limited means to force their mercenaries to honor their contracts. One strategy was to capture and execute disloyal *condottieri*, more of whom died at the hands of their employers than were killed on the battlefield. The first recorded execution of a military captain was that of Fra Moriale in Rome in 1354; the most notorious occurred at Sinigaglia in December 1502, when (with Machiavelli as a fascinated witness), Cesare Borgia arranged for the execution of four of his rebellious captains after inviting them to a banquet of reconciliation. Defamatory images were used, most notably by the Florentines, to humiliate those military captains who they felt had betrayed them. In 1425, a *pittura infamante* of the *condottiere* Niccolò Piccinino was painted on the wall of the palace of the *podestà*. When Niccolò appealed to his employer, the Visconti lord of Milan, to persuade the Florentines to whitewash the portrait, the Signoria responded, "Concerning the depainting of Niccolò Piccinino, we marvel that you would require it, or anyone consent to it. For it would set the worst example and give cause to the captains to be lacking in faith and not concerned with their honor."[63] The uneven performance of *condottieri* during the Quattrocento suggests that they were not particularly concerned about their reputation for loyalty. A handful were renowned for honoring their contracts, for example, the English captain John Hawkwood, who was given a state funeral by the Florentine commune in 1394 and whose equestrian portrait was later painted by Paolo Uccello on the interior wall of the cathedral. The Venetian republic likewise honored three of its loyal captains—Paolo Savelli, Gattamelata, and Bartolomeo Colleoni—with equestrian statues.

The tense adversarial relationships between Italian governments and their mercenaries were replicated in the diplomatic activity between regimes in their negotiations and contacts with each other. The Italian League, formed by the major regional powers after the peace of Lodi in 1454, obligated its members to seek peaceful solutions to their quarrels. But within a few years of signing that pact, these regimes, abandoning any pretense of commitment to collective security, embarked on a series of conflicts which destabilized the peninsula and opened the way to foreign intervention. Republics and despots both ignored sworn oaths to adhere to their commitments. Pope Pius II once observed that "the Florentines and the Venetians consider an oath sacred to the extent that it is useful to maintain it."[64] In her superb analysis of the Italian diplomatic scene in these decades prior to the French invasion of 1494, Melissa Bullard has described "the wariness and heightened sense of uncertainty which permeated Italian relations in the late fifteenth century" and the atmosphere of suspicion and distrust that hovered like a dense cloud over every chancery.[65] The Florentine ambassador in Rome in the 1480s, Guidantonio Vespucci, wrote despairingly to Lorenzo de' Medici that "nowadays no trust was to be had in what was said or written to one, nor in friendship nor in promises made, but only in that which . . . one can see is happening."[66] Lorenzo's view was no less negative: "I have very little trust in the affairs of Rome; there is no solidity there."[67] Lorenzo perceived no more *fede* in his allies than in his enemies. While he did everything in his power to sustain Florence's alliance with her major partner, Lodovico Sforza, the lord of Milan, he regarded *il Moro* with barely disguised contempt, often questioning his judgment, his stability, his honesty, and even (on one occasion) his manhood.[68] Lorenzo occasionally described himself as the only honest man in a coterie of scoundrels: "I govern myself in these matters with as much sincerity and *fede* as any man in the world"; and again, "I follow my free and true nature, and despite what others might say, I will be with signor Lodovico [Sforza] with that trust and commitment that I have always demonstrated."[69]

Melissa Bullard, analyzing the language used in diplomatic correspondence in these years, noted "the close affinity between Italian mercantile and diplomatic correspondence," and she suggests that this bond "illustrates the attempt to impose rules to regularize and hence limit risk" in diplomatic relations.[70] A letter written in 1474 by Lorenzo de' Medici to Galeazzo Maria Sforza, the lord of Milan, illustrates this connection. "Your Excellency knows," Lorenzo wrote, "how important credit and *fede* are to a merchant. It seems strange to me that in the Roman court, where men from every country and nation congregate, anyone would give credence to His Holiness' (Pope Sixtus IV) suspicion that we have ever mismanaged [our business]. In the past we have been [papal] treasurers, and never there or anywhere else, have we been unfaithful and for more than a hundred years, we have been merchants."[71] Lorenzo was perhaps suggesting that the *fede* which the Medici had earned as honest businessmen should be transferred to their political activities.

I have drawn a sharp contrast between the role of trust in the economic and political worlds of late medieval and Renaissance Italy. *Fede* remained a vital element in economic relationships because the penalties for a breach of trust were severe. Perhaps, as Thomas Kuehn has suggested for late Quattrocento Florence, the ethical standards of the past had been eroded to some degree, though this problem merits further study. In the political arena, trust was a shrinking commodity, in very short supply within and between states. The widespread practice of exile manifested the lack of trust within political societies. By the end of the fifteenth century, the swearing of an oath as a guarantee of an obligation had become practically worthless in both domestic and interstate politics. Machiavelli, who understood as well as any of his contemporaries the political world he inhabited, realized how exceptional was his own conduct when he wrote in 1513 to his friend Francesco Vettori (1513) that the Medici "should not doubt my loyalty, for always having kept my word, I have not now learned to break it, and anyone who has been faithful and honest for 43 years, as I have been, cannot change his nature. My poverty is witness to my honesty."[72] As so often, Machiavelli had the last word.

CHAPTER SIX

Florence Redux

When, in November 1952, I made my first tremulous entrance into the reading room of the Florentine Archivio di Stato, I joined a small coterie of researchers that, on any given day, numbered no more than a dozen.[1] That group included two distinguished historians from the United States, Felix Gilbert and Raymond De Roover, and Nicolai Rubinstein from London. The only Italian scholar in daily attendance in the archives was Elio Conti, then in the early stages of his research on fifteenth-century Florentine society. The older generation of Florentine historians had either died (Davidsohn, Caggese, Barbadoro) or were no longer actively engaged in research (Salvemini, Rodolico). Few students from the University of Florence ventured into the archives; their professors (Sestan, Garin, and Cantimori) encouraged them to work instead in the Biblioteca Nazionale. Students of the eminent economic historian Armando Sapori did work in the archives, and members of the staff (Guido Pampaloni, Francesca Morandini, Roberto Abbondanza) published the results of their researches in the *Archivio storico italiano* and in other Tuscan journals. From this very modest nucleus of scholars then working on medieval and Renaissance Florence, it would have been difficult to predict the explosive growth of the field in subsequent years. But already in the 1950s, a cluster of young historians from the Anglo-

Saxon world were coming to the archives to work on their research projects: Louis Marks, Philip Jones, Lauro Martines, Marvin Becker, David Herlihy, George Holmes, Peter Partner. This was the generation that revolutionized Florentine studies.

These scholars came to Florence from varied academic backgrounds. They were not linked to any historical tradition, nor any particular ideology or methodology. The influence of German refugee scholars (Baron, Kristeller, Mommsen, Gilbert) on this generation of Americans has been exaggerated.[2] Though my mentor at Princeton, Theodor Mommsen, did suggest my dissertation topic on fourteenth-century Florence, I was converted to the study of Florentine history by two Oxford scholars: William Deakin and Cecelia Ady. Lauro Martines was visiting Florence to study Renaissance painting when I induced him to explore manuscript sources in the archives. Marvin Becker was planning to write a biography of Walter of Brienne when he began his research in the commune's fiscal records and developed his thesis on the evolution of the Florentine territorial state. David Herlihy came to Florence by way of Pisa and Pistoia and then began his monumental study based on fifteenth-century tax records, the *catasto*. He found his partner in that enterprise, Christiane Klapisch-Zuber, through a chance encounter with Emmanuel LeRoy Ladurie.[3] English and Australian students migrated to Florence through their apprenticeship with Nicolai Rubinstein and Philip Jones, but their choice of research topics was often dictated by their particular interests and encounters with specific archival sources. It was these encounters, often accidental, with those records that fostered the research agendas and kindled the passions of those students. For some, fiscal records provided the raw material for their investigations; for others, the official sources of the commune; for still others, private records: diaries, letters, account books.

This combination of an exceptionally rich documentary record and a group of historians endowed with tenacity and imagination has produced a body of scholarship that has no equal in European urban history before the French Revolution.[4] Hans Baron's *Crisis of the Early Italian Renaissance* is the crown jewel of this corpus, its thesis still hotly debated four decades after its publication.[5] Nicolai Rubinstein has recently published the second edition of his classic work on the Florentine constitution under the Medici.[6] "Marvin Becker's powerful hypothesis regarding the transformation of communal government into . . . the 'territorial state' has continued to reverberate in works devoted to the history of the late medieval state."[7] Books based on the *catasto* records by David Herlihy and Christiane Klapisch-Zuber and by Elio Conti constitute the most thoroughly documented study of the demographic and economic foundations of a Renaissance society.[8] Lauro Martines's two books on Florentine humanists and lawyers developed a sound methodology for studying professional elites in Italian cities.[9] Richard Trexler's pioneering and controversial work on Florentine civic ritual is required reading for students of Italian urban history.[10] Richard Goldthwaite's books and articles on the Florentine economy have established him as the heir of a grand tradition that includes Alfred Doren, Armando Sapori, Raymond de Roover, and Federico Melis.[11] Of the large number of books devoted to family history, the monographs of F. W. Kent and Anthony Molho, and the collection of articles by Christiane Klapisch-Zuber, stand out as works of exceptional quality.[12]

In 1983, I published a review article on Florentine historiography, in which I emphasized the domination of English-speaking scholars, the relatively modest achievement of Italians, and the absence of German historians, who had been so prominent in the field in the prewar period.[13] I noted that in the 1970s, twenty books on medieval and Renaissance Florence had been published in English; that pattern continues today. In the past decade, sixteen history books on Florence have been published by American scholars, seven by British, eleven by Italians, two by Australians, and one each by French and Canadian historians.[14] There has emerged, in the past two decades, a generation of Italian historians, well versed in the literature and methodologies of current scholarship, who are making a significant contribution to Florentine historiography.[15]

A remarkable feature of postwar Florentine historiography is the intense concentration on the fourteenth and fifteenth centuries, and the neglect of the period before Dante. How to explain this lack of interest in the medieval centuries in favor of the period after the Black Death? Where, among Italian medievalists, are the successors of Gaetano Salvemini, Nicola Ottokar, Gioacchino Volpe, Cinzio Violante? Why did Nicolai Rubinstein, who had been a student in Florence of the Russian medievalist Ottokar and wrote his first book on a thirteenth-century topic, decide instead to concentrate on the fifteenth century? Why did David Herlihy, whose first book was a study of thirteenth-century Pisa, and who had written articles on the economy and demography of Carolingian Europe, write his next books on late medieval Pistoia and on fifteenth-century Florence? The history of medieval Florence is essentially that constructed by Robert Davidsohn a century ago.

The concentration of Florentine research on the post-Dante period can be explained primarily by the unparalleled richness of the documentation, both public and private. A prime example is the *catasto*, the volumes of tax reports from 1427 to 1480. These thousand-odd tomes contain information about demographic patterns, births and deaths, marriages and dowries, economic investments; and about such topics as familial relationships; the status of women, orphans, and bastards; illness and disease; literacy. The information contained in these tax records can be supplemented by private letters and diaries (some 150 of the latter from the fifteenth century); by notarial protocols; by court records; and by the deliberations of the civic magistracies established to confront particular problems. These include records of inventories of the property of orphans; guild records furnishing information on the lives of laborers in the cloth industry; as well as data on the identities and lives of prostitutes and on males accused of homosexual acts.[16]

But there is a downside to this massive accumulation of source material. Florentine scholars can become so absorbed in the particular niche that they have carved out for themselves that they do not see the forest for the trees. In a review article published some thirty years ago, Randolph Starn noted this obsession with documents, so characteristic a feature of Florentine historical scholarship.[17] This could lead to tunnel vision, to an unwillingness to look beyond the immediate object of study to search for contexts and connections, or to consider comparisons with other Italian communities. I will cite an example of how deep immersion into the archival sources transformed the scholarship of a major historian. I first met Elio Conti in 1952, when he was embarked on an ambitious enterprise to write a comprehensive history of fifteenth-century Florentine society, based primarily but not exclusively on the *catasto* records. Conti had been encouraged to undertake this project by Gaetano Salvemini, who had returned from exile in the United States to teach at the University of Florence after the war.[18] Conti's plan was to identify the "classes" in Florentine society and to demonstrate how their relations transformed the economy, the political system, and the culture. But while exploring the documentary record, Conti realized that he could not understand urban society without knowledge of the rural world that surrounded and nourished it. He then published three volumes on that agrarian milieu, but he never moved beyond preliminary studies to analyze Florentine urban society, a task that was later undertaken by David Herlihy and Christiane Klapisch-Zuber, with the aid of the computer. Conti and his students edited and published a range of documentary sources: notarial records and deliberations of municipal councils. His last published work before his premature death in 1988 was a study of the Florentine fisc in the fifteenth century, a work of vast erudition, but one that puzzled its readers for its empiricism and its failure to summarize and contextualize its argument.[19] Conti's plan to write a *histoire totale* of Quattrocento Florentine society was ultimately defeated by the "many tons of paper" that he had studied in thirty-five years of research, but which he could not organize and synthesize.

Conti's inability to integrate his material is a symptom of a serious defect in Florentine historiography: the failure to summarize and integrate recent scholarship. In his 1970 review article, Starn observed that "a serious, full-scale history of medieval and Renaissance Florence . . . cannot be expected for a long time."[20] More recently, John Najemy described Florentine historiography as being in a state of disintegration. Reviewing five books on fifteenth-century topics, he stressed the differences in their methods, their interpretations, their "languages," and concluded that their arguments were fundamentally irreconcilable.[21] Felix Gilbert made the same point in an essay describing the various interpretations of three books on Florentine topics, "so different the reader may wonder if the Florence one scholar writes about can possibly be the same city another scholar discusses."[22] Najemy is certainly correct in concluding that controversy, not consensus, reigns in Florentine historiography. Anthony Molho has been sharply critical of what he describes as the "anglophone" tradition of Florentine history, accusing its practitioners of idealizing its republican government and of ignoring the pattern of class conflict and the exploitation of the urban working class and the rural peasantry by the city's dominant elite.[23] One "anglophone" historian, Humfrey Butters, delivered a broadside against his colleagues, who (he claims) have been seduced by the lure of writing "total history" and by the claims of social science to establish historical laws.[24] So on the one hand are scholars who deplore the positivist character of much Florentine historiography and who urge a greater attention to theory;[25] and on the other hand, those who criticize any commitment to theoretical models: whether Marxist or *marxisante*, or *Annaliste*, or Foucauldian.

In some areas of Florentine history, a rough consensus has been achieved, most notably with respect to the city's political development, "from a faction-ridden and ungovernable commune to a guild republic to an oligarchic one."[26] Also generally accepted is the tripartite structure of Florentine society: a small, wealthy elite of entrepreneurs and rentiers; a middling class of artisans and shopkeepers; and a large underclass of the poor and the destitute. Recent scholarship has focused less on class distinctions and more on the bonds (patron-client relations; neighborhood, parish and confraternal associations) that linked together the members of this community.[27] The city's economic development after the Black Death remains a very controversial subject, with some historians emphasizing its growth and prosperity, and others its stagnation and decline.[28] The character and evolution of the Florentine economy is linked to a more fundamental issue that was formulated most dramatically 140 years ago by Jacob Burckhardt when he described Florence as being "the most important workshop of the Italian, and indeed of the modern European spirit." The relative "modernity" of Renaissance Florence—its politics, its economy, its social order, its culture—continues to divide Florentine historians. The most forceful and eloquent exponent of the "modernity" thesis is Richard Goldthwaite, who described his most recent book as "an enlargement of Jacob Burckhardt's classic—and much debated—vision of Renaissance Italy as the birthplace of the modern world; to his formulation about the Italians' discovery of antiquity, nature, man and the individual is here added their discovery also of things."[29] A prominent spokesman for the opposing camp is Anthony Molho, who argues that "an immersion in the Florentine culture of the fifteenth century leads one . . . to an uncompromisingly nonmodern world . . . It was not a bourgeois world but rather one whose values were closer, more akin, to those of a feudal, aristocratic society."[30]

These controversies among Florentine historians over method and interpretation can be seen as evidence of the sustained vitality and dynamism of the field. Michael Rocke's book, *Forbidden Friendships*, is an original, pathbreaking analysis of Florence's homoerotic culture in the fifteenth century. Samuel Cohn's study of Tuscan and Umbrian wills as testimonials of shifting patterns of piety should muffle if not silence those who have criticized the failure of Florentine historians to engage in comparative analysis.[31] Cohn's new book, *Creating the Florentine State*, challenges current orthodoxy on the construction of a regional state in the fifteenth century and throws new light on rebel mountaineers on Florence's northern and eastern frontiers.[32] So long neglected, Florence's religious history has experienced a remarkable revival in recent years.[33] A work in progress that is notable for its scope and depth is the study of the pre-Reformation Florentine church by David Peterson, the most comprehensive analysis of an Italian regional church that has yet been written.[34] Equally impressive for its range and its interdisciplinary character is Dale Kent's *Cosimo de' Medici and the Florentine Renaissance*. No other book on Florence, or indeed on any Italian Renaissance city, has utilized so broad a range of sources, or has integrated so effectively the various strands of cultural activity in the Medici era: oral, literary, visual; Christian, humanist, *popolare*.[35] The occasion of the five hundredth anniversary of the death of Lorenzo de' Medici (1992) unleashed a torrent of publications dedicated to Il Magnifico, whose career has been more fully documented and analyzed than that of any other Florentine with the possible exception of Dante. Together with the corpus of Lorenzo's correspondence and newly discovered sources, these studies will be integrated into F. W. Kent's projected two-volume biography of Lorenzo.[36]

The insularity that once characterized Florentine historiography has been replaced by a sustained effort to integrate the city's history into a broader regional (and peninsular) context, and to develop comparative perspectives. This integration has been a central theme in the series of volumes dedicated to Tuscan ruling elites, and in a collection of articles edited by William Connell and Andrea Zorzi on Florentine Tuscany.[37] The focus of these volumes is the structure of relationships that linked the capital city, provincial towns, and rural villages (and their inhabitants) together. Included in this conceptual framework are the economic relations between Florence and its territory, the political and social bonds between Florentine patrons and their clients and dependents in the dominion, as well as the ties binding members of guilds, confraternities, and neighborhoods. Another distinctive feature of recent scholarship is the interweaving of topics (political, socioeconomic, religious, cultural) that in the past were often treated as autonomous categories. Thus, the production of a work of art is perceived as a complex process "in which Church, state, individual power, intellectual endeavor, artistic propaganda and private delectation come together in the multi-faceted synthesis."[38] Even a conservative field like diplomatic history has been transformed by the felt need to broaden horizons and perspectives. Daniela Frigo describes Renaissance diplomacy as "the arena of action with which the manifold currents of a state's political life flowed: power balances within ruling elites or at court, individual careers and fortunes, the influence of groups and factions, legal and political culture, religious and confessional motives, military force, economic expansion, the degree of consensus enjoyed by the government or dynasty."[39]

In recent years, as Edward Muir has noted, there has been a significant shift in Italian Renaissance historiography away from Florence.[40] Venetian historical writing can match both the quality and the output of its Tuscan rival, and the historians of the Adriatic republic have been more active in synthesizing their research.[41] Of the major Italian cities, only Milan has failed to attract the interest of foreign scholars, who "mostly prefer Florence, Venice and Rome, for various good reasons . . . and for various bad reasons, including snobbery and inertia."[42] Within Tuscany itself, a rich historiography has developed in recent years, focusing on the major cities (Pisa, Siena, Lucca, Arezzo) and also on the smaller provincial towns (Prato, Pescia, Poppi, Pistoia).[43] The multivolume history of Prato has been described as "an enterprise which will surely set a new standard of excellence in the field of European urban history in the early modern age."[44] Florentine historiography could benefit greatly from a comparable enterprise.

While Florence's historiographical hegemony has been weakened in recent years, so too is its status as the primary if not sole creator of Renaissance culture. The city has always been fortunate in the quality and reputation of its panegyrists, from Bruni, Ficino, and Vasari to Burckhardt and Baron.[45] Burckhardt was a particularly influential promoter of the notion that the Renaissance was fundamentally a Florentine achievement. "Not only did Burckhardt frame what remains one of the grandest and clearest expositions of what the Renaissance was, and why it mattered, but he also left a clear trail for those who would follow in his footsteps and decide for themselves whether his large claims were actually true. Burckhardt's advice was simple. If you want to understand the Renaissance, go to Florence."[46] There are few, if any, scholars of Renaissance Italy who today would accept this Burckhardtian axiom. Bruni's claim for Florence's central role in the revival of antiquity has been challenged, as has the general significance of humanism in Italian (and European) cultural history.[47] Giorgio Vasari's hugely influential *Lives of the Most Excellent Painters, Sculptors and Architects* emphasized Florence's preeminence in the artistic revolution, but recent scholarship has given equal weight to the achievements of northern Italian artists, and particularly those working in princely courts.[48] Nevertheless, a case can still be made for Florence's "exceptionalism" and for stressing those dimensions of its historical experience that distinguished it from other Italian urban societies. These unique features include the vital strand of republicanism in its political practices and ideology; the balance of its economic system among its commercial, industrial, banking craft, and agrarian components; the remarkable receptivity by its elite of classicizing influences in literature and art; the symbiotic relationship between elite and popular culture; and the strongly empirical element in that culture.[49]

Today Florence is a museum city that is barely able to survive the phenomenon of mass tourism, while its inhabitants choke on its polluted air. And yet, it continues to work its magic on our imagination and our sensibilities. A recent issue of *The New Yorker* contained a review by the literary critic George Steiner of Michael Levey's book on Florence.[50] Steiner, who noted that he "has walked and walked that city a hundred times over," still finds it "obstinately new." "Florence exceeds its masterpieces," he wrote. "There is about this city, frequently morose, even harsh, a mystery of implosion, as if singular forces of intellect and feeling had been compelled into fruitful collision by the ring of hills, by a climate susceptible of white heat and bone-jarring cold. Genius and civic ferocity were intimately meshed. . . . Out of catastrophes sprang energies that have, in essence, come close to defining Western civilization. As our millennium limps to a close, it does more and more appear as if the foremost poetic intelligence—the preeminent act of shaping thought and philosophy in the Western legacy, were Dante's. There are whole continents that have contributed less to mankind than this one small city."

CHAPTER SEVEN

Living on the Edge in Leonardo's Florence

Leonardo da Vinci was born on April 15, 1452, the product of a liaison between a provincial notary, ser Piero d'Antonio da Vinci, and a peasant girl who is known only by her Christian name, Caterina. At some point in his early childhood, Leonardo's mother was married and the boy was taken into his father's household, where he lived with his legitimate siblings. These scraps of biographical information are found in ser Piero's tax reports. Leonardo himself did not write about his childhood in his voluminous notebooks, save for that one notorious reference to a dream involving a bird, around which Sigmund Freud constructed his fable about the boy's early years. To understand the conditions of life in the small village of Leonardo's boyhood and later in Florence, where he lived and worked as an apprentice in Verrocchio's shop, we have to create images of those rural and urban milieux of the later fifteenth century. We are blessed with a plethora of sources to help us construct these historical scenarios. They include public records—statutes and legislation; acts of civil, criminal, mercantile, and ecclesiastical courts; tax records; and notarial protocols that include documents pertaining to marriages and dowries, property transactions, and testaments. In addition to this vast corpus of public documents, Florentine archives and libraries house the richest collection of private records, most notably, letters and diaries, of any European city in the Renaissance era.

The city's population fluctuated between forty and fifty-five thousand inhabitants.[1] This seems a minuscule figure to us today, but in the fifteenth century, Florence ranked among the five most populous cities in Italy. Florence was a wealthy city, deriving its wealth from industry (primarily cloth making), trade, and banking, as well as agriculture and a large and productive craft sector. But the city's wealth was divided unevenly, with about a hundred very rich men like Cosimo de' Medici, whose fortune of 150,000 florins made him one of the financial giants of Europe and also one of the most important patrons of the arts; an affluent elite made up of a substantial number of well-to-do merchants, cloth manufacturers, bankers, landowners, and lawyers; and a middling category of artisans, retail merchants, and professional men like Leonardo's father, the notary ser Piero da Vinci. This layer of the social hierarchy included nearly all of the painters, sculptors, architects, and goldsmiths with whom Leonardo lived and worked from the mid-1470s until 1482, when he left Florence for Milan. At the bottom of the social scale were the poor, comprising about one-third of the city's population: cloth workers, laborers in the construction industry, servants, street peddlers, mendicants, criminals, prostitutes.

Despite the hierarchy of Florentine society, based on wealth, family status, and political influence, there was considerable interaction between members of the social groups: between, for example, the rich merchants who commissioned the grand palaces being built in these years and the artisans, masons, sculptors, and painters who constructed and decorated them.[2] The barriers separating social groups were somewhat less rigid than in most other Italian cities or in communities across the Alps, with legally defined, privileged nobility.

Florence, though nominally a republic, since 1434 had been under the control of a coalition of prominent families led by the Medici—first Cosimo, then Piero, and finally Lorenzo, who succeeded his father as head of the government in 1469 when he was only twenty, and when the seventeen-year-old Leonardo was still an obscure apprentice. Florence was also the capital of a large regional state, one of five major powers in Italy, with a total population of some three hundred thousand. But this Tuscan state was the weakest of the major powers in the peninsula, less populous and less wealthy, and during the last decades of the fifteenth century, Florentines became acutely aware of their vulnerability.

My central theme in this chapter is that sense of vulnerability, the awareness of grave perils that threatened Florence's security and prosperity during Leonardo's lifetime. In titling it "Living on the Edge," I mean to suggest a state of extreme anxiety that we in California associate with natural disasters (earthquakes, fires, floods) and now terrorism. The dangers threatening Florentines in the fifteenth century included natural disasters but also two scourges over which they had no control: poor harvests and the food shortages which caused starvation and social unrest; and the epidemics of plague that struck city and countryside on average once a decade. The plague inspired the greatest fear and dread because it attacked, so unpredictably, both its cause and cure unknown. While the majority of the plague's victims were children and the elderly, the disease also struck adults, including heads of households. Alessandra Strozzi (d. 1471) lived through five visitations of the plague which claimed the lives of her husband, three of her children, and several other relatives. She described the sense of loss and desperation experienced by the remnants of the family who survived these epidemics, which threatened their livelihood and their status in the city.[3]

Political crises and upheavals, both internal and external, contributed to the atmosphere of tension and anxiety in Florence. The Medici regime, never stable, was threatened by rivalries among its leaders and also by challenges from citizens who had been excluded from office and power. In 1478 a group of conspirators led by members of the Pazzi family, wealthy bankers, attempted to assassinate Lorenzo de' Medici, and while failing in that goal, they did manage to kill his younger brother Giuliano. The conspirators then rode on horseback through the city, seeking the citizenry's support for their rebellion. But enraged Medici partisans captured the conspirators, and four of the ringleaders were hanged from the windows of the palace of the Signoria.[4] The intense political passions unleashed by this conspiracy were revealed gruesomely when a band of adolescent boys disinterred the body of one of the executed plotters, Messer Jacopo de' Pazzi, dragged it through the city, and threw it into the Arno river, where it floated downstream all the way to Pisa. The Pazzi rebellion ignited a conflict between Florence and her enemies, Pope Sixtus IV and the king of Naples, and for two years, soldiers hired by the pope and the king ravaged the Florentine countryside south of the city. In his tax report for the year 1480, Manente Buondelmonti described his losses in the Chianti region, where "the mill was destroyed by our own soldiers, and all of the harvest taken. Our stores, our buildings and the land have been so badly damaged that we have lost everything we worked for this year. . . . The parish church and all of the cottages are deserted, occupied only by soldiers who drank about fifty barrels of our wine."[5] This destruction was a foretaste of that wrought by foreign armies unleashed in the peninsula, beginning with the French invasion of 1494.

During the last decade of Lorenzo's life, from 1482 to 1492, Il Magnifico (as he was called) tightened his hold on the government and worked to promote his image as a wise statesman primarily responsible for the city's prosperity and for maintaining peace in Italy. Many Florentines accepted that image, for example, Lorenzo's business partner, Giovanni Tornabuoni, who commissioned Domenico Ghirlandaio to paint a famous fresco cycle dedicated to the Virgin Mary and St. John the Baptist in the Dominican church of S. Maria Novella. Inscribed in one scene from that cycle was this legend: "The year 1490, when this most beautiful city, renowned for abundance, victories, arts and noble buildings, enjoyed salubrity and peace."[6] But behind this facade of well-being were clear signs of serious trouble for the Medici, for Florence, and for the whole of Italy. The Medici bank, which was a critical element in that family's power, was teetering on the edge of bankruptcy. And despite Lorenzo's efforts to maintain peace, relations between the major Italian powers deteriorated in these years. The major villain in the events leading to the French invasion of 1494 was the ruler of Milan, Lodovico Sforza, who was also Leonardo's employer and patron from 1482 to 1499. Lodovico invited Charles VIII, the king of France, to invade Italy and conquer the territory of his enemy, the king of Naples. The French monarch accepted this invitation and in the summer of 1494 led an army of thirty thousand soldiers across the Alps into Italy.

Piero de' Medici had replaced his father, Lorenzo, as head of the Florentine government upon the latter's death in 1492. Piero was young, inexperienced, and headstrong, and he had alienated many prominent citizens who had been his father's allies. When the French army approached the city, these men organized a coup d'état, expelling the Medici and inviting the French to enter the city as friends and allies. Charles VIII accepted the invitation, and on November 4, 1494, the first contingent of French troops marched through the gate of S. Gallo on the northern edge of the city. The chronicler Piero Parenti, an eyewitness to this occupation, wrote that the French soldiers "marched through the streets, entering the most elegant houses, forcing their inhabitants to vacate, and marking those occupied houses with chalk." The civic authorities notified citizens that they should open their homes to the soldiers and not remove any furniture or goods. Fearing trouble, many Florentines left the city with their money and jewelry, finding refuge in their country villas.

Negotiations between the French king and the Florentine authorities over a treaty agreement stalled at one point, when one of the city magistrates, Piero Capponi, threw down the gauntlet to Charles. "You can sound your trumpets," he told the king, "and we will ring our bells." The ringing of the bells would signal the citizenry to assemble with their arms in the piazza della Signoria to attack the invaders. The king then agreed to a settlement by which he accepted a cash payment of 100,000 florins, and in return promised to protect the city and to restore the rebellious town of Pisa to Florentine control, a promise he did not keep. Florentines witnessed the departure of the French army on November

28 with an enormous sense of relief that was overshadowed by their increased awareness of the city's vulnerability. The French, who had moved south to occupy the kingdom of Naples, were soon forced to abandon their conquest and retreat to their homeland. Passing through Tuscany in the spring of 1495, the French army (according to Piero Parenti) "robbed and looted the rural districts, while in the city, fears of another assault swept through the streets and squares."[7] "The bells began to ring" (this is still Parenti's account) "and rumors circulated that the French army was approaching the city walls." Once again, the inhabitants sought to hide their possessions and their daughters and "ran through the streets like people possessed, not realizing where they were going or why."[8] The first foreign invasion was short-lived, but it was followed by others: another French army invaded Milan in 1499; Spanish troops occupied part of the Neapolitan kingdom in 1502; a German force invaded Friuli in 1508.

In this febrile atmosphere, Florentines endeavored to govern themselves, to preserve their depleted territory, and to raise money for military needs. The political situation in the city remained tense and unstable. The republican regime had to contend with opposition from supporters of the exiled Medici and also with an impoverished laboring class. Unemployment in the cloth industry was widespread, trade routes having been interrupted by the invading armies. The ravages of the soldiery had reduced the supply of grain available to feed the urban population, and a spate of rainy weather in the summer of 1496 created famine conditions in city and countryside. The druggist Luca Landucci reported that the price of wheat tripled during the autumn and winter of 1496–97. The city's churches, monasteries, and charitable foundations were overwhelmed by the throngs of hungry and destitute people. Landucci described the tragic fate of one poor peasant who had come into the city to find food for his family. Returning to his cottage in the country, he discovered that his wife and three children had died of starvation, and overwhelmed by despair and remorse, he committed suicide. Landucci also reported how a crowd of poor women who went to the palace of the Signoria to demand bread and then ran through the streets, frightening the shopkeepers, who immediately shut down their stores, leaving the citizens without access to food. Famine conditions meant malnutrition, which invariably led to epidemics, as the germs that thrived in this crowded and unsanitary urban environment invaded weakened bodies. The plague followed famine as night follows day, and Landucci reported that during the spring of 1497, one hundred inhabitants died each day.[9]

The late fall, winter, and spring of 1497–98 also witnessed the climax of the Savonarola story, one of the most traumatic moments in the city's history. Girolamo Savonarola, a Dominican friar and a native of Ferrara, had achieved fame and a large following in Florence through his preaching and his prophecies. His message was simple and dramatic. The church, the papacy, and Italian society were all corrupt and in drastic need of reform. God had chosen him, Savonarola, to warn Italians to cleanse themselves and their society or face destruction. The particular target of Savonarola's wrath was the Borgia pope, Alexander VI, and the papal court, which he described as a cesspool. Savonarola limited neither his message nor his activities to the religious sphere but involved himself in the city's political life. He denounced the Medici as tyrants and favored a broad-based republican government that included artisans and shopkeepers (but not wage laborers) as well as merchants and bankers. His supporters formed a party to promote his political program, which included an agenda for improving civic morality by attacking gambling, prostitution, and homosexuality. From his base in the convent of S. Marco, he exhorted his followers to enact his program and to strive for the reformation of the city, which he called the "New Jerusalem." His Dominican colleagues organized groups of boys and girls to patrol the city, to identify malefactors, and to eradicate vice. These children were responsible for the famous "bonfires of the vanities," the collections of paintings, books, musical instruments, and women's finery that were burned in the city squares.[10]

Savonarola's preaching and his political agenda attracted a large and enthusiastic following in the city, men and women from the great aristocratic families as well as members of the lower classes: artisans, shop-keepers, day laborers. These disciples flocked to his sermons; they came to S. Marco to talk to him and his fellow Dominicans, to pray, to confess, to hear mass, to receive the Eucharist. Savonarola's appeal to women and adolescents was particularly strong, and these groups constituted some of his most loyal supporters. But the friar also made enemies among the ecclesiastical hierarchy headed by Pope Alexander VI, and among members of other religious orders, notably the Franciscans and the Augustinians, who were jealous of the friar's influence. In secular society, Savonarola was opposed by supporters of the Medici and by members of the elite who disliked his involvement in politics and his program of reform. Savonarola had polarized the city to such a degree that one speaker in a council meeting complained that wives were alienated from their husbands, and fathers from their sons. Two of the shrewdest observers of contemporary politics, Niccolò Machiavelli and Francesco Guicciardini, held opposing views on Savonarola. After hearing one of the friar's sermons in the cathedral, Machiavelli wrote to a friend that "in my judgment, the friar colors his lies and suits them to the occasion." Guicciardini, in contrast, praised Savonarola's work: "His labors for morality were most holy and wonderful; and never had Florence witnessed such virtue and such faith as in his years here."[11]

The issue that most sharply divided the citizenry was Savonarola's claim to be a prophet and the authentic voice of God. In May 1497 the friar had been excommunicated by Pope Alexander VI, but a year later (February 1498) he returned to the pulpit in the cathedral. When the pope threatened to place the city under interdict, the Signoria ordered the friar to cease preaching. A Franciscan friar then challenged Savonarola's colleague, Fra Domenico da Pescia, to an ordeal by fire, in which each would walk between two burning pyres of wood to determine who enjoyed divine favor. Thousands of citizens flocked into the piazza della Signoria to witness this ordeal, which never took place. Savonarola's opponents, sensing that public opinion had shifted against the friar, seized him in S. Marco, and forced him to confess under torture that he was a false prophet. Though he later recanted his confession, he was sentenced to death and with two of his close associates, was hanged, and his body burned in the piazza della Signoria. Luca Landucci, who had been a fervent disciple of the friar, expressed his disillusionment and despair when he wrote that many like himself had believed that Savonarola was truly an agent of God, with a divine mandate to reform society, cleanse the church, and introduce a new order into the world. But after the friar's confession, Landucci felt betrayed, though he did admit that thousands of his fellow citizens continued to believe that the friar had been a true prophet of God.[12] Though they could not publicly express their opinions, these *frateschi*, or *piagnoni* (as they were called), met secretly to pray, to sing hymns, and to share their memories of the man whom they revered. They remained a force in the city's political life, promoting the friar's agenda for years after his death.[13]

In 1499, a year marked by a poor harvest and food shortages, Leonardo da Vinci returned to Florence from Milan, where his patron, Lodovico Sforza, had been imprisoned by an invading French army. "The duke lost his state and his property," Leonardo wrote, "and none of his works were completed for him."[14] Those works included Leonardo's clay model for an equestrian statue of Lodovico's father, Francesco Sforza, which was pulverized by French soldiers, who used it for target practice. The early 1500s were not a prosperous time for the Florentines, or for Leonardo, who in 1502 was hired as a military engineer by Cesare Borgia, the son of Pope Alexander VI, who was then attempting to carve out a state for himself in central Italy. In 1501, Cesare had led an army into Florentine territory. According to the chronicler Bartolomeo Masi, Borgia's troops ravaged the countryside west of Florence between Empoli and Prato.[15] Throngs of peasants fled into the city for protection. Fearing for their lives, the nuns cloistered in convents outside the city sought refuge within the walls. Borgia's army eventually moved out of Florentine territory, but his depredations were followed by two major rebellions in the subject towns of Pistoia and Arezzo. These revolts revealed the Florentine government's weakness and its tenuous hold on its own territory. Nature contributed to the tribulations of the city, which in the winter and spring of 1504–5 experienced the worst food shortage in living memory, with grain selling for four times the normal price. Even with communal subsidies to provide cheap grain, hundreds died of starvation.[16] Then in the summer of 1510, Florence was shaken by an earthquake, "so frightening" (reported Bartolomeo Masi) "that the inhabitants fled from their houses and spent the night in the streets." Masi also wrote of a cold spell in the winter of 1510, with huge snowfalls and freezing temperatures that damaged olive trees and vines, and reduced the supply of oil and wine.[17]

Food shortages and famine, threats of military attacks, visitations of the plague, and political unrest had little immediate impact on Florentine cultural activity. The republican regime, though heavily burdened by military expenditures, found the resources to build the hall of the Great Council in the palace of the Signoria, and to commission Leonardo and Michelangelo to decorate the walls with frescoes of battle scenes (only copies of which have survived). The government also commissioned Michelangelo's statue of David in 1501, and Leonardo worked on his most famous portrait, the Mona Lisa, in these years. But eventually, the unstable political and economic conditions in Florence took their toll on cultural activity. Artists depend on patrons for their sustenance, and patrons, whether individuals or corporations, prefer stability to disorder and chaos. Leonardo never felt any close bond to his native city. Lacking any substantial commissions, he left Florence for Milan in 1506, to work for the French king, Louis XII, and eventually he moved to France as a protégé of Louis's successor, Francis I. Michelangelo was much more closely attached to his family and to Florence, but he too found greater opportunities elsewhere, living and working in Rome from 1508 to 1515, and again from 1534 until his death in 1564.

The republican regime established in 1494 managed to survive until 1512,[18] when it foundered in the context of the struggle between the rulers of France and Spain to dominate the Italian peninsula. Florence, though an ally of the French monarch, Louis XII, sought to remain neutral in that contest. But in the late summer of 1512, a Spanish army in support of the exiled Medici invaded Tuscany and moved toward Florence. Some four thousand militia were sent to defend the town of Prato, about ten miles northwest of the city, but these troops were no match for the professional soldiers of the Spanish army. The Spaniards breached the walls of Prato and entered the town, according to Bartolomeo Masi, "killing whoever sought to defend himself, and killing those who fled, some into houses, some into churches, so that there was not a single church where mass could be sung, on account of the blood of the victims who had been massacred. During three hours that evening, the enemy killed some six thousand victims. . . . And those who survived were taken prisoner, and tortured to reveal where they had hidden money and treasure. The soldiers pillaged the entire city: the houses and the churches and the monasteries. They killed priests and friars and nuns and they violated the women and stole chalices from the churches, and whatever they could not carry away, they sold. And the pillaging began on the 29th of August and it continued until the 19th of September. Finally the Spanish army abandoned Prato, and the value of their booty was estimated at one million florins. They took with them more than one thousand prisoners, some of whom they sought to ransom and some women and girls whom they took by force."[19]

Bartolomeo Masi described the effect of this calamity on the Florentines: "Everyone was petrified with fear, as they sought to hide their valuables, some in monasteries and convents, some in other places which they hoped would not be discovered. Peasants abandoned the countryside, flocking into the city with their possessions. Every house in Florence was occupied by eight or ten or twenty peasants who had fled from their farms to escape the enemy troops." In times past, soldiers would not have risked their souls by invading sacred places like convents, but the experience of Prato indicates that these sanctuaries were no longer safe. In these turbulent conditions, adherents of the Medici were able to seize the city and to establish a regime under that family's control. Supporters of the republican regime went into exile, were imprisoned, or were harassed by the Medici. One of their victims was Niccolò Machiavelli, who lost his position in the government and was later accused of conspiracy and tortured before being exiled to the village of S. Casciano, south of Florence, where he wrote his most famous work, *The Prince.*

The restoration of the Medici solved none of Florence's major problems, though the election of a Medici pope, Leo X, in 1513 did benefit those clients of the family who obtained lucrative offices in the papal government.[20] But the Medici exploited the city's resources to subsidize the papacy's military operations.[21] The chronicler Giovanni Cambi, describing conditions in the years 1522–23, wrote that the cloth industry shut down when factory owners closed their shops and fled to their country villas to escape the plague. And so, Cambi wrote, "the poor workers were unemployed, and forced to sell their belongings—clothing, bedding, shoes, kitchen utensils, to buy food for their starving families."[22] Unlike the poor, the well-to-do could escape by fleeing the city, but they were beset by other problems. Cambi described the plight of aristocratic fathers with a large number of nubile daughters. The problem was the escalation of dowries, which in times past had amounted to 500 florins, but were now in the range of 2,000 to 3,000 florins. Cambi reported that "there are more than 3,000 girls in the city between the ages of eighteen and thirty who cannot marry because their parents cannot pay these dowries."[23] To preserve their patrimonies, aristocratic families devised a system of permitting only one son and one daughter to marry. The other girls were placed in convents, though they had no religious vocation, and the other sons either entered the church or remained in a permanent state of bachelorhood.[24] As a result, most of these lineages were biologically extinct by the nineteenth century.

The late 1520s marked the climax of these years of turmoil, not only for Florence but for all of Italy. In 1525, a Spanish army defeated its French opponents in a decisive battle near the city of Pavia in Lombardy, capturing the French monarch, Francis I, who was forced to relinquish his claims to Milan and to pay a huge ransom. Instead of accepting his defeat, Francis immediately organized a league of Italian states to oppose the Spanish monarch, Charles V. The second Medici pope, Clement VII, joined that alliance. The Spanish monarch sent an army into Italy, which besieged and then sacked Rome in the spring of 1527, a horrible scene witnessed by the pope from the ramparts of the Castel Sant'Angelo. The looting, burning, and killing continued for ten days before some semblance of order was established, but the occupation of Rome by this army lasted for nine months. Within days, the news of the Rome disaster reached Florence, where it sparked a revolt against the Medici regime and the establishment of that city's last republican government. It survived for three years, succumbing to a siege by a Spanish army in August 1530.

The story of that siege has been told and retold by those who experienced the ordeal, and later by chroniclers and historians: the bombardments of the Spanish artillery; the destruction of the houses, villas, and convents outside the city walls; and as food supplies were cut off, the slow but inexorable strangulation of the city, which eventually forced its surrender. A recently published source, the correspondence of Michelangelo's father and his brothers, provides an intimate perspective on this crisis and its impact on one Florentine family. The artist himself had been appointed to supervise the city's defenses, a task he performed creditably, except for an unauthorized trip to Venice in the early stages of the siege. Michelangelo's father, Lodovico, and his three brothers (Buonarroto, Giansimone, and Gismondo) were in constant communication with each other, and their letters graphically testify to the city's parlous condition. In June 1528, even before the siege began, Buonarroto wrote that "here in Florence there is no business activity because of the plague, and every day there is yet another house infected. There is fear of war, and all of the poor are dying of hunger."[25] The twin themes of plague and food shortages run through this correspondence. By the spring of 1528, the price of wheat had risen to 100 *soldi* a bushel, four times its normal price. Once the siege began, the food supply shrank further and the inhabitants all faced starvation. The plague continued to claim its victims, including Michelangelo's brother Buonarroto and a two-year-old nephew. And whereas in the past the city's aristocrats could flee to their villas to escape the plague, this option was no longer open. Writing in late September 1529, Michelangelo's brother Gismondo wrote to his father, who held an administrative post in the *contado:* "We are living here in very dire straits and in great danger. We are confined here and we cannot leave the city without a license from the authorities."[26] Gismondo also informed his father that his sister, Francesca, a nun in a convent outside the walls, had managed to enter Florence through the gates. In a letter sent before the siege ended, Buonarroto wrote: "I will be silent on our condition here and the difficulties that we face. . . . You should thank God that you are not here, for there is no food and the plague continues to strike."[27]

Our story ends in 1530, with the termination of the siege, the demise of the last republic, and the restoration of the Medici to power. Within a few years, the destruction wrought by the siege was gradually repaired, and the city embarked upon another and very different phase of its history. Under the Medici dukes, the turbulent politics of the republican era was replaced by an authoritarian but stable regime. The city's aristocrats preserved their status and much of their wealth by accepting Medici rule and the perquisites that derived from it. The Florentine economy remained quite prosperous for several decades before losing its dynamism and ceasing to play a significant role in the European market. As ever, Florence was prone to sporadic food shortages and periodic visitations of the plague, the most lethal being that of the early 1630s, which killed tens of thousands of inhabitants and effectively destroyed the city's cloth industry. But under the aegis of the Medici court, cultural life continued to flourish. The city added a rich musical dimension to the achievements of its painters, sculptors, architects, and other craftsmen. If in these centuries there were no literary giants to compare to Dante, Boccaccio, or Petrarch, there were erudite scholars and scientists, like Galileo, of international distinction.

CHAPTER EIGHT

Florentine Cathedral Chaplains in the Fifteenth Century

This essay focuses on a little studied group within the ranks of the Florentine clergy: the corps of chaplains who serviced the chapels in the cathedral and who also participated in the liturgical functions of the metropolitan church. The sources consulted for this study are primarily documents found in the Archivio di Stato, and particularly notarial protocols and tax records. I have not had the opportunity to consult the archives of the Opera del Duomo, although Margaret Haines has provided me with valuable information, for which I thank her warmly. This is a preliminary study, based on incomplete documentation, which will explain why some of the issues raised have not been completely resolved. Still, it has been possible to sketch an image of this clerical community, to know something about the social and economic background of the chaplains, their education and training, their stipends and benefits, their career patterns, their duties and responsibilities.

The most important fact concerning the chaplains is the dramatic increase in their numbers during the fifteenth century. A communal provision of 1373 cites the total number of cathedral chaplains (as distinct from the canons) at nineteen.[1] That number did not expand significantly during the next half-century. A tax survey of cathedral personnel in 1431 records a total of twenty-two chapels, together with twenty-seven canonries.[2] Ninety years later, an archepiscopal visitation of the cathedral (1514) recorded a total of fifty-six chapels serviced by chaplains and supported by a group of thirty-three salaried clerics, and an additional thirty without stipends who were available to fill vacated posts.[3] This doubling of the number of endowed chapels was a testimonial to the powerful impulse—by individuals, families, and corporate bodies—to invest heavily in the liturgical services of the metropolitan church.

Who were these chaplains? What can we learn of their background, their families, their education? By what process did they obtain their positions in the cathedral? From the notarial records, I have compiled a list of some three hundred chaplains who served in the cathedral during the fifteenth century. Their names provide few clues to their background: ser Antonio di Jacopo, ser Ammannato di Barnaba, ser Matteo Pucci. The majority of these chaplains were recruited from the middle ranks of Florentine society. Their fathers were artisans and shopkeepers from the lower guilds, minor officials in the city's bureaucracy, or small landowners and merchants from the towns and rural districts of the dominion. The 1480 tax records identify certain of these young clerics who were enrolled in the cathedral school: Biagio, aged thirteen, and Giovanbattista, aged nine, the sons of Andrea di Biagio, a messenger *(mazziere)* employed by the Signoria; Matteo, aged sixteen, the son of a ropemaker, Girolamo di Piero; and Bartolomeo, aged nine, the son of Filippo di Bartolo, a carpenter.[4] These adolescents came from families of modest status but whose fathers were literate and willing to invest in an education for their sons to pursue an ecclesiastical career. A substantial number of cathedral chaplains were natives of towns in the Florentine dominion—Prato, Arezzo, Scarperia, Empoli, Volterra, Colle, Montevarchi—where they had been trained in *grammatica* in the free civic schools established in those communities.[5] Only six of the three hundred chaplains were members of prominent Florentine lineages: Strozzi, Davanzati, Pandolfini, Alberti, and two Castellani. Some of the Florentine aristocracy regarded a chaplain's position as beneath their dignity, comparable to occupying a rural benefice in the dominion.[6] For their sons, they aspired to obtain a canonry in Florence, Fiesole, Pisa, or Pistoia, or a lucrative office in the Roman curia.[7] The competition for such high clerical offices was intense, as illustrated by a letter sent by the Florentine ambassador in Rome, Guidantonio Vespucci, to Giovanni Lanfredini: "If your son is four years old, as you state, it will be difficult to obtain a benefice for him, even without the cure [of souls], since he could not take ecclesiastical orders at that age, and it is not customary to give benefices to laymen."[8]

For young men of modest birth and status who sought to enter the ranks of the Florentine clergy, the major obstacle was the cost of a Latin education. Even though school teachers in Florence were badly paid, the expense of schooling was a heavy charge on the resources of artisan and shopkeeper families. One solution to the problem was to send boys to study with a priest, who would teach his pupils the rudiments of Latin in exchange for serving in the church. Thus, Margherita, the widow of a bricklayer reported (1480) that her twelve-year-old son Benedetto "is staying with a priest to become a cleric."[9] In 1435, a cathedral school for clerics was established by Pope Eugenius IV. The papal bull creating this school stipulated that the total complement of students was fixed at fifty-three, of which number thirty-three were to be subsidized by stipends of 9 florins annually.[10] Thus, boys from poor families could attend the school while living at home, and make a small contribution to their family's budget. These scholars were obligated to serve in the cathedral for ten years, and then to be qualified at age twenty-five for ordination and to fill vacancies in the cathedral chapels. The bull further stipulated that clerics who received these scholarships should not be required to pay any fees for their ordination. While no lists of these scholars have survived, it is plausible to assume that the majority of cathedral chaplains were graduates of the Collegio Eugenianum.

The documents shed some light on the process by which clerics were selected to fill the cathedral chaplaincies. The cathedral canons were patrons of eleven chapels (c. 1500), and they customarily chose clerics who were graduates of the cathedral school and who, like ser Jacopo di Gratia da Castro San Giovanni, "had served in this church as an acolyte" when he was promoted in 1447.[11] The consuls of the Lana guild were patrons of ten chapels, and they too tended to select clerics from among that pool of scholars whom they, together with the archbishop, had originally selected to places in the school. But some twenty-four chapels were endowed by families or individuals, and these patrons were more likely to appoint outsiders to officiate in their chapels. Some of these chaplains were blood kin of the patrons; for example, in 1514, the chapels of the Corbizi, the Biancardi, the Ricci, the Zambelli. Others were clients of chapel patrons, who exercised their rights to appoint these dependents.

For a small majority of chaplains, their appointment to a cathedral chapel was a lifelong career. Some twenty chaplains served in the cathedral for twenty years or more; the longest recorded tenure was that of ser Piero di Lorenzo del Fornaio, who obtained a chaplaincy in 1470 and was still active in 1514. But for the majority of chaplains, their cathedral service was limited to two, three, or five years. These highly visible positions in the cathedral did provide some chaplains with the opportunity to obtain a more lucrative benefice, as rector of an urban church or a baptismal church in the dominion. In 1449, a cathedral chaplain, ser Anselmo di Giovanni, was elected by the parishioners of the urban parish of S. Maria Nepotecosa to be their rector; another chaplain, ser Giovanbattista Tomasi, was promoted to a canonry in the urban church of S. Maria Maggiore.[12] No cathedral chaplain was ever promoted to a canonry in the metropolitan church; these high offices were reserved for the sons of the Florentine and Tuscan aristocracy. Two chaplains, however, were chosen as canons in other Tuscan dioceses: ser Antonio di Francesco Naldini to the cathedral of Arezzo, and ser Gabriele di Filippo degli Albizzi, appointed in 1482 by Lorenzo de' Medici to fill a vacant canonry in Fiesole.[13]

Some chaplains were salaried employees of their patrons,[14] while the majority received the income from the endowments of the chapels which they served. In addition to these basic revenues, they (together with the canons) obtained a share of the daily distributions from the chapter's endowment. These daily payments were suspended whenever a chaplain failed to perform his liturgical duties. No evidence has yet been found to determine the amount of that daily subsidy. In the collegiate church of S. Lorenzo, canons received between 4 and 5 *soldi* daily for their participation in the services at the main altar, while chaplains were given one-half of that amount, about 2 *soldi*.[15] That pittance was about one-fifth of the daily wage of an unskilled laborer in the construction industry.[16] Since lay burials were prohibited in the cathedral except in very rare circumstances, the chaplains did not receive any income from that important source of revenue which clerics in other churches and monasteries enjoyed. But they did receive small fees of 1 or 2 *soldi* for participating in the funerals of cathedral clergy.[17] Cathedral canons and chaplains were also invited regularly to participate in religious ceremonies in other Florentine churches. But in 1457, the cathedral canons voted to refuse to participate in any service in a local church unless they received collectively a minimum fee of 30 *lire*. They did stipulate, however, that the cathedral chaplains were obligated to attend these ceremonies, for which they presumably received a smaller fee.[18] Probably the most important source of supplementary income for cathedral chaplains derived from the coins which were given to them by worshippers at their chapels or altars. Chaplains were obligated to turn over offerings from boxes located in their chapels, but they were allowed to accept certain gifts from the faithful, and particularly for their role as confessors during Lent.[19] The coins collected in the boxes were divided among the *operai del Duomo*, the chapter and individual clerics governed by rules that were incorporated in the constitutions.[20] S. Lorenzo's constitution of 1369, which could have served as a model for the cathedral, described in elaborate detail the income which was reserved for the treasury and which could be retained by the chaplains.[21]

Motivated by either necessity or greed, some cathedral chaplains increased their income by servicing chapels in other churches or by obtaining a second benefice. A cathedral chaplain, ser Matteo di Giovanni, serviced a chapel in S. Lorenzo for two years and two months in the late 1460s, for which labor he received a stipend of 43 florins.[22] In 1486, a cathedral canon, Messer Dino Corbizi, rented his baptismal church in Poggibonsi to a cathedral chaplain, ser Bartolomeo d'Andrea Jacobi.[23] The chaplain received a stipend of 130 *lire* annually, and in addition, was entitled to 60 bushels *(staiora)* of wheat, 45 barrels of wine, and 3 1/2 barrels of oil each year. To service this church, ser Bartolomeo was obligated to hire two chaplains and an acolyte, responsible for conducting services at the main altar and in the endowed chapels. Though holding plural benefices required the approval of the archbishop and the cathedral canons, such permission was rarely if ever refused, even by the austere archbishop Antoninus. Ser Fruosino di Lorenzo de Vulparia held two rural benefices in addition to his cathedral chaplaincy: S. Maria de Carpineto and S. Giusto ad Ema.[24] Two other chaplains, ser Antonio Masaini and ser Giuliano d'Antonio, were canons in the collegiate church of S. Appollinare.[25] Ser Lapo Martini was the rector of the urban church of S. Benedetto; his colleague, ser Angelo di ser Jacopo d'Arezzo, occupied the benefice of S. Leo.[26] In addition to his cathedral chaplaincy, ser Bartolo d'Andrea held a similar office in the collegiate church of SS. Apostoli.[27] Ser Bindo d'Antonio da Empoli was an assiduous collector of income-producing benefices. He serviced three chapels in the cathedral in the 1460s, while also holding the rectorship of the rural church of S. Martino a Pontormo.[28] Ser Dino di Niccolò di ser Dino served as cathedral chaplain for almost thirty years (1486–1514), and he also rented the urban parish church of S. Cristoforo in 1493.[29]

Since the income of these chaplains derived from several sources, mostly undocumented, it is not possible to draw any firm conclusions about their total annual value. It seems likely that these priests were not as well remunerated as were the city's beneficed clergy, three-quarters of whom received income from church property that was above the minimum (35 florins annually) needed for a cleric's sustenance.[30] The chaplain of the urban church of S. Cecilia reported in 1427 that the endowment of his chapel was only 204 florins, with an annual income of 14 florins. He noted that this paltry sum was only one-half of the amount required for his livelihood.[31] Cathedral chaplains were housed rent-free

in the *canonica*, and they were not obligated to pay for the physical maintenance of their chapels or altars, as were the parish clergy. Their basic
expenditures were for food, clothing, and the salaries of any domestic
servants in their employment.[32] The most burdensome expense for the
cathedral clergy (archbishop, canons, chaplains) were the taxes imposed
by both secular and ecclesiastical authorities throughout the fifteenth
century.[33] In 1431, during the war with Lucca, the commune levied a tax
of several thousand florins on the Florentine clergy, of which 100 florins
was assessed on fifteen cathedral chapels.[34] Fifty years later, at the time
of the Pazzi conspiracy and the war with Pope Sixtus IV, forty chapels
were assessed a total of 146 florins.[35] Submitting his report to the tax officials in 1427, the prior of the collegiate church of SS. Apostoli spoke
for many of his clerical colleagues when he wrote: "There are taxes
levied by the pope, by the commune and by the archbishop; and there
are so many expenses that one could speak of the devil incarnate! Every
day there are more accursed taxes to pay."[36]

The duties and responsibilities of the cathedral chaplains were defined in two basic sources: (1) the constitutions of the cathedral chapter,
which were compiled and revised by the canons and approved by the
archbishop; and (2) the specific contracts drawn up by the patrons of the
chapels. The chapter's constitutions described the role of the chaplains
in the cathedral's religious services, while the patrons' contracts focused
specifically on their particular responsibilities in the chapels that they
served. While neither of these sources for the cathedral have yet been
discovered, their general content can be inferred from surviving records
of the church of S. Maria Impruneta. In 1465, Pope Paul II issued a bull
authorizing the establishment of nine chaplaincies in that baptismal
church, which housed the renowned image of the Virgin.[37] The occupant of that benefice drafted a constitution defining the duties of these
chaplains, based upon the system that regulated the functions of the
cathedral chaplains. The key provision in that constitution is the section
describing the schedule of the chaplains' participation in divine services.
The names of the chaplains were recorded on a tablet, with each priest

obligated to celebrate mass at his turn in the rotation and to participate regularly in other liturgical functions. Those priests who failed to attend services on work days were to be fined 5 *soldi* for each infraction and 10 *soldi* on Sundays and feast days. Chaplains who sought a leave of absence from their duties were required to obtain the approval of their superior and to furnish a substitute. Other provisions of the constitution regulated the activities of the chaplains in ministering to the sick and dying, in hearing confessions, and in baptizing infants.

S. Maria Impruneta also provides an example of a contractual agreement between patrons and chaplains. In 1431, Cardinal Antonio Casini endowed two chapels in the cathedral and a third in the baptismal church of S. Maria Impruneta.[38] Casini funded the cathedral chapels by purchasing shares of the communes' funded debt *(monte)* for 1,300 florins; the annual income for each chapel was estimated at 40 florins. The priests officiating in the cathedral chapels were to be chosen by the officials of the *monte*, the four oldest canons and the consuls of the wool guild. Casini formulated very precise instructions for the priest who serviced his Impruneta chapel. While he was allowed to acquire additional benefices, these could only be held in the region of Impruneta and Florence. He was obligated to reside in the cloister of the Impruneta church and to participate in the liturgical services of that church. In the chapel that Casini had endowed, the priest was to celebrate mass according to a schedule, and on the feast day of the apostles Simon and Jude, he was to celebrate a commemorative mass in which all clerics attached to the church would participate. The cardinal authorized the expenditure of 10 florins for this ceremony: 6 florins for oil; 2 florins for candles; and 2 florins for *pietanza*, the commemorative meal provided for the participating clergy.[39]

Only in the most general sense could the cathedral chaplains be considered a homogeneous group or category. Within their ranks there developed a hierarchy as rigidly structured as that of the metropolitan church itself: archbishop, vicar general, archdeacon, canons, chaplains, and the clerics who participated in the liturgical services while hoping for a promotion to a chaplaincy. At the top level of this hierarchy of chaplains were those clerics who serviced the most richly endowed and most popular chapels, and who usually enjoyed the longest service in the cathedral. There was a wide disparity in chapel endowments, ranging in 1427 from 860 to 53 florins.[40] In a tax assessment imposed by the commune on the clergy in 1431, fourteen cathedral chapels were assessed between 1 and 15 florins, while eleven other chapels were so poorly endowed that their chaplains paid no tax.[41] The gulf between rich and poor chapels continued throughout the fifteenth century. Among the richest and most popular chapels were those dedicated to S. Zenobi, to S. Stefano, the patron saint of the wool guild, to the Virgin Mary, located near the south door, and to the chapels dedicated to the Holy Trinity and the Conception of the Virgin, located on either side of the main cathedral entrance facing the baptistry.[42] These chapels attracted the largest crowds of the faithful, and their chaplains received a disproportionate share of offerings. In 1455, the cathedral *operai* elected ser Angelo di ser Jacopo d'Arezzo to service the altar of the Virgin adjacent to the holy water font by the canons' door, which had attracted large numbers of worshippers. The *operai* stipulated that ser Angelo was to receive no salary, apparently assuming that his income from gratuities would be adequate for his livelihood.[43]

The career of ser Angelo illustrates the cleavage within the ranks of the cathedral chaplains. He belonged to a small group of clerics whose service in the cathedral could be counted in decades and not years. The illegitimate son of an Arezzo priest, he received a dispensation in 1428 to be admitted to holy orders and to hold benefices.[44] From that moment until his death in 1467, he served as a cathedral chaplain while holding two other benefices: the parish church of S. Leo in Florence, and a rural church in the diocese of Arezzo.[45] The annual income from his cathedral chapel dedicated to S. Matteo and the church of S. Leo was estimated at 49 florins, comparable to the average for the city's parish churches.[46] Ser Angelo's lengthy tenure of some forty years enabled him to establish contacts with the cathedral canons, who were his chapel's patrons, and with the influential guildsmen who filled the office of the *operai del Duomo*. Having learned the traditions and routines of the metropolitan church, he could play a role as patron and teacher of the younger clergy. Together with other senior clerics, he was a prime candidate for the offices to which chaplains could be elected by the canons, and for which they received small stipends.[47] Cathedral chaplains were also chosen as officials of the "societas presbiterorum civitatis Florentine," which maintained a hospital for the city's clergy in the Via S. Gallo.[48] Cathedral chaplains possessed their own hospital in the *canonica*, called *la carità dei cappellani*, which had been endowed by Pope Eugenius IV in 1435, and which was administered by the chaplains.[49] The most valued privilege enjoyed by chaplains like ser Angelo was the right of burial in the cathedral crypt.[50] In their testaments, chaplains often stipulated that the cathedral clergy were to participate in their funeral rites;[51] some provided money for masses to be sung on the anniversary of their death. An entry in an account book of *la carità dei cappellani* (1564) states that "we are obligated once a year to celebrate a mass for the soul of ser Agostino di Jacopo Lapini, our chaplain and brother still alive, and for the souls of his father, mother, brothers and sisters dead and alive, and for all of his relatives, and for all those individuals who were in his mind when he ordered this act of charity."[52] Like their colleagues in other Florentine churches and monasteries, the cathedral clergy were spending more time in prayers for the dead, though not so intensively as the chaplains in the New Sacristy of S. Lorenzo, whose offices were created by Pope Clement VII in 1532. Four priests were obligated to say three masses each day and to recite the Psalter with alternating prayers, "twenty-four hours a day for eternity."[53]

Only a small minority of cathedral chaplains enjoyed the lengthy tenure and privileges of ser Angelo d'Arezzo. The employment and emoluments of most chaplains were no more stable or secure than that of a poor chaplain in the urban church of S. Niccolò, who wrote in his tax report (1438) that "since my salary is insufficient, on certain days of work I officiate in a number of Florentine churches, and so am barely able to survive."[54] Security of employment for chaplains was jeopardized by the fact that they were under the control and discipline of several masters. Those whose chapels were endowed by lay patrons could be dismissed at any time by their employers. For failing to fulfill their religious responsibilities, they could be terminated by the cathedral canons and by the *operai del Duomo*, the commission of wool guild members authorized to regulate the cathedral clergy. In the 1430s, several chaplains were expelled from their posts and from their lodgings in the *canonica* by the *operai*. Among those discharged was the well-known storyteller Piovano Arlotto, who lost his chaplaincy in 1431.[55] Three chaplains were deprived of their positions in the 1460s by the archbishop, for reasons that were not specified in the documents.[56] In 1483, a cathedral chaplain, ser Giovanbattista de Cortigiani of Empoli, confessed to the papal penitentiary that he was the father of two children born to a Dominican nun. He received absolution from Pope Sixtus IV that prohibited any further disciplinary action against him.[57]

Cathedral chaplains performed their religious functions before a much larger audience than did their clerical colleagues in other urban churches and monasteries. They gained financial and psychological benefits from living and working in one of the most splendid churches in Christendom, an obligatory stop for every visitor to Florence, from poor peasants coming from the Mugello or the Valdipesa, to popes, cardinals, and princes. The chaplains would have witnessed such momentous events as the consecration of the cathedral by Pope Eugenius IV (1436), the ceremony uniting the Latin and Greek churches (1439), the funeral service for the venerated archbishop Antoninus (1459), and the assassination (1478) of Giuliano de' Medici, the brother of Lorenzo the Magnificent. But working conditions in the cathedral were less than ideal in the fifteenth century. It was a site of continuous construction and remodeling, not only the cupola and its lantern, but the sacristies and the chapels. The *operai del Duomo* contributed to the disorder by dismantling altars and constructing others, and by shifting chapels from one site to another.[58] So polluted by dust and debris was the cathedral interior in 1439 that chaplains experienced difficulty in celebrating mass in their chapels.[59] Nature also played a role in fomenting chaos, when, for example, lightning bolts struck the cupola's lantern in April 1492, showering the cathedral interior with fragments of marble and causing so much damage that (one observer reported) it would take five years to repair.[60] Living conditions in the *canonica* must have been very crowded, with the large increase in the numbers of both canons and chaplains. It is most unlikely that cathedral chaplains enjoyed living quarters as spacious as those of their colleagues at Impruneta, each of whom was provided with a house, with a porch, dining room, living room, kitchen, and cellar.[61]

The most difficult times for the cathedral clergy were those years (1494–98) when the Dominican friar Girolamo Savonarola was a dominant figure in Florence's religious and political life. It was from the cathedral pulpit that Savonarola articulated his powerful message of reform and regeneration, before vast throngs estimated at fifteen thousand. These sermons, and other religious celebrations orchestrated by the friar and his supporters, disrupted the normal liturgical routines in the cathedral.[62] They also focused the attention of Florentines upon the failures and shortcomings of the clergy, not only the papal curia in Rome, but the local hierarchy, from archbishop and canons to parish priests and chaplains. The cathedral clergy who were present at the friar's Lenten sermons of 1498 heard themselves excoriated for their tepid religiosity and their preoccupation with money. Savonarola claimed that "the altar had become the *bottega* of the clergy" and that priests regarded the laity solely as a source of income: "What do you want to give me and I'll say a mass for you?" The cathedral clergy would not have appreciated Savonarola's assertion that there were too many priests in Florence officiating at too many ceremonies that they organized solely for profit.[63] A greater peril for the clergy was Pope Alexander VI's excommunication of Savonarola and his warning (February 1498) to the cathedral canons and chaplains not to celebrate mass whenever the friar preached there. In their appeal to the Signoria to prohibit Savonarola from preaching in the cathedral, the canons expressed their fear that they would lose their prebends if the pope's warning was ignored.[64] The cathedral clergy played no significant role in the dramatic events that culminated in Savonarola's downfall in the spring of 1498. But they were surely relieved by his removal from the scene, and by the end to the turbulence that had characterized the friar's brief Florentine career. The establishment of the Medici principate created a more stable environment for the Florentine church, which was perceived as an essential prop for that authoritarian and hierarchical regime.

APPENDIX 1

List of cathedral chapels in 1427 with endowments

(Archivio di Stato, Florence, Catasto, 194, i, fols. 15v–22v)

The hospital of the chapel of Sᵃ Maria del Fiore (860 fl.)

Chapel of Sᵃ Maria e S. Zanobi (257 fl.)

Chapel of S. Tommaso di Chonturbie (405 fl.)

Chapel of Sᵃ Maria della Misericordia (301 fl.)

Chapel of the Pecori family (500 fl.)

Chapel of S. Lorenzo (228 fl.)

Chapel of S. Andrea (53 fl.)

Chapel of S. Giovanni Evangelista (457 fl.)

Chapel of S. Marco and S. Antonio (293 fl.)

Chapel of S. Zanobi (243 fl.)

Chapel of S. Antonio (556 fl.)

Chapel of Sᵃ Cicilia (203 fl.)

APPENDIX 2

Cathedral chapels, chaplains, and patrons in 1514

(Archivio arcivescovile, Florence, Visita pastorale 1514, fols. 4r–5v)

Chapel of _____; ser Piero di Lorenzo (chapter of cathedral)

Chapel of S. Bartolomeo; Maestro Bartolomeo di Francesco (heirs of ser Giovanni and Antonio de Prato Veteri)

Chapel of S. Niccolò; D. Francesco di Domenico Boscheri (consuls of Lana guild; hospitaler of S. Maria Nuova; heirs of D. Jacopo Ugolini)

Chapel of Sᵃ Agnese; ser Stefano di Giovanni da Ancona *(ut supra)*

Chapel of _____; ser Antonio di Enfrosinio (captains of the Bigallo)

Chapel of S. Gregorio; D. Dino Corbizi (Corbizi family)

Chapel of S. Lorenzo; ser Francesco di Cristoforo (Corsini family)

Chapel of S. Giuliano; ser Dino di Niccolò di ser Dino (consuls of Lana guild)

Chapel of S. Tommaso de Conturbie; ser Leonardo di Domenico (chapter of cathedral)

Chapel of Sᵃ Maria Magdalena; ser Antonio Ghiebuzzeni (heirs of ser Francesco da Romena)

Chapel of S. Geronimo; ser Domenico Castellani (Tornabuoni family)

Chapel of S. Zanobi; ser Jacopo di Barnaba (chapter of the cathedral)

Chapel of Sᵃ Maria and S. Zanobi; ser Jacopo de Zettis (Medici family)

Chapel of the Conception of the Virgin Mary; ser Michelangelo de Bracchis (consuls of Lana guild; officials of the *Monte*)

Chapel of _____; ser Buonsignore Buonsignori (consuls of Calimala guild)

Chapel of S. Geronimo; ser Piero di ser Riccardo (chapter of the cathedral; *operai del Duomo*)

Chapel of _____; ser Giovanbattista de Goteschi (Vinacezzi family; Velluti family)

Chapel of S. Stefano; ser Francesco di Andrea de Bighazzis (Lana guild)

Chapel of S. Antonio; ser Lorenzo da Filicaia (Lana guild; Giraldi family)

Chapel of S. Giovanni Evangelista; ser Antonio di Girolamo (chapter of cathedral)

Chapel of S. Donato; ser Benedetto de Zambellis (Zambelli family)

Chapel of the Trinity; ser Vincenzo di Antonio (heirs of Alessandro de' Pecori)

Chapel of _____; ser Niccolò di Domenico (chapter of the cathedral)

Chapel of S. Michele and S. Niccolò; ser Jacopo Bonaiuti (Lana guild)

Chapel of S. Matteo; ser Alberto de Bettini (chapter of the cathedral)

Chapel of Sᵃ Maria and S. Giovanni Battista; ser Tommaso Gherardi (confraternity of S. Zenobi)

Chapel of S. Gregorio; ser Bartolomeo da Pistoia (Benivieni family)

Chapel of S. Cosimo and S. Damiano; ser Giovanni di Francesco d'Antonio (Medici family)

Chapel of _____; ser Giovanni di Zenobi (_____)

Chapel of the Conception of the Virgin Mary and Sᵃ Barbara; ser Mariano de Mori (heirs of D. Tommaso de Bordella)

Chapel of _____; ser Raphaelo di Piero (chapter of the cathedral)

Chapel of S. Jacopo; ser Geronimo de Biancardi (Biancardi family)

Chapel of the Conception of the Virgin Mary; ser Gandello Manelli (Lana guild)

Chapel of S. Stefano; ser Lorenzo Guasconi (Lana guild)

Chapel of S. Giovanni Cristosomo; ser Francesco de' Ricci (Ricci family)

Chapel of S. Stefano and S. Zanobi; ser Giuliano de' Sagginochi (heirs of Vanni Rucellai)

Chapel of Sª Maria and S. Zanobi; ser Marco Faville (captains of Or San Michele)

Chapel of S. Sigismondo and Sª Maria; ser Luca di Lando de Gomaglis (hospital of S. Maria Nuova; *operai del Duomo*)

Chapel of S. Andrea, S. Jacopo e S. Filippo; ser Michele di Giovanni (Sapiti family)

Chapel of Sª Caterina; ser Filippo d'Antonio (Bischeri family)

Chapel of Sª Cecelia; ser Giovanni di Francesco (chapter of the cathedral)

Chapel of S. Lorenzo; ser Paolo Luti (chapter of the cathedral)

Chapel of S. Piero; ser Antonio Adimari (*operai del Duomo*; parish of S. Piero Zelorum)

Chapel of Sª Maria e S. Zanobi; ser Jacopo di Giovanni (chapter of the cathedral)

Chapel of S. Giovanni; ser Leonardo di Francesco (Capponi family)

Chapel of S. Lorenzo; ser Niccolò di Domenico (Lana guild; Corsini family)

Chapel of S. Antonio; ser Filippo de' Giannis (captains of Parte Guelfa)

Chapel of Sª Maria and S. Zanobi; ser Lorenzo di Luca (society of S. Zanobi)

Chapel of Sª Maria and S. Gaudenzio; ser Matteo di Giovanni (Lana guild)

Chapel of the Annunciation of the Virgin Mary; ser Mariotto de' Rossi (Lana guild; Taddei family)

Chapel of Sª Caterina; ser Niccolò de Zeta; (*operai del Duomo*; Carnonali family)

Chapel of S. Andrea; ser Battista da Bibbiena (Pecori family)

Chapel of S. Piero and S. Paolo; D. Antonio Zeni (Antonio Zeni)

CHAPTER NINE

The Pope, the Pandolfini, and the *Parrochiani* of S. Martino a Gangalandi (1465)

In the middle decades of the fifteenth century, Messer Carlo Pandolfini was one of Florence's most prominent citizens. He belonged to the inner circle of Medici partisans who, in the words of the chronicler Benedetto Dei, was one of the "major figures in the state and the regime."[1] Carlo's father, Agnolo, had been prominent in Florentine politics in the early decades of the century, and one of the city's richest men.[2] Carlo's knighthood entitled him to wear golden spurs and a sword, and to be escorted by servants in public "and to maintain a lifestyle and dress as befits a knight."[3] He occupied all of the city's major offices, internal and external, participated regularly in civic debates, and was sent on important diplomatic missions. In 1451, he was a member of the Florentine delegation accompanying the emperor-elect, Frederick III, on his way to Rome and his coronation.[4] Carlo's father and his cousin Pandolfo were members of the city's influential humanist community, which added to the family's reputation. The Pandolfini were relatively recent immigrants to Florence (early fourteenth century) and so did not enjoy the status of the most ancient lineages: Albizzi, Buondelmonti, Corsini, Peruzzi, Alberti, Medici. They belonged instead to that middling upper-class stratum defined by Piero Guicciardini (1484): "though not yet noble, still not completely ignoble."[5]

Messer Carlo and his kinfolk were allies of the Medici, and their social status and political influence depended, to a significant degree, on the survival of that unstable regime. But their place in Florence's political and social hierarchy was also threatened by economic and demographic realities. Agnolo Pandolfini's fortune had been significantly depleted by mid-century. Carlo's assets in 1458 were estimated to be 8,446 florins, while those of his two cousins, Jacopo and Pandolfo di Giannozzo, totaled 5,819 florins.[6] These were substantial assets, but paltry compared with Agnolo's fortune in 1427 (32,689 florins).[7] This shrinkage of Pandolfini wealth was due in part to the heavy tax burden imposed on the Florentine citizenry in the first half of the Quattrocento, and also to their withdrawal from that entrepreneurial activity which had initially created their fortune.[8] In 1480, Carlo's son Bartolomeo (aged forty-five) reported that he was not involved in any business activity; his real estate holdings (1,609 florins) provided him with a modest annual income of 107 florins.[9] During the first half of the fifteenth century, the Pandolfini lineage comprised only two households, and so faced the risk of biological extinction in that demographically fragile age.[10] Agnolo Pandolfini had two sons, Carlo and Giannozzo, who survived to maturity; his brother Giovanni died without heirs. In his *catasto* report of 1469, Carlo listed his four legitimate sons: Domenico (aged forty, married and the father of five children); Bartolomeo (aged thirty-six and the father of three small children); Meglo (aged twenty-four, unmarried), and Alessandro (aged twenty, unmarried).[11] Another son, Giuliano, was a cleric with a doctorate in canon law; he had obtained a canonry in the Florentine cathedral in 1460.[12] Only two of Carlo's legitimate sons had reached adulthood and established their own families by the 1490s.[13] Giannozzo sired five sons (Niccolò, Jacopo, Pandolfo, Pierfilippo, and Priore), who had reached maturity by mid-century.[14] This small contingent of adult males limited the lineage's opportunity to contract marriage alliances and to fill civic offices. With so few blood kin living in the city, the Pandolfini were also restricted in their ability to obtain financial support, or *fideiussori*, to furnish guarantees for offices.

Carlo Pandolfini could not have foreseen his nephew's death and its negative impact on his lineage, when a year earlier (October 1464) he traveled to Rome as a member of the Florentine embassy to congratulate the newly elected pope, Paul II, on his promotion to the Holy See. That mission had been given instructions by the Signoria to make specific requests to the pontiff: the protection of the Vallombrosan order from exploitation by curial bureaucrats; a tax exemption for the convent of S. Brigida; and the canonization of a local cleric, the *beato* Andrea Corsini.[15] Carlo Pandolfini had his own agenda, which was described in a papal *breve* sent (December 1464) to a canon of the Florentine cathedral, Messer Salvino Salvini. The focus of Pandolfini's strategy was the priory of S. Martino a Gangalandi near Signa, a village some ten miles west of Florence in the Arno valley. This zone was the ancestral home of the Pandolfini; Carlo's father, Agnolo, had lived in the family villa near Signa for the last decade of his life.[16] Carlo petitioned the pope to grant him and his heirs the patronage rights (*giuspatronatus*) to S. Martino, to authorize him to appoint the prior instead of the church's parishioners. According to Carlo's estimate, the annual income of the benefice was 100 florins; he promised to add 200 florins to the church's property and thus increase its annual revenue to 125 florins. His patronage would not only improve substantially the church's financial condition, but would also increase the likelihood of a resident prior and would reduce the quarrels and tensions among parishioners arising from the absenteeism of its rectors.[17]

Carlo Pandolfini's effort to gain control of S. Martino was an initial step to insert his lineage into the ecclesiastical structure of his ancestral base, and more broadly, into the Tuscan church. This strategy had long been pursued by older, more established lineages: the Buondelmonti in the zone around Impruneta, the Medici in the Mugello, the Machiavelli in the Valdipesa, the Ricasoli in the Chianti region.[18] The benefits of this penetration were substantial. The income from church property could be siphoned off into the family's coffers; parcels of the church's holdings might be integrated into the patrimony.[19] The lineage's coat of arms carved into the church's fabric was a symbol of its influence in the region,[20] as was its burial chapel, filled with the tombs of family members. Moreover, a priory like S. Martino could be filled by a clerical kinsman, providing him with a comfortable income. Carlo's son Giuliano and nephew Niccolò di Messer Giannozzo were the first two members of the family to pursue ecclesiastical careers in the 1450s. Giuliano was the rector of S. Maria Descho in the diocese of Fiesole in 1459, and in the following year he obtained a canonry in the Florentine cathedral.[21] His cousin Niccolò became an avid collector of benefices, culminating (January 1475) in his promotion to the bishopric of Pistoia.[22] Messer Piero di Taddeo Pandolfini held several benefices in the diocese of Pistoia in the 1470s and 1480s; his kinsman Giannozzo was promoted to the bishopric of Tropea in 1484, a post that he held until his death in 1525.[23] Writing to her son Filippo in December 1464, Alessandra Strozzi made a reference to a Pandolfini, who had sought to gain possession of an oratory whose patrons once had been Strozzi. Alessandra described this benefice hunter in unflattering terms: "He appears to be a blockhead; for many years he has not lived with his father or his brother. He does nothing but engage in litigation with priests and friars. He does have powerful friends at the [papal] court."[24] Such litigious tactics appear to have been typical of the Pandolfini in their aggressive pursuit of lucrative church offices.[25]

Roberto Bizzocchi has demonstrated that the transfer of *giuspatronato* from parishioners of rural churches to aristocratic lineages was a common phenomenon in the Florentine dominion during the Quattrocento.[26] The rationale for this shift from parochial to private control was usually the poverty of the parishioners, who could not afford to maintain the church's fabric or to enlarge its property holdings. In May 1448, Pope Nicholas V received a petition from a prominent Medicean, Francesco di Nerone Dietisalvi, to obtain the patronage rights of the church of S. Cresci a Maciuole in the diocese of Fiesole. Dietisalvi asserted that the church fabric was in very poor condition, and its annual income only 50 florins. He owned property in the region and he promised to spend 250 florins to repair the church if he and his heirs were granted patronage rights.[27] Members of the large Strozzi family were very active in obtaining possession of churches in their rural neighborhoods. Wealthy merchant Filippo Strozzi was granted the *giuspatronato* of the church of S. Piero de Ripoli after he promised to purchase land worth 500 florins to augment the church's income.[28] In January 1493, eleven parishioners of the church of S. Maria de Travalli (diocese of Florence) voluntarily transferred their patronage rights to Francesco di Vanni Strozzi. They were too poor to repair the church's crumbling fabric, and they noted that Francesco and his father had made generous contributions to the restoration of the church.[29] In a few cases, parishioners resisted the efforts of wealthy and influential neighbors to gain patronage rights over their church. In July 1451, Luigi di Giovanni Soderini claimed to be the patron of the church of S. Martino de Corella, whose resident priest had just died. He selected a kinsman, Francesco Soderini, to replace the deceased incumbent and petitioned Archbishop Antoninus to ratify the appointment. But the parishioners of S. Martino protested this move, claiming that Francesco Soderini had not been ordained and that the Soderini claim to the church's patronage was fraudulent.[30]

Carlo Pandolfini could not legitimately claim that the church of S. Martino a Gangalandi was impoverished, since its property had been valued at over 1,500 florins in 1427, with an annual income of 160 florins. It was one of the wealthiest churches in the Valdarno Superiore, capable of supporting two priests, an acolyte to assist in the liturgical services, and a cook. The salaries of these employees were calculated at 60 florins annually, and in addition, the holder of the benefice was obligated to pay a papal *decima* of 35 florins annually.[31] But the income from other sources (tithes; fees for baptisms, burials, and confessions; offerings at the altars) would have provided the prior with a substantial income. In the early sixteenth century, over one thousand parishioners came to the church for confession during the Lenten season.[32] Since 1432, the occupant of this benefice had been Leon Battista Alberti, who had never resided in S. Martino but lived in Rome, where he held a curial post as *abbreviator.* Like hundreds of other absentee holders of Tuscan benefices, Alberti hired clerics to perform the liturgical duties at S. Martino.[33] Although no rental contract between Alberti and his surrogates has survived, the model of such agreements can be determined from examples in the notarial record. Alberti may have leased the benefice for a specified number of years for an annual rental payment, or he may have divided the revenues and the expenses between himself and his lessee.[34] He did appoint procurators, in Rome and Florence, to represent his interests as the incumbent of S. Martino and to collect revenues from the benefice. One of those procurators was Marco Parenti, whose relationship with Alberti is documented from 1447 until 1468.[35]

Alberti appointed Marco Parenti as his legal representative to challenge Carlo Pandolfini's effort to obtain the patronage rights to S. Martino, and he was joined in this effort by ser Domenico da Figline, the procurator for a group of the church's parishioners. On 15 December 1464, Parenti appeared before Canon Salvini to argue that no action on the Pandolfini petition should be taken, since neither he nor ser Domenico had received copies of the papal *breve.* Salvini agreed to postpone a decision in the case and to provide the procurators with copies of the papal letter. Two days later, at a formal session in the cathedral, Carlo Pandolfini's son Domenico repeated his father's proposal to invest 200 florins in S. Martino's property holdings and asked Salvini to reject the challenge submitted by Parenti and his colleague. On 19 December, Parenti and ser Domenico presented their arguments before Canon Salvini. They challenged the assertion of Carlo Pandolfini and his son that the church and its property were in poor condition: "not only a rector but a great prelate could live there decently and comfortably." The church's fabric and its property did not require any repairs. The procurators also labeled as totally false the assertion by the Pandolfini that the parishioners of S. Martino supported their petition to obtain patronage rights to the church. But fearing the power of Messer Carlo, they did not dare to voice their opposition. The procurators stated further that the Pandolfini had never been major benefactors of S. Martino. The parishioners had spent large sums of money on the construction and the repairs of the buildings, but they would cease to contribute if the Pandolfini obtained patronage rights. Nor did the procurators give any credence to the claim that an increase of 20 florins in the church's annual revenue would induce its rectors to reside in the church. In their closing argument, Marco Parenti and ser Domenico listed a number of procedural violations which (they argued) invalidated the Pandolfini case and obligated Salvini, the apostolic delegate, to quash the petition.[36]

Before reaching a decision, Canon Salvini interviewed two witnesses produced by Domenico Pandolfini, acting as procurator for his father, Carlo. Marco di Filippo, a Florentine barber, and Francesco d'Antonio, from Ponte Greve, in the *contado*, testified that the majority of the parishioners of S. Martino favored the bestowal of patronage rights on Messer Carlo Pandolfini and his heirs. The witnesses stated that they had discussed the issue with several parishioners, some of whom had come to Florence to express their wishes to Canon Salvini.[37] The challenges to the Pandolfini petition were quickly dismissed by the canon, who labeled them "frivolous." He then authorized the implementation of the papal *breve* awarding patronage rights to Carlo Pandolfini and his heirs, with the stipulation that within one year, the new patron should spend 200 florins "for the benefit and utility of that church" so that its income would be increased by 25 florins annually.[38]

In this dispute over the future of a large and wealthy *contado* church, Carlo Pandolfini enjoyed the potent support of the Roman curia, the local ecclesiastical establishment, and his Medici allies.[39] That some (the majority?) of the parishioners of S. Martino would oppose this transfer of patronage is comprehensible, even though they could not compete with their prepotent neighbors in power and influence. Leon Battista Alberti's decision to oppose the Pandolfini is more problematical, since his possession of the benefice was not threatened by this transfer of patronage rights.[40] Perhaps he was concerned about the potential loss of any privilege to name his successor to the benefice. In August 1464, Alberti had been dismissed from his curial post as *abbreviator,* and the loss of that office with its lucrative income may have intensified his anxiety over his benefice at S. Martino.[41] Eventually, Alberti was restored to his curial post,[42] and upon his death in Rome in February 1472, he was still the rector of S. Martino. On 25 April 1472, Carlo Pandolfini submitted the nomination of Alberti's successor to the archiepiscopal curia in Florence, "the baptismal church being vacant due to the recent death of the venerable Messer Battista Alberti, the last incumbent."[43]

The acquisition of patronage rights to S. Martino by Carlo Pandolfini did not terminate that family's relationship with the distinguished occupant of the church. Alberti continued to receive income from the benefice, and his loan of 500 ducats to Messer Carlo may have been the source of the latter's investment in S. Martino's property, which was required by the settlement.[44] In his last testament, Alberti instructed his executors to complete the construction of the chapel that he had founded in S. Martino.[45] And so, unless Alberti arranged for his own hired chaplain to celebrate anniversary masses for his soul, that service was performed by the rector nominated by Pandolfini. That family continued to pursue its strategy of infiltration into the ecclesiastical structure of its ancestral base. In 1473, ser Jacopo di ser Carlo Pandolfini obtained the baptismal church of SS. Giovanni e Lorenzo de Signa.[46] But for reasons unknown, the Pandolfini did not retain control of S. Martino, which, in 1514, was described as being in the possession of the archbishop of Florence.[47] The final episode in the Alberti-Pandolfini connection occurred in the late sixteenth century, when Senator Filippo Pandolfini discovered a copy of the third book of Alberti's *Della Famiglia* in his family library. He attributed the work to his ancestor, Agnolo di Filippo, substituting the Pandolfini name for that of the Alberti interlocutors. The mistake in authorship was not discovered until the mid-nineteenth century.[48]

CHAPTER TEN

Alessandra Strozzi (1408–1471)

The Eventful Life of a Florentine Matron

In the spring of the year 1422, a marriage was celebrated in Florence between Matteo Strozzi, a member of one of the city's most distinguished lineages, and Alessandra Macinghi, the daughter of a less prominent family, but a girl (she was only fourteen) whose wealthy father could afford a very substantial dowry of 1,600 florins. Matteo was twenty-five, eleven years older than his child bride, who did not conceive until four years after the marriage. But from 1426, when her first child, Andreuola, was born, until 1436, she gave birth to eight children. All of these babies were fed by wet nurses, a common practice among upper-class Florentine families; and all of them survived their infancy, which was quite unusual in a city where one-fifth of all babies died before their first birthday. The young couple had lived in Florence for twelve years, when a political crisis disrupted their lives. In 1434, the Medici family emerged as the dominant force in Florentine politics, and their enemies (including some members of the Strozzi clan) were penalized by fines and by sentences of exile. Matteo Strozzi was exiled to Pesaro on the Adriatic coast, where Alessandra joined him with their brood. In 1436, the plague claimed the lives of Matteo and three of the children. Alessandra then returned to Florence with the remainder of her family to face with the formidable task of reconstructing her life as the widow of a citizen who had suffered political disgrace.[1]

Alessandra was only twenty-eight years old when she returned to Florence, and she might have considered the option of remarriage. But that would have involved the abandonment of her five children, who (as was customary in those circumstances) would have been reared by her husband's Strozzi relatives. So she chose to remain a widow and to devote the remainder of her life to rearing her children and preserving her property, which consisted of a house in Florence, farms in the country that provided much of her household's food, and a modest investment in municipal bonds. Her kinfolk supported her both morally and materially: her brother Zanobi until his death in 1452; and her late husband's first cousins: Jacopo, Filippo, and Niccolò di Leonardo Strozzi. These three brothers, also forced into exile in 1434, had established mercantile companies in Bruges, Barcelona, and Naples. They gave Alessandra's adolescent sons, Filippo and Lorenzo, a home in Naples as well as the mercantile training they would need to become fully fledged members of Florence's entrepreneurial elite, which held such a dominant position in European international commerce and banking. Alessandra's first surviving letter, written in August 1447, was sent to her son Filippo, then nineteen years old, in Naples, where he was employed in his uncle's firm. Its contents and its tone are those of a letter written by any mother to a young son away from home. Alessandra tells her son to work hard and obey his uncle Niccolò; "Think what he has done for you and be worthy to kiss the ground he walks on."[2] Alessandra also warned her son to be careful with his money and avoid the temptations that he would encounter in Naples. This was the first of seventy-two letters that Alessandra wrote to her sons, which were preserved and brought back to Florence by Filippo when his sentence of exile was finally cancelled in 1466. So we owe the existence of this cache of letters—the most extensive and most informative collection written by a woman in Renaissance Italy—to the political and economic circumstances affecting this family in Medicean Florence.

Perhaps the most striking feature of these letters is their sense of authenticity and spontaneity. Most surviving vernacular letters from this period were written by merchants and politicians. Their correspondence, laconic and reserved, usually discussed such topics as markets, exchange rates, and political machinations. By contrast, Alessandra was open and candid in expressing her feelings and her moods; and these were often anxious, fearful, occasionally depressed. She described her difficult economic situation, her problems with tax collectors, and her fears about the recurrence of plague, that terrible disease which struck so frequently and unpredictably, and for which there was no cure. In the early years of her widowhood, when her sons had not yet established themselves in business, Alessandra was particularly concerned about her economic circumstances. Her estate was modest, as was the income from her property; and the supply of grain, wine, and oil from her farms was dependent on the vagaries of the weather. Her rural property was rented to sharecroppers *(mezzadri)*, and both she and the peasants who cultivated her land suffered when an unseasonable frost, or floods, or drought damaged the harvest. Alessandra was a tough, even ruthless, landlady who scrutinized carefully the work of her peasants and insisted upon her half-share of the yield. When an elderly couple, Piero and Cilia, who had cultivated her farm at Pazzolatico became too ill to work the land, she evicted them and wrote to Filippo that "if these two people do not die, they will have to go begging." Writing later to her son, she noted that Piero was still alive (apparently his wife had died), and (she wrote), "He will have to become a beggar; I can do no more than is possible. The best that could happen is that God would call him to himself."[3] There is a defensive note in this account, and Alessandra's behavior strikes us as callous, and sharply in contrast to the Christian ideal of charity, which, in other contexts, she did advocate and practice.

The city's tax officials were particularly harsh and vindictive in treating families—like Alessandra's—that were at odds with the Medici regime. In her letters to Filippo and Niccolò, Alessandra complained bitterly about her taxes, which she viewed as excessive and punitive. "I have

tax debts of 240 florins," she wrote in August 1447, "and I have been mo-
lested by no less than four separate tax collectors, and for the past six
months I have done nothing but go from one office to another," as she
sought to reduce her obligations.[4] Three years later, her tax bill had risen
to 400 florins, but she was able to obtain a reduction of that amount to
just 90 florins.[5] Her laments over the "outrageous" levies were a constant
refrain; in 1459 she wrote to Filippo that her assets and his were being
consumed by taxes; "and to pay them, I would have to dip into capital;
and if I don't, then there is more trouble; and so whatever I decide to do,
it will be bad for us."[6] Alessandra was as reluctant to settle debts as she
was to pay taxes. She complained to Filippo (in January 1465) that for several months she had been harassed by a pork butcher from the town of
Borgo San Lorenzo to pay a debt of nine florins that had been incurred
by her husband more than thirty years before. She insisted, correctly, that
she was not obligated to satisfy claims against her husband's estate with
money from her dowry. But when the pork butcher threatened to have
her excommunicated, and thus damage her reputation and honor, she relented and finally agreed to a settlement of the debt.[7]

Having sent her two oldest sons abroad to learn the skills necessary
for a mercantile career, Alessandra was left with the care of her youngest
son, Matteo, and his two sisters, Caterina and Alessandra. She turned
her attention first to arranging marriages for her daughters, an arduous
task in the best of times, but made more difficult by the tarnished reputation of this branch of the Strozzi lineage. Alessandra's first surviving
letter to her son Filippo in Naples in 1447 informed him of the marriage
that she had arranged between his sister Caterina and Marco Parenti,
the son of a prosperous silk manufacturer whose family was less distinguished than the Strozzi. Alessandra agreed to pay a dowry of 1,000
florins to her son-in-law, and she explained to Filippo the rationale for
her action. "If I hadn't taken this decision, Caterina wouldn't have been
married this year, because he who marries is looking for cash, and I
couldn't find anyone who was willing to wait for the dowry until next
year. . . . We've taken this decision for the best because she was six-

teen and we didn't want to wait any longer to arrange a marriage. And we found that to place her in a nobler family with greater political status would have needed 1400 or 1500 florins, and this would have ruined both of us."[8] Alessandra also noted that Marco was so pleased with his bride that he showered her with gifts of clothing and jewelry. "When Caterina goes out," she noted with pride, "she will have more than 400 florins on her back." Alessandra's intuition that her daughter "will be as well placed as any girl in Florence" proved to be correct. When Marco wrote in his diary concerning his wife's death in 1481, he stated that their marriage "had been very joyous and happy." "May God have received her soul," he added, "as I certainly believe because of her kindness and the worthiness of her life and the great honesty and grace of her ways."[9] This marriage also brought Alessandra an unexpected bonus: a son-in-law who was devoted to her and her family and became her most loyal and trustworthy counselor.

Alessandra's choice of a husband for her younger daughter and namesake, Alessandra, was not so fortunate, though she described the bridegroom, Giovanni Bonsi, in very positive terms when writing to Filippo in 1451. He was, she wrote, "a respectable, well-behaved young man, and quite acceptable and he has so many good qualities. Judging by what I have heard about him, and what I saw last summer, I'm very pleased with him."[10] Giovanni Bonsi received a dowry of 1,000 florins, and he appeared to be (at the time of the marriage) a successful businessman in Rome. But as a reminder (if one were needed) that not all Renaissance Florentines were successful as merchants, or bankers, or manufacturers, Bonsi's entrepreneurial career was a depressing story of failure and loss. He returned to Florence from Rome to operate a woolen cloth factory but the enterprise did not prosper, and he was in such dire financial straits that by 1466 he was barely able to feed and clothe his family, which consisted of his wife, Lessandra, and six children. Writing to Filippo in January 1466, Alessandra described Bonsi's parlous situation. He had asked Filippo to lend him money to pay off his debts, amounting to 200 florins, and to enable him to invest capital in a cloth factory.

Though Alessandra was usually willing to help her relatives in financial difficulties, she did not support this request for a loan to Bonsi because "I don't know whether he will be able to repay you when it's due, because I don't see him being in a position in a year's time to lay his hands on that amount of cash. And that being the case, if he was not able to pay, it would disgrace him. So it might be better not to get involved."[11] Clearly, for Alessandra, there were limits to charity for kinfolk.

With her two daughters married, Alessandra had to consider the future of her youngest child, Matteo. Filippo urged his mother to send the boy to Naples, where he would be trained for a mercantile career in the family business. But Alessandra resisted this pressure, citing the boy's fragile health and her own needs. She wanted Matteo to stay with her for company, for running errands, and for writing her letters. "I've brought him up," she wrote to Filippo, "thinking that nothing but death could part him from me." Finally, however, she relented, knowing that Matteo would be forced to leave Florence and go into exile when he was sixteen. "I decided not to consider the fact that out of three sons, I'll have none to look after me, but to do what's best for you instead,"[12] she wrote to Filippo in the summer of 1449. Matteo was only thirteen when he left Florence, and Alessandra's letters to Filippo were replete with expressions of anxiety about the boy's health and his life and work in Naples. She urged Filippo to treat his brother gently, to correct his mistakes firmly yet without violence.[13] There is a five-year gap (from 1453 to 1458) in Alessandra's correspondence, so we have no direct evidence concerning the relationship between her and her youngest son in those years. But shortly after her correspondence resumed, in September 1459, Alessandra received word that Matteo had died in Naples, at the age of twenty-three. She had not seen him during the ten years since his departure from Florence. Her poignant letter to Filippo, describing her emotions upon learning of Matteo's death, is worth quoting at length.[14]

My dear son. On the 11th of August, I received your letter of July 29th, with the news that my dear son Matteo had become ill, and since you didn't tell me the nature of his malady, I became worried about him. I called Francesco and sent for Matteo di Giorgio, and they both told me that he had a tertian fever. I gained some comfort from this, for if some other malady does not develop, one does not die from malaria. Then I heard from you that he was getting better so my spirits rose. I then learned that on the 23rd, it pleased God who gave him to me to take him back. Being sound of mind, he received all of the sacraments as a good and faithful Christian. I am deeply grieved to be deprived of my son; by his death I have suffered a bitter blow, greater than the loss of filial love; and so have you, my two sons, reduced now to such a small number. I praise and thank our Lord for everything which is his will, because I am sure God took him when he saw his soul was healthy. I see from what you've written that you've resigned yourself to this hard and bitter death. . . . Although the pain in my heart is like nothing I ever felt before, I've taken comfort from two things. First, he was with you so I'm certain he had doctors and medicines and everything was done for his well-being, and any remedies which could be used were used and nothing was neglected to keep him alive, but that nothing was any help to him and it was the will of God that it should be so. The other thing which has comforted me is that Our Lord gave him the opportunity while he was dying to free himself from sin, to ask for confession and communion and extreme unction, and all of this, I gather, he did with piety. We can hope from these signs that God had prepared a good place for him. And knowing we must all take this journey and not knowing how and not being sure of doing so in the way my beautiful son Matteo had . . . gives me peace, keeping in mind that God could have done far worse to me, because those who die suddenly who are cut to pieces . . . they lose their body and soul together. . . . I hope God doesn't let me live long enough to go through this again.

There can be no question of the depth and intensity of Alessandra's anguish over the death of her son, who had survived the dangerous years of infancy, childhood, and adolescence only to succumb to a malarial fever in his early twenties. Alessandra's grief was intensified by the thought that she might have been able to see Matteo before he died: "You should have told me the first day Matteo was sick," she wrote, "and I could have jumped on a horse and been there in a few days."[15] Death was so common, so much a part of everyday life in that world that some have argued that surviving parents had become inured to the loss of their children. Alessandra's letter is powerful evidence to challenge this view. Her letter does reflect the Christian belief that all human lives were in God's hands, and that individuals could do little to protect themselves in a world in which their vulnerability was so apparent. The most lethal disease in that age was the so-called Black Death, which had first struck Europe with deadly force in the mid-fourteenth century. It had killed between one-fourth and one-third of all Europeans in a two-year epidemic.[16] The plague continued to strike Florence, Tuscany, and the rest of Italy (and Europe) at irregular intervals, every ten or fifteen years. Alessandra had herself survived plague epidemics, in 1417, when she was nine and again in 1424, when she was a young bride. She lost her husband and three of her children to the plague in Pesaro in 1436. After her return to Florence, she lived through two major visitations of the plague, in 1449–50, and again in 1463–65. The only practicable response to these epidemics was to leave the city for rural areas where the plague had not spread. So Alessandra and her household spent several months in country villas, waiting for the disease to loosen its grip on the city. During these stays in the country, she reported to her sons in Naples the number of victims who succumbed: from forty or fifty per day at the height of the plague to just two or three when the epidemic was subsiding and Florentines felt safe enough to return to their homes in the city.[17]

Among the plague victims were, inevitably, Alessandra's relatives, friends, and neighbors, who had provided her with support and services. She noted, for example, in June 1450 that she had rented one of her farms to a "rich and worthy peasant," the head of a large household of seventeen, of whom twelve had died in the plague. "So many have died," she wrote to Filippo, "that the farmhouses are empty and the land remains uncultivated and fallow."[18] A few months earlier, in December 1449, she reported the deaths of several members of the Strozzi family, as well as the demise of her first cousin with two of her children, "so this time our immediate family has been hit."[19] The death of her husband's cousin, Benedetto Strozzi, was described by Alessandra as a grievous loss, "first, to his immediate family, and then and to all of us, and to all the Strozzi. Everyone turned to him for help and there's no one else in the family who would be missed as much as he will be."[20] Alessandra was particularly sensitive to the deaths of fathers who left behind widows and orphans living in poverty. When the widow of Soldo Strozzi appealed desperately to Filippo on behalf of her two daughters, being without dowries, and "the most damaged and the most endangered by their father's death," Alessandra urged him to assist the children.[21] The death (in October 1465) of Pandolfo Pandolfini, a friend and distant relative, prompted this comment by Alessandra: "I haven't been so upset about the death of a relative since my son died, as I've been about this. I'm very upset for his young wife's sake, and because he is leaving so many children; it's as if the whole Pandolfini family were dying. And I'm sorry for your sake, because you had revived your relationship with him. . . . Had he been alive he could have been a big help to you because he was in the good graces of the leading citizens [that is, the Medici and their partisans] and that was what you needed."[22]

The carnage wrought by the plague, and by other maladies for which medical knowledge at that time had no cure, prompted Alessandra to put pressure on her sons in Naples to marry, to raise families, and to insure the survival of their branch of the Strozzi clan. This was no simple or easy task. Negotiating upper-class marriages was a complex, frustrating, and time-consuming business that invariably required the services of a marriage broker. Arranging marriages for Filippo and Lorenzo was complicated by two factors: their reluctance to give up their bachelor lifestyle and their status as exiles unable to live in Florence. Writing to Filippo in the spring of 1464, Alessandra stated that "I find it easy to understand why you want to put off getting married . . . and why you're so slow in finding a wife. You behave like a man who wants to put off dying or paying his debts for as long as you can. At the moment you've only got one woman in the house, and you're well looked after but when you get married, there'll be lots of them and you wonder how you'll get on. . . . You must make up your mind eventually."[23] A year later, Filippo decided to marry and asked his mother to begin searching for a suitable bride. The first serious prospect was a seventeen-year-old girl, the daughter of Francesco Tanagli, with a dowry of 1,000 florins. Alessandra commissioned Marco Parenti, her son-in-law, to conduct negotiations with the girl's father. Marco was invited to meet the girl and he reported to Alessandra that "she looks beautiful and she seems quite suitable . . . We've been told that she has the right ideas and is capable and that she runs the household because there are twelve children . . . and according to what I hear she runs it all because her mother is always pregnant and doesn't do much."[24] In her next letter to Filippo, Alessandra reported her own visual impressions of the Tanagli girl, whom she saw when both were attending mass in the cathedral. "Not knowing who she was, I sat on one side of her and had a good look at her. She seemed to me to have a beautiful figure and to be well put together. She has a long face and her features aren't very delicate but they're not like a peasant's . . . It seemed to me, from looking at her face and how she walks, that she isn't lazy, and altogether I think that if the other considerations suit us she wouldn't be a bad deal and will do us credit."[25] But the delays caused by the need to refer the matter to Filippo in Naples eventually persuaded the girl's father to terminate negotiations. That news annoyed Alessandra, who wrote to Filippo that "I don't know when I've been more upset, because it seemed to me that she suited us better than anyone else we might find . . . This one was just what we needed."[26]

Alessandra's intense desire to arrange marriages for her sons was reflected in nearly every letter that she wrote to them. "Having two sons who have worked so hard for so long, and not seeing any children of yours, sometimes makes me wonder: 'Who are they doing all this work for? If they go on as they are, they'll harden their hearts and stay as they are, and they'll keep me in these negotiations for so long that I'll die."[27] Marriage, for Alessandra, was strictly a business arrangement. She wrote to Filippo that "we should leave the Tanagli girl alone and buy the Adimari girl first"; and later to Lorenzo, when urging him to accept a marital agreement: "You must go ahead with your purchase so that you can see that the devil's not as black as he's painted." To carry this mercantile metaphor further, Alessandra referred to Fiametta Adimari, who had become the favorite candidate for Filippo's wife: "I've seen her and I'm pleased with her and she doesn't seem so ordinary to me. She's good meat with lots of flavor."[28] Though Alessandra did feel that compatibility was an important element in a successful marriage, she did not place a high priority on what we today would call "love." She deplored the behavior of a Strozzi cousin who had married a young girl after his first wife died. "The wonder was at him, the silly old fool," she wrote, "that he let her do what she liked and was so besotted with her that she brought shame on both herself and him. Men, when they have such a feather-brained wife have to hold them in check, and a man, when he is a real man, makes his wife a wife, and he can't do that if he is infatuated with her."[29]

Alessandra's travail over her sons' marriage prospects finally ended in 1466, when the Medici regime cancelled the sentence of exile for Filippo and Lorenzo. Filippo returned to Florence in the autumn of 1466, and once the stigma of political disfavor had been removed, his marriage to the sixteen-year-old Fiametta Adimari was quickly arranged. Filippo received her dowry of 1,500 florins in February 1467 and the marriage was celebrated in March.[30] Their firstborn child, Alfonso, was born in December of that year, and his birth was followed by six others during the next decade. Fiametta died in childbirth in 1476, and Filippo then married Selvaggia Gianfigliazzi, by whom he had three children. Alessandra lived long enough to enjoy her first grandson, Alfonso, and granddaughter, Lucrezia, who was born in 1469, two years before her death.

The scenario of Lorenzo's marriage was more complicated than that of his older brother. His first choice of a bride was a distant cousin, Marietta di Lorenzo Strozzi, but Filippo strongly opposed that alliance. He noted that Marietta's uncle, Giovanfrancesco Strozzi, had suffered bankruptcy, and thus loss of reputation, and that he was also an exiled opponent of the Medici. So Lorenzo abandoned that plan and instead married Antonia Baroncelli, a girl from an old and respected Florentine lineage, in the spring of 1470. Antonia brought to the marriage a dowry of 1,400 florins. Her first child, Matteo, was born in 1471, shortly after Alessandra's death.[31]

In her feelings about her children, their progeny, and the importance of preserving her family's wealth and social rank, Alessandra was quite conventional, reflecting the mentality of her class. She accepted without question or reservation the hierarchical structure of Florentine society, and she also accepted its patriarchal ethos, based on the conviction that women were inherently inferior to men. In the negotiations for marriage partners for her children, she focused on the status of their families, which was determined by a complex calculation of rank based on antiquity (how long had they been established in the city), on wealth, on political influence and reputation. She agreed to the marriage of her daughter Caterina to Marco Parenti, who was wealthier than her own family but was willing to accept a smaller dowry in exchange for a socially advantageous marriage.[32] Though she became very fond of her son-in-law, who proved to be a stalwart defender of her interests, she complained about his relatives, and particularly his mother, who (she implied) had not learned how to behave in their social milieu and did not properly acknowledge services done for them by their kinfolk.[33] She disdained those families who, like the Pucci, had been lowly artisans but had then risen rapidly in the social hierarchy through their close ties with the Medici. When she learned that her son's patron, King Ferrante of Naples, had agreed to write a letter on Filippo's behalf to Antonio Pucci, an influential member of the Medici government, she commented: "I know that it will be humiliating for the king to write to a man of such lowly condition."[34] And when informing Filippo of the membership of the city's supreme executive, the Signoria, she commented: "These are people that one does not know.[35]

Alessandra was no feminist, nor was she a Renaissance Mother Teresa, as her comments about the elderly peasant couple she evicted from her farm indicate. Her view of her social inferiors was a combination of indifference and contempt; they were doomed by their fate to be the hewers of wood and the carriers of water. She voiced little concern or apprehension about a plague epidemic whose victims were from the lower classes and "did not touch respectable people."[36] Alessandra had bought a slave girl named Cateruccia who proved to be a source of grief and discord. "I have never beaten her, even though she has behaved abominably toward me and my daughters. . . . For several months now, she has said that she doesn't want to stay with us, and she is so perverse that I can't do anything with her." This letter was written while Alessandra was arranging the marriage of her daughter Lessandra, and while she was tempted to sell the slave girl, she decided to wait until Lessandra had moved into her husband's house, for fear that Cateruccia would spread tales about the girl and jeopardize the marriage. "She treats me so badly," Alessandra wrote, "that it would appear that I am the slave and she is the mistress."[37] Cateruccia was still living in the house five months later, when another slave girl arrived from the household of a Strozzi cousin in Barcelona. Fourteen years later (1465), Alessandra was still complaining about Cateruccia, her frequent illnesses and her indolence.[38]

Alessandra was typical of her class and gender, her values and opinions reflecting the mentality of upper-class Florentine women. But in one respect, her strong interest in Florentine politics, she was unique. That preoccupation would not have been shared by her female friends and relatives, for whom politics was an activity that concerned their menfolk but not themselves. But Alessandra was forced to pay attention to affairs in the Palazzo Vecchio and in the streets and squares since the status and fortunes of her sons were at stake. She was acquainted with, and related by blood and marriage ties to, many of the major figures in the Medici regime. Her son-in-law Marco Parenti was not a Medici partisan but instead favored a return to the republican regime that had governed the city prior to the Medici. Alessandra shared Marco's reservations about the Medici, and she was frequently critical of the regime's leadership, noting on one occasion their fickle and inconstant behavior. "One day," she wrote, "they are prepared to send each other into exile, and then next day they kiss and make up. They behave like children, changing their minds daily like leaves in the wind."[39] She described in rich detail the serious political crisis of 1466, when a group of Medici leaders plotted to take over the regime from Piero de' Medici, who had succeeded his father, Cosimo, just two years before. But that coup failed, and the Medici remained in control of the regime and the city. A profoundly disenchanted Marco Parenti attributed this failure to restore an authentically republican regime to the triumph of private over public interest. In his memoir describing these events, he wrote: "Those citizens considered their own private advantage and chose to follow it, forgetting the city and its civil regime, public honor and the dignity of a free republic."[40]

Though she was not a friend of the Medici, Alessandra was impressed by their ability to seize and hold onto power in Florence. Writing to Filippo in 1462, she made this very shrewd and prescient comment: "Let me remind you that whoever joins with the Medici prospers, and whoever joins their enemies is ruined."[41] Alessandra had learned that Filippo had become friendly in Naples with a wealthy banker, Piero de' Pazzi, who was a rival of the Medici. She urged her son to break off his connection with the Pazzi "for you will lose more than you might gain."[42] Sixteen years after she made this prophetic observation, in 1478, the Pazzi organized a conspiracy against Lorenzo de' Medici, the failure of which led to the death of some seventy conspirators, including three members of the Pazzi family and their allies from the prominent Baroncelli and Salviati families.

Alessandra's two sons and their Strozzi relatives made their fortunes as merchants and bankers, active in the international economy that for centuries had been a primary source of Florentine wealth.[43] Alessandra was not privy to the details of her sons' business affairs, but she was well aware of the risky nature of their operations. It would be difficult to overemphasize the volatile nature of Florentine entrepreneurial activity in this period, so unstable were the markets and so unpredictable the business climate. Filippo's success as a merchant banker in Naples depended heavily on the favor of his prince, King Ferrante, but that support could evaporate overnight. Alessandra described to her sons the business failure of their cousins Lodovico and Gianfrancesco Strozzi, whose bankruptcies resulted in their loss of honor, which (she feared) would be a lasting blemish on the reputation of the entire lineage.[44] A tax report by a bankrupt merchant, Andrea Vecchietti, sent to prison by his creditors, described the shame and humiliation resulting from such financial disasters. "To escape from this misery," he wrote, "many times every day I have prayed for death."[45] The business activity that carried the greatest shame was usury—the illicit charge of interest on loans. Not only was usury seen as an offense against society, punishable by fines and imprisonment, but it was also viewed by the church as a mortal sin. Usurers, like suicides, could not be buried in consecrated ground, and their heirs could be prosecuted by church courts to restore the illegal profits they had inherited. But the church's definition of what constituted usury was unclear, and ecclesiastical authorities disagreed on this controversial issue. For example, the Dominican order took a strict position on the question, while their Franciscan rivals were more flexible, approving of certain financial transactions that the Dominicans regarded as usurious. Whoever lent or borrowed money could be guilty of usury, and so many Florentine businessmen emulated Cosimo de' Medici, who (so reported his biographer, Vespasiano da Bisticci) "had prickings of conscience that certain portions of his wealth—where it came from I cannot say—had not been righteously gained, and to remove that weight from his shoulders, he held conference with Pope Eugenius IV, who was then in Florence, as to the load which lay on his conscience."[46] The pope suggested to Cosimo that he could allay his anxiety by building a monastery, and so Cosimo spent 40,000 florins to reconstruct and decorate the Dominican convent of San Marco, which stands today as one of the great monuments of Medicean largesse, with its splendid frescoes by Fra Angelico.

Like Cosimo, and like thousands of her Florentine contemporaries, Alessandra was a devout Christian. She accepted church's teachings that she had absorbed as a child; these were reinforced by the hundreds of sermons that she had heard in the churches she attended over the years. As Heather Gregory, the translator of her letters, has noted, Alessandra believed that good works helped secure the soul's salvation and that God rewarded good Christians in this life. She commended her son Filippo for helping the son of an enemy who was in dire straits in Naples. "You gave Brunetto's son food to eat and clothes to wear," she wrote, "and you gave him shelter and money and sent him back here; out of the seven acts of mercy you have performed three. You have done very well and you didn't hold what his father had done to you against him. God will help you prosper even more, because whoever is charitable can only meet with good in return."[47]

Among the good works that she believed beneficial for her salvation were pilgrimages. She considered a trip to Rome in 1450 to obtain the indulgences offered during that jubilee year, but in the end she did not go.[48] She described how a prominent citizen, Antonio Pucci, had been cured of the plague: "He was very afraid and gave a lot of money to God, rescuing prisoners from the Stinche [the city prison]. He did so much, he was given the grace to recover."[49] In a letter of 1465, Alessandra informed Filippo that she had spent 5 florins "to have masses said and alms given on behalf of the souls of your father and my son, and the other departed members of our family."[50] She admitted that for some years she had neglected to make these propitiatory gestures on All Saints' Day, perhaps because of her anxiety over her financial situation.

The last letter of Alessandra's to have survived was written to Filippo in Naples in April 1470, just one year before her death.[51] Its tone was somber and it describes some of the perils of living in this city that seemed never to be stable or serene. First, Alessandra described a prison riot and breakout, which was finally suppressed when the three ring-leaders were publicly executed. Then she wrote that a group of exiles had seized control of the nearby town of Prato and were planning an assault on Florence. "Oh," she wrote, "don't ask about the confusion that reigned in this city; for two hours there was complete chaos with people running about the streets and particularly around the Medici palace." Then news arrived that the exile group had all been captured, and on the following day, they were led into Florence, where they were beheaded. "All the people have been frightened and it seems a very dreadful thing, with so many people dead and tortured." This event was followed by an earthquake, which further terrified the inhabitants. "Between one fear and another," Alessandra confessed, "I seem to have been half beside myself; I thought we were close to the end of the world. . . . May God keep us from further troubles." For Alessandra, the lesson to be gained from these crises was "to put your soul in order and be ready." We must assume that on her deathbed a few months later, she was prepared to meet her Maker.

Alessandra did not live to witness the dramatic triumphs and tragedies of her progeny in the decades after her death. Of the triumphs, the most notable and visible was her son Filippo's decision to build a splendid palace, "more grand than that of Lorenzo the Magnificent," as one contemporary reported. This grandiose structure was begun in 1489 and was not completed until many years after Filippo's death in 1491. One of the largest and finest palaces of the Quattrocento, it was designed, so Filippo's son Lorenzo wrote, as a building "which should bring renown to himself and to all his kinsmen in Italy and abroad."[52] Reared in this palace was Filippo's son and namesake, Filippo the Younger, whose career combined both triumph and tragedy.[53] Like his father, he was a successful merchant and banker, with firms established in Naples, Rome, and Florence. He married the granddaughter of Lorenzo the Magnificent, and was a close associate of the Medici during the pontificates of Pope Leo X and Pope Clement VII. But in the 1530s, he broke with the Medici and organized a military force against the young duke Cosimo. His army was defeated at the battle of Montemurlo in the summer of 1537, and Filippo was taken prisoner. After eighteen months of imprisonment, he died, either by assassination or by his own hand. His sons and brothers migrated to France, where they served the French crown as bankers and military commanders throughout the sixteenth century. But other members of the Strozzi lineage survived in Florence and played important roles in the governance of the Medici grand duchy from the sixteenth to the eighteenth century.

NOTES

INTRODUCTION

1. G. Brucker et al., *History at Berkeley. A Dialog in Three Parts* (Berkeley and Los Angeles, 1998), p. 21.

2. G. Brucker, "Hero Worship," *The Green Caldron* (Urbana, October 1942): 1–2.

3. J.-S. Bailly, *Revolutionary Mayor of Paris, 1789–91* (Urbana, 1950).

4. G. Brucker, *Renaissance News and Notes* 7 (1994): 1–3.

5. F. W. Kent, unpublished paper delivered at the Harvard Center for Italian Renaissance Studies (Villa I Tatti), June 1995.

6. A. Molho, *Marriage Alliance in Late Medieval Florence* (Cambridge, MA, 1994), pp. viii–ix.

7. G. Brucker, ed., *The Society of Renaissance Florence: A Documentary Study* (New York, 1971).

8. G. Brucker, *Giovanni and Lusanna: Love and Marriage in Renaissance Florence* (Berkeley and Los Angeles, 1986).

9. G. Brucker, *Renaissance Florence: Society, Culture and Religion* (Goldbach, Germany, 1994).

10. Archivio di Stato, Florence; Notarile avanti il Principato, 694, fol. 158v; 10 October 1463; 13511, no. 257, 25 January 1450/51; Provvisioni, Registri, 154, fols. 4v–5r, 29 March 1463.

11. S. Cohn, *Creating the Florentine State. Peasants and Rebellion, 1348–1434* (Cambridge, 1999).

12. R. Fubini, *Quattrocento fiorentino. Politica, diplomazia, cultura* (Pisa, 1996).

13. D. Kent, *Rise of the Medici: Faction in Florence 1426–1434* (Oxford, 1978).

14. J. Najemy, "Linguaggi storiografici sulla Firenze rinascimentale," *Rivista storica italiana* 97 (1985): 144–45.

15. R. Goldthwaite, *Architectural History* 28 (1980): 307.

16. A. Molho, review of *Giovanni and Lusanna. Love and Marriage in Renaissance Florence*, by G. Brucker, *Renaissance Quarterly*, 40 (1987): 99.

17. A. McIntyre, *New York Review of Books*, 7 March 1974.

18. D. Cannadine, *In Churchill's Shadow. Confronting the Past in Modern Britain* (Oxford, 2003), p. ix.

CHAPTER ONE

1. A. Brown, *The Renaissance*, 2nd ed. (London and New York, 1999), pp. 2–3.

2. J. Burckhardt, *The Civilization of the Renaissance in Italy* (New York, 1958), p. 143.

3. Ibid., p. 175.

4. Ibid., p. 389.

5. A central theme in C. Klapisch-Zuber, *Women, Family and Ritual in Renaissance Italy* (Chicago, 1985).

6. F. W. Kent et al., *A Florentine Patrician and His Palace*, vol. 2 (London, 1981), p. 66.

7. G. Brucker, *Renaissance Florence* (Berkeley and Los Angeles, 1983), pp. 100–101.

8. N. Machiavelli, *The Prince*, chap. 17, trans. M. Musa (New York, 1964), p. 139.

9. J. McManners, *Church and Society in Eighteenth Century France* (Oxford, 1999), 1: 96.

10. P. J. Jones, "Florentine Families and Florentine Diaries in the Fourteenth Century," in *Studies in Italian Medieval History Presented to Miss E. M. Jamison* (Rome, 1956), p. 183.

11. E. Muir, "The Sources of Civil Society in Italy," *Journal of Interdisciplinary History* 29 (1999): 381.

12. Ibid., p. 384.

13. R. de Roover, *The Rise and Decline of the Medici Bank, 1397–1494* (Cambridge, MA, 1963), p. 28.

14. A. Perosa, ed., *Giovanni Rucellai ed il suo Zibaldone*, 1 (London, 1960), p. 121.

15. G. Brucker, ed., *The Society of Renaissance Florence: A Documentary Study* (New York, 1971), p. 27.

16. E. Panofsky, "Renaissance and Renascences," *Kenyon Review* 6 (1944): 201–26.

17. L. Martines, *Power and Imagination. City States in Renaissance Italy* (New York, 1979), chap. 11.

18. A. Grafton and L. Jardine, *From Humanism to the Humanities. Education and the Liberal Arts in Fifteenth- and Sixteenth-Century Europe* (Cambridge, MA, 1986).

19. W. Bouwsma, *A Usable Past. Essays in European Cultural History* (Berkeley and Los Angeles, 1990), p. 228.

20. R. Fubini, *Quattrocento fiorentino. Politica, diplomazia, cultura* (Pisa, 1996), p. 167.

21. F. Guicciardini, *Storia d'Italia* (Bari, 1929), 1: 2.

22. M. Baxandall, *Painting and Experience in Fifteenth Century Italy* (Oxford, 1972), pp. 111–15.

23. G. Brucker, *Florence: The Golden Age, 1138–1737* (Berkeley and Los Angeles, 1998), pp. 19–21.

24. P. Findlen et al., eds., *Beyond Florence* (Palo Alto, 2001).

25. J. R. Hale, ed., *A Concise Encyclopedia of the Italian Renaissance* (Oxford, 1981), p. 183.

26. L. Goldschneider, *Leonardo da Vinci* (Oxford, 1948), p. 17; J. P. Richter, ed., *The Literary Works of Leonardo da Vinci* (London, 1970), p. 395; A. R. Turner, *Inventing Leonardo* (New York, 1993), p. 187.

27. J. R. Hale, *War and Society in Renaissance Europe, 1450–1620* (Baltimore, 1985), p. 179.

28. N. Machiavelli, *Lettere*, ed. F. Gaeta (Milan, 1981), p. 279.

29. R. Klein and H. Zerner, *Italian Art 1500–1600* (Englewood Cliffs, NJ, 1966), pp. 119, 122–24, 129–32.

30. Quoted by J. Kirshner, in his introduction to E. Cochrane, *Italy 1530–1630* (London and New York, 1988), p. 2.

31. P. Burke, *The European Renaissance: Centres and Peripheries* (Oxford, 1998), chaps. 2, 3.

32. W. Bouwsma, *Climax and Waning of the Renaissance* (New Haven and London, 2001).

33. J. Donne, *An Anatomy of the World* (Cambridge, 1951).

CHAPTER TWO

1. R. Putnam, with R. Leonardi and R. Nanetti, *Making Democracy Work: Civic Traditions in Modern Italy* (Cambridge, MA, 1993), pp. 121–62.

2. Ibid., pp. 181, 174.

3. F. C. Lane, *Venice and History* (Baltimore, 1966), p. 520.

4. D. Waley, *The Italian City-Republics* (London, 1969), pp. 221–39; P. J. Jones, "Economia e società nell'Italia medievale: la leggenda della borghesia," in *Einaudi Storia d'Italia*, ed. R. Romano and C. Vivanti (Turin, 1978), 1: 185–372; Romano, "Una tipologia economica," and Vivanti, "Lacerazioni e contrasti," in ibid., 1: 253–304, 867–948.

5. For recent surveys of the literature, see G. Brucker, *The Civic World of Early Renaissance Florence* (Princeton, 1977), pp. 3–13; J. Najemy, "Linguaggi storiografici sulla Firenze rinascimentale," *Rivista storica italiana* 97 (1985): 102–59; Leonardo Bruni, "On the Florentine Constitution," in *The Humanism of Leonardo Bruni*, ed. G. Griffiths, J. Hankins, and D. Thompson (Binghamton, NY, 1987), pp. 171–74.

6. Bruni, "Florentine Constitution," p. 171.

7. Gregorio Dati, *Istoria di Firenze dall'anno MCCCLXXX all' anno MCC-CCV* (Florence, 1735), trans. in *The Society of Renaissance Florence: A Documentary Study*, ed. G. Brucker (New York, 1971), pp. 75–78.

8. J. Najemy, "The Dialogue of Power in Florentine Politics," in *City States in Classical Antiquity and Medieval Italy*, ed. A. Molho, K. Raaflaub, and J. Emlen (Stuttgart, 1991), p. 278.

9. Archivio di Stato, Florence (hereafter ASF), Catasto, 17, fol. 749r; 18, fol. 806r; 21, fol. 88r.

10. For examples of regulatory legislation and its enforcement, see Brucker, *Society of Renaissance Florence*, pp. 179–212; ASF, Deliberazioni dei Signori e Collegi (ordinaria autorità), 99, unpaginated, 25 February 1497/98.

11. ASF, Giudice degli Appelli, 75, fols. 201r–201v, 80, fol. 282r.

12. The main themes in this paragraph, and the one preceding, are discussed in detail in Brucker, *Civic World*, pp. 248–507; and in D. Kent, *The Rise of the Medici: Faction in Florence 1426–1434* (Oxford, 1978).

13. On Medicean electoral strategies, see N. Rubinstein, *The Government of Florence under the Medici 1434–1494* (Oxford, 1966); on the fisc, E. Conti, *L'imposta diretta a Firenze nell'Quattrocento 1427–1494* (Rome, 1984); on the judicial system, L. Martines, *Lawyers and Statecraft in Renaissance Florence* (Princeton, 1968), pp. 387–404; on the issue of "free speech," Rubinstein, *Government of Florence*, pp. 156–57.

14. For descriptions of Lorenzo's network, see Lorenzo de' Medici, *Lettere*, ed. R. Fubini et al. (Florence, 1977–), 9 vols. to date. For a succinct summary, see F. W. Kent, "Patron-Client Networks in Renaissance Florence and the Emergence of Lorenzo as 'Maestro della Bottega'," in *Lorenzo de' Medici: New Perspectives*, ed. B. Toscani (New York, 1991), pp. 279–313.

15. F. W. Kent, *Household and Lineage in Renaissance Florence* (Princeton, 1977), p. 212; "Lorenzo and Oligarchy," in *Lorenzo il Magnifico e il suo mondo*, ed. G. Garfagnini (Florence, 1994), p. 46.

16. A. Perosa, ed., *Giovanni Rucellai ed il suo Zibaldone* (London, 1960), p. 9; Leon Battista Alberti, quoted in R. Weissman, *Ritual Brotherhood in Renaissance Florence* (New York, 1982), p. 29. Weissman's first chapter, "Judas the Florentine," pp. 1–41, describes the agonistic character of Florentine society.

17. F. W. Kent, "Un paradiso habitato da diavoli": Ties of Loyalty and Patronage in the Society of Medicean Florence," in *Le radici cristiane di Firenze*, ed. A. Benvenuti (Florence, 1994), p. 198; G. Brucker, "Florentine Voices from the Catasto, 1427–1480," *I Tatti Studies* 5 (1993): 22–32.

18. Kent, *Household and Lineage*, p. 83; "Patron-Client Networks," p. 294.

19. Weissman, *Ritual Brotherhood*; J. Henderson, *Piety and Charity in Late Medieval Florence* (Oxford, 1994); N. Eckstein, *The District of the Green Dragon: Neighborhood Life and Social Change in Renaissance Florence* (Florence, 1995), p. 217.

20. A. Brown, "Lorenzo and Public Opinion in Florence," in Garfagnini, ed., *Lorenzo il Magnifico*, pp. 61–85.

21. F. Gilbert, *Machiavelli and Guicciardini* (Princeton, 1965), p. 19. The phrase *vivere popolare* was commonly used by contemporaries, for example, Luca Landucci, *Diario fiorentino dall 1450 al 1516* (Florence, 1883), pp. 97, 110.

22. Gilbert, *Machiavelli and Guicciardini*, pp. 7–104; H. Butters, *Governors and Government in Early Sixteenth Century Florence 1502–1519* (Oxford, 1985), pp. 1–165.

23. The quotations in this paragraph are from D. Fachard, ed., *Consulte e Pratiche della Republica fiorentina 1498–1505* (Geneva, 1993), pp. 1–9.

24. Lodovico Alamanni, quoted in R. von Albertini, *Das Florentinische Staats-bewusstsein im Übergang von der Republik zum Prinzipat* (Bern, 1955), p. 370.

25. Kent, "Patron-Client Networks," p. 302.

26. *The Autobiography of Benvenuto Cellini*, trans. G. Bull (Baltimore, 1956), pp. 21–22.

27. The impact of a devastating plague in the early 1630s is described by G. Calvi, *Histories of a Plague Year* (Berkeley and Los Angeles, 1989). Political instability ensued not only in the city but also in the territory; G. Spini, *Cosimo I de' Medici e la indipendenza del principato mediceo* (Florence, 1945), pp. 178–87. The elaborate celebration of a Medici marriage is described by J. Saslow, *The Medici Wedding of 1589: Florentine Festival as Theatrum Mundi* (New Haven, 1996).

28. E. Cochrane, *Florence in the Forgotten Centuries* (Chicago, 1973), pp. 43, 64; Benedetto Varchi, quoted in F. Diaz, *Il Granducato di Toscana: I Medici* (Turin, 1987), p. 74; Cochrane, *Florence*, p. 40.

29. Weissman, *Ritual Brotherhood*, p. 198. See also K. Eisenbichler, "Italian Scholarship on Pre-Modern Confraternities in Italy," *Renaissance Quarterly* 50 (1997): 567–80; Diaz, *Granducato*, p. 201.

30. N. Machiavelli, *Discorsi*, bk. 1, chap. 55, in *Tutte le opere di Niccolò Machiavelli*, ed. G. Mazzoni and M. Casella (Florence, 1929), p. 127. Machiavelli mistakenly included Lombardy and the papal states in his catalogue of regions that had never experienced republican government. Landucci, *Diario fiorentino*, p. 371: "Si cominciò a lasciare la portatura de' capucci, e nel 1532 non se ne vedeva pure uno, che fu spenta la usanza, e scanbiò di capuccio si porta berrette e cappegli. . . . e or cominciossi a portare la barba" (Florentines no longer wore hoods on their cloaks, and by 1532, there were none to be seen. Instead of hoods, they wore caps, and they also began to grow beards).

31. The definitive study of these *ottomati* is B. Litchfield, *Emergence of a Bureaucracy: The Florentine Patricians, 1530–1790* (Princeton, 1986).

32. Diaz, *Granducato*, p. 3: "La libertà civile, in quanto tutela dei diritti individuali, e sempre stata . . . ignorata dalle 'democrazie' communali" (Civil liberty, in the sense of protecting individual rights, had always been ignored by communal "democracies"). For the legislation that flooded granducal Tuscany, see *Legislazione toscana raccolta e illustrata da Lorenzo Cantini* (Florence, 1800–1807), 30 vols.

33. Diaz, *Granducato*, p. 133.

34. P. Ginsborg, "The Italian Republic in the Face of the Future," in *Italian History and Culture* (Florence, 1966), 2: 4.

35. J. C. Waquet, *Corruption: Ethics and Power in Florence, 1600–1770*, trans. L. McCall (University Park, PA, 1991), p. 17. G. Delille, quoted in D. Sella, *Italy in the Seventeenth Century* (New York, 1997), p. 83.

36. Sella, *Italy in the Seventeenth Century*, pp. 80–81.

37. J. Bossy, "The Counter-Reformation and the Peoples of Catholic Europe," *Past and Present* 47 (1970): 51–70; W. Hudon, "Religion and Society in Early Modern Italy—Old Questions, New Insights," *American Historical Review* 101 (1996): 783–804. The plight of the confraternities is a major theme in Bossy's seminal article "Counter-Reformation," pp. 54–59, but his statement that confraternities were no longer an obstacle to uniform parochial observance "because they ceased to exist" is too extreme. See Sella, *Italy in the Seventeenth Century*, pp. 137–42.

38. Diaz, *Granducato*, p. 194.

39. Sella, *Italy in the Seventeenth Century*, pp. 52–62; S. Woolf, *A History of Italy 1700–1860: The Social Constraints of Political Change* (New York, 1991), pp. 21–26.

40. Sella, *Italy in the Seventeenth Century*, pp. 154–55. An illustration of the survival of this mentality in the nineteenth century involved Bettino Ricasoli, the "enlightened" Tuscan statesman and landowner: "Whenever there was the least hesitant attempt to change customary relationships, with the peasants hinting at the existence of wishes diverging from those of their master, Ricasoli reacted swiftly, conveying to his factor at Brolio that he was master, that the property was his, and that he alone could decide how to manage it, and the first peasant that dared to speak ill of him would be dismissed"; F. Chabod, *Italian Foreign Policy. The Statement of the Founders*, trans. W. McCuaig (Princeton, 1996), p. 293.

41. R. Carr, *Times Literary Supplement*, 15 October 1993, p. 4. See also E. Gellner, *Civil Society and Its Rivals* (New York, 1996); Woolf, *History of Italy*, pp. 69–74, 93–111; A. Mola, *La massoneria nella storia d'Italia* (Rome, 1981), pp. 21–57; E. Cochrane, *Tradition and Enlightenment in the Tuscan Academies, 1690–1800* (Chicago, 1961), pp. 3–47.

42. Woolf, *History of Italy*, p. 476; M. Nolan, "Against Exceptionalism," *American Historical Review* 102 (1997): 772–73.

CHAPTER THREE

1. *Times Literary Supplement*, 9 July 1993, p. 5.

2. N. Machiavelli, *The Prince*, trans. Mark Musa (New York, 1964), chap. 26.

3. F. Gilbert, "The Concept of Nationalism in Machiavelli's *Prince*," *Studies in the Renaissance* 1 (1954): 38–48; and his *Machiavelli and Guicciardini* (Princeton, 1965), pp. 325–26.

4. D. Hay, *The Italian Renaissance in Its Historical Background*, 2nd ed. (Cambridge, 1977), chap. 3.

5. These passages are cited by D. Waley, *The Italian City-Republics* (London, 1969), pp. 7–8.

6. J. Hale, *Machiavelli and Renaissance Italy* (New York, 1960), p. 87.

7. D. M. Bueno de Mesquita, "Ludovico Sforza and His Vassals," in *Italian Renaissance Studies*, ed. E. F. Jacob (London, 1960), pp. 214, 216.

8. F. Guicciardini, *History of Italy*, trans. S. Alexander (New York, 1979), p. 191.

9. Ibid., p. 273.

10. Machiavelli, *The Prince*, chap. 25.

11. N. Machiavelli, *The Discourses*, in *The Portable Machiavelli*, ed. and trans. P. Bondanella and M. Musa (New York, 1979), bk. 1, chap. 12, p. 212.

12. E. Cochrane, *Histories and Historiography in the Italian Renaissance* (Chicago, 1981), bks. 4–5.

13. E. Cochrane, *Italy 1530–1630* (Chicago, 1988), pp. 243–44; A. Stussi, "Lingua, dialetto e letteratura," in *Einaudi Storia d'Italia*, 1 (Turin, 1972), pp. 677–728. At the time of unification (1860), "only 2.5 per cent of the population could confidently speak the national language—Italian"; S. Woolf, *A History of Italy 1700–1860* (London, 1979), p. 476.

14. F. Venturi, "L'Italia fuori d'Italia," in *Einaudi Storia d'Italia* (Turin, 1973), 3: 987–96.

15. Ibid., 3: 1007.

16. Woolf, *A History of Italy 1700–1860*, pp. 75–91.

17. *Einaudi Storia d'Italia, Annali* (La chiesa e il potere politico dal Medioevo all'eta' contemporanea) (Turin, 1986), 9: 198–216, 721–66.

18. Woolf, *A History of Italy 1700–1860*, p. 150.

19. Quoted in ibid., p. 225.

20. Ibid., p. 161.

21. Ibid., p. 205.

22. Quoted in F. W. Artz, *Reaction and Revolution 1814–1832* (New York, 1934), p. 4.

23. D. Mack Smith, ed., *The Making of Italy 1796–1870* (New York, 1968), pp. 42–50, 220–23, 263–65.

24. Woolf, *A History of Italy 1700–1860*, p. 332.

25. Ibid., pp. 361–406.

26. G. Tomasi di Lampedusa, *The Leopard*, trans. A. Colquhoun (New York, 1960), pp. 203–6, 214.

27. See C. Vivanti, "Lacerazioni e contrasti," in *Einaudi Storia d'Italia*, 1: 867–948.

28. Ibid., 1: 916.

29. Woolf, *A History of Italy 1700–1860*, p. 476.

30. Ibid., p. 421.

31. Ibid., p. 479; R. Putnam, *Making Democracy Work* (Princeton, 1993), pp. 133–44, 174–81; C. Tullio-Atran, *La nostra Italia* (Milan, 1986).

CHAPTER FOUR

1. *The Oxford Dictionary of Nursery Rhymes*, ed. I. Opie and P. Opie (Oxford, 1973), pp. 324–25. Herbert (d. 1633) included only the first three lines of the poem in his *Jacula Prudentum* (Outlandish Proverbs): the final lines were added later by unknown hands.

2. J. Adamson, "England without Cromwell: What if Charles I Had Avoided the Civil War?" in *Virtual History*, ed. N. Ferguson (London, 1997), pp. 91–124.

3. J. M. Roberts, *Times Literary Supplement*, 11 July 1975, p. 782.

4. F. Braudel, *The Mediterranean and the Mediterranean World in the Age of Philip II*, trans. S. Reynolds (New York, 1976), 1: 21.

5. Quoted in Ferguson, *Virtual History*, p. 6.

6. T. Judt, *The New York Review of Books*, 3 December 1998, pp. 51–52.

7. Roberts, *Times Literary Supplement*, p. 782.

8. E. Muir, "The Fall of Renaissance Italy," unpublished paper.

9. E. Duffy, *Saints and Sinners. A History of the Popes* (New Haven and London, 1997), chaps. 2, 3.

10. P. J. Jones, *The Italian City-State, 500–1300. From Commune to Signoria* (Oxford, 1997), p. 341.

11. D. Abulafia, *Frederick II: A Medieval Emperor* (London, 1988), p. 368.

12. D. Hay and J. Law, *Italy in the Age of the Renaissance 1380–1530* (London, 1989), pp. 199–200.

13. G. Brucker, *The Civic World of Early Renaissance Florence* (Princeton, 1977), p. 316; Duffy, *Saints and Sinners*, p. 132; G. Barraclough, *The Medieval Papacy* (London, 1968), p. 162.

14. Tierney, quoting K. Morrison; "Communication," *American Historical Review* 103 (1998): 1758.

15. Brucker, *Civic World*, p. 423.

16. Duffy, *Saints and Sinners*, p. 148. Several ultramontane cardinals did not travel to Rome for the 1492 conclave.

17. R. Fubini, "The Italian League and the Balance of Power at the Accession of Lorenzo de' Medici," in *The Origins of the State of Italy, 1300–1600*, ed. J. Kirshner (Chicago, 1996), pp. 171–73.

18. Ibid., p. 187.

19. N. Machiavelli, *The Prince*, trans. M. Musa (New York, 1964), chap. 7.

20. Duffy, *Saints and Sinners*, p. 148.

21. Fubini, "The Italian League," pp. 167, 182–84.

22. M. Bullard, *Lorenzo il Magnifico. Image and Anxiety, Politics and Finance* (Florence, 1994), pp. 65–79, 87–94.

23. T. Dean and D. Chambers, *Clean Hands and Rough Justice. An Investigating Magistrate in Renaissance Italy* (Ann Arbor, 1997).

24. H. Butters, "Politics and Diplomacy in Late Quattrocento Italy: The Case of the Barons' War (1485–86)," in *Florence and Italy. Renaissance Studies in Honour of Nicolai Rubinstein*, ed. P. Denley and C. Elam (London, 1988), p. 15.

25. J. Burckhardt, *The Civilization of the Renaissance in Italy*, trans. S. Middlemore (New York, 1958), p. 34.

26. A. Ryder, "The Angevin Bid for Naples, 1380–1480," in *The French Descent into Renaissance Italy, 1494–95*, ed. D. Abulafia (Aldershot, 1995), p. 68.

27. A. Lovett, *Early Hapsburg Spain 1517–1598* (Oxford, 1986), p. 10.

28. Ibid., pp. 24, 27.

29. M. Mallett, "Personalities and Pressures: Italian Involvement in the French Invasion of 1494," in *The French Descent*, pp. 152–53.

30. Ibid., p. 163.

31. J. R. Hale, *War and Society in Renaissance Europe* (Leicester, 1985).

32. D. Laven, "Machiavelli, italianità and the French Invasion of 1494," in *The French Descent*, p. 357.

33. Ibid., pp. 361–62.

34. R. Mackenney, *Sixteenth Century Europe: Expansion and Conflict* (New York, 1993), p. 224.

35. D. Chambers, "Francesco II Gonzaga, marquis of Mantua, 'Liberator of Italy'," in *The French Descent*, pp. 224–29.

36. J. Najemy, *Discourses of Power and Desire in the Machiavelli-Vettori Letters of 1513–1515* (Princeton, 1993), p. 160.

37. Ibid., p. 170.

38. F. Guicciardini, *Maxims and Reflections of a Renaissance Statesman*, trans. M. Domandi (New York, 1965), p. 48.

39. E. Chamberlin, *The Sack of Rome* (London, 1979), p. 196.

40. P. Prodi, *The Papal Prince. One Body and Two Souls: The Papal Monarchy in Early Modern Europe*, trans. S. Haskins (Cambridge, 1987), p. 20.

41. G. Parker, *Europe in Crisis 1598–1648* (Ithaca, 1979), p. 50.

42. J. R. Hale, *Machiavelli and Renaissance Italy* (New York, 1963), p. 87.

CHAPTER FIVE

1. M. Villani, *Cronica*, ed. F. Dragomanni (Florence, 1846), bk. 3, chap. 16.

2. *New York Review of Books*, 10 August 2000, p. 47.

3. R. Weissman, *Ritual Brotherhood in Renaissance Florence* (New York, 1982), chap. 1. Cf. T. Cohen, "A Long Day in Monte Rotondo: The Politics of Jeopardy in a Village Uprising," *Comparative Studies in Society and History* 33 (1991): 651–52: "In an insecure world of tight and wary solidarities, *fede* was at once cherished, rare and precarious."

4. P. J. Jones, *The Italian City-State, 500–1300. From Commune to Signoria* (Oxford, 1997) p. 174.

5. S. Epstein, *Genoa and the Genoese 958–1528* (Chapel Hill, 1996), p. 65.

6. Jones, *Italian City-State*, p. 230.

7. Ibid., p. 33.

8. A. Astorri, "Note sulla Mercanzia fiorentina sotto Lorenzo dei Medici," *Archivio storico italiano* 150 (1992): 968.

9. Ibid., p. 972.

10. A. Strozzi, *Lettere di una gentildonna fiorentina ai figliuoli esuli*, ed. C. Guasti (Florence, 1877), p. 354.

11. T. Kuehn, "Multorum fraudibus occurrere," *Studi senesi* 93 (1981): 312.

12. L. De Angelis et al., eds., *La civiltà fiorentina del Quattrocento* (Florence, 1993), pp. 94–95.

13. B. Machiavelli, *Libro di ricordi*, ed. C. Olschki (Florence, 1954), pp. 26–31.

14. Ibid., p. 156.

15. Astorri, "Note sulla Mercanzia," p. 973.

16. R. de Roover, *The Rise and Decline of the Medici Bank 1397–1494* (Cambridge, MA, 1963), p. 74.

17. Kuehn, "Multorum fraudibus occurrere," p. 323.

18. Ibid., pp. 342–50.

19. R. Mueller, *The Venetian Money Market. Banks, Panics and the Public Debt 1200–1500* (Baltimore and London, 1997), p. 36.

20. Ibid., p. 122.

21. Ibid., p. 124.

22. F. Braudel, *The Mediterranean and the Mediterranean World in the Age of Philip II* (New York, 1972), 1: 500.

23. R. Goldthwaite, *American Historical Review* 103 (1998): 500.

24. A. Calabria, "Finanzieri genovesi nel Regno di Napoli nel Cinquecento," *Rivista storica italiana* 101 (1989): 578–613.

25. Braudel, *The Mediterranean*, 1: 507.

26. E. Muir, *Ritual in Early Modern Europe* (Cambridge, 1997), p. 43.

27. R. Marshall, *The Local Merchants of Prato* (Baltimore and London, 1999).

28. *Selected Letters of Alessandra Strozzi*, ed. and trans. H. Gregory (Berkeley, Los Angeles, and London, 1997), pp. 125–27.

29. Kuehn, "Multorum fraudibus occurrere," p. 312; Mueller, *The Venetian Money Market*, p. 125.

30. An excellent analysis of the role of *fede* in medieval Italian commercial activity has recently been published by G. Dahl, *Trade, Trust and Networks: Commercial Culture in Late Medieval Italy* (Lund, 1998).

31. P. Prodi, *Il sacramento del potere* (Bologna, 1992).

32. E. Muir, "The Sources of Civil Society in Italy," *Journal of Interdisciplinary History* 29 (1999): 380–81.

33. Ibid., p. 383.

34. G. Guidi, *Ii governo dells città repubblica di Firenze di primo Quattrocento* (Florence, 1981) p. 228; A. Doren, *Le arti fiorentine* (Florence, 1940), 1: 124.

35. D. Kent, *The Rise of the Medici. Faction in Florence 1426–1434* (Oxford, 1978), p. 243.

36. Archivio di Stato, Florence (hereafter ASF), Consulte e Pratiche (hereafter CP), 49, fol. 124r, 21 February 1431.

37. G. Brucker, *The Civic World of Early Renaissance Florence* (Princeton, 1977), pp. 69–71.

38. ASF, CP, 54, fol. 13r.

39. A. Molho, "Tre città-stato e i loro debiti pubblici," in *Italia 1350–1450: tra crisi, trasformazione, sviluppo* (Pistoia, 1991), p. 200.

40. ASF, Carte Strozziane, ser. 3, 178, no. 6.

41. D. Peterson, "Out of the Margins: Religion and the Church in Renaissance Italy," *Renaissance Quarterly* 53 (2000): 853.

42. ASF, Catasto, 18, fol. 806r.

43. F. Pellegrini, *Sulla repubblica fiorentina a tempo di Cosimo il Vecchio* (Pisa, 1880), p. 37.

44. E. Muir, review of Crouzet-Pavan, "Sopra le acque salse," in *Speculum* 69 (1994): 1150. Cf. Crouzet-Pavan, "Toward an Ecological Understanding of the Myth of Venice," in *Venice Reconsidered. The History and Civilization of an Italian City-State*, ed. J. Martin and D. Romano (Baltimore and London, 2000), pp. 39–66.

45. Muir, "Sources of Civil Society," p. 386.

46. E. Muir, "Was There Republicanism in the Renaissance Republics? Venice after Agnadello," in *Venice Reconsidered*, p. 150.

47. Details in Epstein, *Genoa and the Genoese*, pp. 325–27.

48. M. Bullard, *Lorenzo il Magnifico. Image and Anxiety, Politics and Finance* (Florence, 1994), p. 92.

49. C. Shaw, *The Politics of Exile in Renaissance Italy* (Cambridge, 2000), p. 1.

50. Kent, *Rise of the Medici*, pp. 339–45, 355–57.

51. Shaw, *Politics of Exile*, p. 62.

52. Ibid., p. 40.

53. Ibid., p. 238.

54. L. Pye, "Civility, Social Capital and Civil Society in Asia," *Journal of Interdisciplinary History* 29 (1999): 380.

55. Lorenzo de' Medici, *Lettere*, ed. M. Mallett (Florence, 1998), 7: 380.

56. *Cronica domestica di Messer Donato Velluti*, ed. I. del Badia and G. Volpi (Florence, 1914), p. 281.

57. Villani, *Cronica*, bk. 3, chap. 96.

58. Ibid., bk. 4, chap. 14.

59. G. Brucker, *Florence. The Golden Age, 1138–1737* (Berkeley and Los Angeles, 1998), p. 13.

60. W. Cafarro, *Mercenary Companies and the Decline of Siena* (Baltimore and London, 1998), p. 89.

61. M. Stefani, *Cronica fiorentina*, ed. N. Rodolico, in *Rerum Italicarum Scriptores*, 2nd ed., vol. 30, pt. 1 (Città di Castello, 1903), rub. 847.

62. M. Mallett, *Mercenaries and Their Masters: Warfare in Renaissance Italy* (London, 1974), p. 102.

63. Kent, *Rise of the Medici*, p. 473.

64. R. Trexler, *Public Life in Renaissance Florence* (New York, 1980), p. 279.

65. Bullard, *Lorenzo Il Magnifico*, p. 87.

66. H. Butters, "The Politics of Protection in Late Fifteenth Century Italy," in *The French Descent into Renaissance Italy, 1494–95*, ed. D. Abulafia (Aldershot, 1995), p. 143.

67. Bullard, *Lorenzo Il Magnifico*, p. 99.

68. Ibid., p. 91.

69. Ibid., p. 100.

70. Ibid., pp. 89–90.

71. Lorenzo de' Medici, *Lettere*, 2: 72–74.

72. *The Portable Machiavelli*, ed. and trans. P. Bondanella and M. Musa (New York, 1979), pp. 70–71.

CHAPTER SIX

1. G. Brucker, "Researching the Renaissance: An American in Florence, 1952," *Renaissance News and Notes* 7 (1994): 1–3.

2. Cf. E. Muir, "The Renaissance in America," *American Historical Review* 100 (1995): 1113; A. Molho, "The Italian Renaissance, Made in the USA," *Imagined Histories. American Historians Interpret the Past*, ed. A. Molho and G. Wood (Princeton, 1994): 271–74.

3. C. Klapisch-Zuber, "Ripensando al catasto," *Archivio storico italiano* 152 (1994): 182.

4. Muir, "The Renaissance in America," p. 1113.

5. H. Baron, *The Crisis of the Early Italian Renaissance*, 2nd ed. (Princeton, 1966); R. Witt, J. Najemy, C. Kallendorf, and W. Gundersheimer, "Hans Baron's Renaissance Humanism," *American Historical Review* 101 (1966): 107–44.

6. N. Rubinstein, *The Government of Florence under the Medici* (1434 to 1494), 2nd ed. (Oxford, 1997).

7. A. Molho, "The State in Public Finance," in *The Origins of the State in Italy 1300–1600*, ed. J. Kirshner (Chicago, 1996), p. 100, n. 9.

8. D. Herlihy and C. Klapisch-Zuber, *Les Toscans et leurs familles* (Paris, 1978), English trans. (New Haven and London, 1985); E. Conti, *La formazione della struttura agraria moderna nel contado fiorentino*, 2 vols. (Rome, 1965); *I catasti agrari della Repubblica fiorentina e il catasto particellare toscano (secoli XIV–XIX)* (Rome, 1966).

9. L. Martines, *The Social World of the Florentine Humanists 1390–1460* (Princeton, 1963); *Lawyers and Statecraft in Renaissance Florence* (Princeton, 1968).

10. R. Trexler, *Public Life in Renaissance Florence* (New York, 1980).

11. R. Goldthwaite, *Private Wealth in Renaissance Florence* (Baltimore, 1968); *The Building of Renaissance Florence* (Baltimore, 1980); *Wealth and the Demand for Art in Italy 1300–1600* (Baltimore, 1993).

12. F. W. Kent, *Household and Lineage in Renaissance Florence* (Princeton, 1977); A. Molho, *Marriage Alliance in Late Medieval Florence* (Cambridge, MA, 1994); C. Klapisch-Zuber, *Women, Family and Ritual in Renaissance Italy*, trans. L. Cochrane (Chicago and London, 1985).

13. G. Brucker, "Tales of Two Cities: Florence and Venice in the Renaissance," *American Historical Review* 88 (1983): 599–616.

14. In this survey, I have counted important collections of articles on Florentine topics.

15. G. Ciappelli, *Una famiglia e le sue ricordanze: I Castellani a Firenze nel Tre-Quattrocento* (Florence, 1995); *Carnevale e Quaresima: comportamenti sociale e cultura a Firenze nel Rinascimento* (Rome, 1997); L. Fabbri, *Alleanza matrimoniale e patriziato nella Firenze del '400* (Florence, 1991); F. Franceschi, *Oltre il "Tumulto": i lavoratori fiorentini dell' Arte della Lana fra Tre e Quattrocento* (Florence, 1993); A. Stella, *La révolte des Ciompi* (Paris, 1993); A. Zorzi, *L'amministrazione della giustizia penale nella Repubblica fiorentina: aspetti e problemi* (Florence, 1988).

16. Utilized by M. Mazzi and S. Raveggi, *Gli uomini e le cose nelle campagne fiorentine del Quattrocento* (Florence, 1983); Franceschi, *Oltre il "Tumulto"*; Mazzi, *Prostitute e lenoni nella Firenze del Quattrocento* (Milan, 1991); M. Rocke, *Forbidden Friendships. Homosexuality and Male Culture in Renaissance Florence* (Oxford, 1996).

17. R. Starn, "Florentine Renaissance Studies," *Bibliothèque d'humanisme et Renaissance* 32 (1970): 679.

18. A. Molho, 'Società e fisco nell interpretazione di Elio Conti," *Nuovi studi storici* 29 (1995): 41.

19. L. Martines, "Forced Loans: Political and Social Strain in Quattrocento Florence," *Journal of Modern History* 60 (1988): 300–311.

20. Starn, "Florentine Renaissance Studies," p. 679.

21. J. Najemy, "Linguaggi storiografici sulla Firenze rinascimentale," *Rivista storica italiana* 97 (1985): 102–59.

22. F. Gilbert, "The Medici Megalopolis," *New York Review of Books*, 21 January 1982, pp. 61–66.

23. A. Molho, "Cosimo de' Medici: Pater Patriae or Padrino?" *Stanford Italian Review* 1 (1979): 9–19.

24. H. Butters, *Governors and Government in Early Sixteenth Century Florence 1502–1519* (Oxford, 1985), pp. ix–x.

25. A. Molho, review of *Giovanni and Lusanna. Love and Marriage in Renaissance Florence*, by G. Brucker, *Renaissance Quarterly* 40 (1987): 96–100; S. Cohn, "David Herlihy—il ricordo di uno studente," *Archivio storico italiano* 152 (1994): 192–201.

26. Muir, "The Renaissance in America," p. 1112.

27. Cf. A. Molho, "Il padronato a Firenze nella storiografia anglofono," *Ricerche storiche* 15 (1985): 5–16; A. Stella, *La révolte des Ciompi*.

28. G. Brucker, "The Economic Foundations of Laurentian Florence," in *Lorenzo de' Medici e il suo mondo*, ed. G. Garfagnini (Florence, 1994): 3–15.

29. Goldthwaite, *Wealth and the Demand for Art in Italy*, p. 5.

30. Molho, *Marriage Alliance in Late Medieval Florence*, p. 347.

31. S. Cohn, *The Cult of Remembrance and the Black Death. Six Renaissance Cities in Central Italy* (Baltimore and London, 1992).

32. S. Cohn, *Creating the Florentine State: Peasant Rebellion and the Mountains from the Black Death to the Return of Cosimo de' Medici* (Cambridge, 1999).

33. T. Verdon and J. Henderson, eds., *Christianity and the Renaissance* (Syracuse, 1990).

34. D. Peterson, *From the "Eight Saints" to Saint Antoninus: The Church in Florence, 1375–1460*, 2 vols. (Baltimore and London, forthcoming).

35. D. Kent, *Cosimo de' Medici and the Florentine Renaissance* (New Haven and London, 2000).

36. A. Brown, *The Medici in Florence. The Exercise of Language and Power* (Florence and Perth, 1992); *Lorenzo de' Medici, New Perspectives*, ed. B. Toscano (New York, 1993); *Lorenzo de' Medici e il suo tempo*, ed. G. Garfagnini (Florence, 1993); *Lorenzo de' Medici e il suo mondo*, ed. G. Garfagnini (Florence, 1994); M. Bullard, *Lorenzo de' Medici. Image and Anxiety, Politics and Finance* (Florence, 1994); *Lorenzo the Magnificent: Culture and Politics*, ed. M. Mallett and N. Mann (London, 1996).

37. *Convegni di studi sulla storia dei ceti dirigenti dal medioevo alla fine del Granducato*, 4 vols. (Pisa and Impruneta, 1981–83); W. Connell and A. Zorzi, eds., *Florentine Tuscany: Structure and Practices of Power* (Cambridge, 2000).

38. M. Kemp, "Not So Eccentric," review in *Times Literary Supplement*, 11 November 1994, p. 12.

39. D. Frigo, ed., *Politics and Diplomacy in Early Modern Italy. The Structure of Diplomatic Practice* (Cambridge, 1999), p. 11.

40. Muir, *"The Renaissance in America,"* p. 1115.

41. E.g., *Storia di Venezia dalle origini alla caduta della Serenissima*, 8 vols. (Rome, 1992–98).

42. Starn, review in *Apollo* 144 (1996): 71.

43. E.g., *Prato: storia di una città*, 2 vols., ed. E. Fasano Guarini (Florence, 1986); J. Brown, *In the Shadow of Florence: Provincial Society in Renaissance Pescia* (Oxford, 1982); G. Benadusi, *A Provincial Elite in Early Modern Tuscany* (Baltimore and London, 1996); W. Connell, *La città dei cruci* (Campo Bisenzio, Italy, 1999).

44. A. Molho, "Recent Works on the History of Tuscany: Fifteenth to Eighteenth Centuries," *Journal of Modern History* 62 (1990): 63.

45. G. Brucker, *Florence: The Golden Age, 1138–1737* (Berkeley and Los Angeles, 1998), pp. 7–11.

46. A. Graham Dixon, *Renaissance* (London, 2000), p. 3.

47. K. Gouwens, "Perceiving the Past: Renaissance Humanism after the 'Cognitive Turn'," *American Historical Review* 103 (1998): 58–63.

48. E. Welch, *Art and Society in Italy, 1350–1500* (Oxford, 1997).

49. Brucker, *Florence: The Golden Age*, pp. 7–22.

50. G. Steiner, "Stones of Light: How Florence Created Civilization amid Catastrophe," *The New Yorker*, 13 January 1997, pp. 76–77.

CHAPTER SEVEN

1. For a demographic and economic analysis of early fifteenth-century Florence, see D. Herlihy and C. Klapisch-Zuber, *Tuscans and Their Families* (New Haven and London, 1985).

2. R. Goldthwaite, *The Building of Renaissance Florence* (Baltimore and London, 1980), chap. 6.

3. See below, note 10.

4. The most recent account of the Pazzi conspiracy is L. Martines, *April Blood: Florence and the Plot against the Medici* (Oxford and New York, 2003).

5. G. Brucker, *Florence: The Golden Age, 1138–1737* (Berkeley, Los Angeles, and London, 1998), p. 98.

6. M. Levey, *Florence: A Portrait* (Cambridge, MA, 1996), p. 218.

7. P. Parenti, *Storia fiorentina*, ed. A. Matucci (Florence, 1994), p. 116.

8. Ibid., p. 239.

9. L. Landucci, *Diario fiorentino dal 1450 al 1516*, ed. I. del Badia (Florence, 1883), pp. 138–46.

10. The most authoritative account of Savonarola's Florentine career is D. Weinstein, *Savonarola and Florence: Prophecy and Patriotism in the Renaissance*

(Princeton, 1970). See also D. Weinstein and V. Hotchkiss, eds., *Girolamo Savonarola: Piety, Prophecy and Politics in Renaissance Florence* (Dallas, 1994).

11. N. Machiavelli, *Tutte le opere di Niccolò Machiavelli*, ed. G. Mazzoni and M. Casella (Florence, 1929), p. 877; F. Guicciardini, *Storie fiorentine dal 1378 al 1509*, ed. R. Palmarocchi (Bari, 1931), p. 157.

12. Landucci, *Diario fiorentino dal 1450 al 1516*, pp. 176–78.

13. L. Polizzotto, *The Elect Nation: The Savonarolan Movement in Florence 1494–1545* (Oxford, 1994).

14. *The Notebooks of Leonardo da Vinci*, ed. E. MacCurdy (New York, 1938), 2: 587.

15. *Ricordanze di Bartolomeo Masi calderaio dal 1478 al 1526*, ed. G. Corazzini (Florence, 1906), pp. 47–48.

16. G. Cambi, *Storia fiorentina*, in *Delizie degli eruditi toscani*, ed. I. di San Luigi (Florence, 1785–86), 21: 204–9.

17. *Ricordanze*, pp. 74–75.

18. Florentine politics in these years are analyzed by H. Butters, *Governors and Government in Early Sixteenth Century Florence 1502–1519* (Oxford, 1985).

19. *Ricordanze*, pp. 94–97.

20. Butters, *Governors and Government*, pp. 212–16.

21. M. Bullard, *Filippo Strozzi and the Medici. Favor and Finance in Sixteenth Century Florence and Rome* (Cambridge, 1980), chap. 6.

22. Cambi, *Storia fiorentina*, pp. 217–28.

23. Ibid., pp. 133, 253–57.

24. B. Litchfield, "Demographic Characteristics of Florentine Patrician Families: Sixteenth to Eighteenth Centuries," *Journal of Economic History* 29 (1969): 191–205.

25. *Il carteggio di Michelangelo. Carteggio indiretto*, ed. P. Barocchi (Florence, 1988), l: 308.

26. Ibid., 1: 321.

27. Ibid., 1: 328.

CHAPTER EIGHT

1. Archivio di Stato di Firenze (hereafter ASF), Provvisioni Registri 61, fol. 15v.

2. ASF, Catasto, 425, fols. 3r–v.

3. Archivio arcivescovile, Florence, Visita pastorale (1514), fols. 4r–5v.

4. A. Verde, *Lo Studio fiorentino 1473–1503. Richerche e documenti* (Pistoia, 1977–85), 3: 1104, 1122–23, 1200.

5. For the free schools in Arezzo, see R. Black, "Humanism and Education in Renaissance Arezzo," *I Tatti Studies. Essays in the Renaissance* 2 (1987): 174–229.

6. Giuliano Tornabuoni petitioned Lorenzo de' Medici for his support in obtaining a benefice for his nephew, "so that he will not have to become a priest in the country"; Verde, *Studio*, 3: 48.

7. In 1479 Alamanno di Bernardo de' Medici requesting help in obtaining a Volterra canonry for his son Luigi; Verde, *Studio*, 3: 48.

8. Biblioteca Nazionale di Firenze, II, V, 12, fols. 189r–v, 2 September 1484.

9. Verde, *Studio*, 3: 1013. On this common practice, see *Motti e facezie di Piovano Arlotto*, ed. G. Folena (Milan, 1953), pp. 87–88.

10. G. Richa, *Notizie istoriche delle chiese fiorentine divise ne' suoi quartieri* (Florence, 1754–62), 6: 103–5.

11. ASF, Notarile Antecosmiano (hereafter NA), 6200, fols. 17v–18r. The record of an election to a chaplaincy by cathedral canons is in NA, 6212, fol. 145r, 24 July 1467.

12. NA, 11108, unpaginated, 23 August 1449; 10085, fol. 184v.

13. NA, 6209, fol. 219r; 6220, fol. 39v.

14. An example of a salaried chaplain: in 1446, the members of the Merchants' Court (Mercanzia), elected a chaplain, ser Andrea de Rischo, to officiate in their chapel at an annual salary of 30 florins; H. Saalman, *Filippo Brunelleschi. The Cupola of S. Maria del Fiore* (London, 1980), p. 278.

15. R. Goldthwaite, *The Building of Renaissance Florence* (Baltimore, 1980), pp. 435–39.

16. N. Cianfogni, *Memorie istoriche dell' Ambrosiana R. Basilica di S. Lorenzo di Firenze* (Florence, 1804), pp. 166–67.

17. The testament of a cathedral chaplain, ser Antonio Masaini, stipulated that the clerics who participated in his funeral service would receive two candles and 2 *soldi*; NA, 20752, 15 October 1457.

18. NA, 6204, fol. 205r.

19. Archbishop Antoninus's constitution: "Item niuno cherico debba o posse chiedere alchuna cosa per gli sacramenti della chiesa. Ma quello che lgle' è offerto, può acceptare per limosina." R. Trexler, "The Episcopal Constitutions of Antoninus of Florence," *Quellen und Forschungen aus Italienischen Archiven und Bibliotheken* 59 (1979): 269.

20. Dr. Margaret Haines has graciously provided me with citations from the records of the Opera del Duomo recording income received from offerings at

altars and from boxes attached to pillars; Opera del Duomo VIII, 3–9, fols. 2r, 4r–v, 6r (February–April 1469).

21. Cianfogni, *S. Lorenzo*, p. 169.

22. NA, 10084, fol. 142r, 24 March 1470.

23. NA, 10087, fol. 146r.

24. NA, 6204, fols. 38r, 145r.

25. NA, 20752, unpaginated, 15 October 1457, 12 April 1458.

26. NA, 11093, unpaginated, 12 December 1468; 20753, fol. 347r.

27. NA, 10086, fol. 369r.

28. NA, 6206, fol. 270r; 10083, fol. 156r.

29. NA, 10088, fol. 451r.

30. G. Brucker, "Urban Parishes and Their Clergy in Quattrocento Florence: A Preliminary *Sondage*," *Renaissance Sudies in Honor of Craig Hugh Smyth* (Florence, 1985), p. 20.

31. Catasto, 194, i, fol. 22v.

32. Brucker, "Urban Parishes," p. 21.

33. R. Bizzocchi, *Chiesa e potere nella Toscana del Quattrocento* (Bologna, 1987), pp. 309–40.

34. Catasto, 425, fol. 3r.

35. ASF, Estimo, 341, fol. 1v.

36. E. Conti, *I catasti agrari della Repubblica fiorentina* (Rome, 1966), p. 120.

37. NA, 6210, unpaginated, 5 July 1465. Two documents from the notarial records contain information about the organization of religious services in the cathedral; NA, 13512, no. 53, 26 March 1454; 6212, fols. 70v–72r, 14 January 1466/67.

38. Casini's endowment (March 1431) is in G. Lami, *Sanctae Ecclesiae Florentinae Monumenta* (Florence, 1758), 1: 144–46.

39. For specific descriptions of a chaplain's duties in other churches, see NA, 6207, fol. 403r, c. 1450; 6208, fol. 419v, 14 February 1465.

40. Catasto, 194, i, fols. 15v–23v.

41. Catasto, 425, fols. 3r–v.

42. G. Poggi, ed., *Il Duomo di Firenze. Documenti sulla decorazione della chiesa e del campanile tratti dell'Archivio dell'Opera* (Berlin, 1909), 1: nos. 106, 215–16, 221; M. Haines, *The Sacrestia delle Messe of the Florentine Cathedral* (Florence, 1983), pp. 42, 123, 217.

43. Poggi, *Duomo*, 1: no. 208.

44. NA, 7943, fol. 53r.

45. The benefices are recorded in NA, 20753, unpaginated, 9 April 1463; 11091, unpaginated, 16 January 1452/53. Ser Angelo died in the spring of 1467; his chaplaincy was then occupied by ser Giovanni de Vico; NA, 13078, fol. 163v, 13 April 1467.

46. The income is reported in Catasto, 987, fol. 420r.

47. Two of these salaried posts were the "officium distributorum" and the "officium sacriste"; NA, 6206, fols. 61v–62r, 30 May 1459.

48. Notarial references to cathedral chaplains serving as officials of this society: NA, 10084, fol. 382v; 10086, fols. 60v, 156r, 187r; 10087, fols. 41v, 63r, 130v, 211v–212r, 228r. The history of this society is described by W. Bowsky, "The Confraternity of Priests and San Lorenzo of Florence: A Church, a Parish and a Clerical Brotherhood," *Ricerche storiche* 27 (1997): 53–92.

49. W. Paatz and E. Paatz, *Die Kirchen von Florenz* (Frankfurt am Main, 1940–54), 3: 423.

50. Poggi, *Duomo*, 2: no. 134.

51. See the testaments of ser Santi di Godenzo and ser Antonio Masaini; NA, 15115, unpaginated, 4 November 1450; 20752, unpaginated, 15 October 1457.

52. *Diario fiorentino di Agostino Lapini*, ed. O. Corazzini (Florence, 1900), p. xiv.

53. R. Gaston, "Liturgy and Patronage in San Lorenzo, Florence, 1350–1650," in *Patronage, Art and Society in Renaissance Italy*, ed. F. W. Kent and P. Simons (Oxford, 1987), p. 129.

54. Catasto, 602, fol. 299r.

55. Haines, *Sacrestia*, pp. 39–40.

56. NA, 6206, fols. 341r, 369r–v; 10084, fols. 97v–98v.

57. NA, 10096, fols. 382v–383r. Cf. R. Bizzocchi, "Chiesa e aristocrazia nella Firenze del Quattrocento," *Archivio storico italiano* 142 (1984): 227–29.

58. The most comprehensive study of the building of the sacristy is Haines, *The Sacrestia delle Messe*. In August 1436, the consuls of the wool guild and the *operai del Duomo* issued a decree to build a lantern for the cupola, to cover the three tribunes, "et de novo edificari certas cappellas a quolibet navium dicte ecclesie, que cappelle erunt catene totius ecclesie" ; C. Guasti, *La cupola di Santa Maria del Fiore* (Florence, 1857), pp. 89–90. For examples of translations of chapels and altars, see Haines, *Sacrestia*, p. 217; Poggi, *Duomo*, 1: no. 371, 372, 1031, 1032, 1034, 1065, 1076, 1144.

59. Poggi, *Duomo*, 2: no. 1081.

60. *Ricordanze di Bartolomeo Masi*, ed. G. Corrazini (Florence, 1906), pp. 16–17.

61. NA, 6210, unpaginated.

62. L. Landucci, *Diario fiorentino dal 1450 al 1516, continuato da un anonimo fino al 1542*, ed. I. Del Badia (Florence, 1883), pp. 124–26.

63. R. Trexler, *Public Life in Renaissance Florence* (New York, 1980), pp. 472–73.

64. D. Weinstein, *Savonarola and Florence. Prophecy and Patriotism in the Renaissance* (Princeton, 1970), p. 283.

CHAPTER NINE

1. B. Dei, *La Cronica*, ed. R. Barducci (Florence, 1984), p. 87.

2. G. Brucker, *The Civic World of Early Renaissance Florence* (Florence, 1977), pp. 381–89; L. Martines, *The Social World of the Florentine Humanists 1390–1460* (Princeton, 1963), pp. 313–14.

3. Archivio di Stato di Firenze (hereafter ASF), Catasto, 829, fol. 20r (1458, tax declaration of Messer Guglielmo Tanagli).

4. L. Martines, *The Social World of the Florentine Humanists*, p. 188.

5. N. Rubinstein, *The Government of Florence under the Medici (1434 to 1494)* (Oxford, 1966), p. 323.

6. A. Molho, *Marriage Alliance in Late Medieval Florence* (Cambridge, MA, and London, 1994), pp. 397–98.

7. Molho, *Marriage Alliance*, p. 397; R. de Roover, *The Rise and Decline of the Medici Bank 1397–1494* (Cambridge, MA, 1963), p. 26.

8. Vespasiano da Bisticci noted the large amount paid by Agnolo in taxes: *Renaissance Princes, Popes and Prelates. The Vespasiano Memoirs* (New York, 1963), p. 247.

9. A. Verde, *Lo Studio fiorentino 1473–1503. Ricerche e documenti* (Pistoia, 1973–85), 3: 303. Additional income came from Bartolomeo's investment in the commune's funded debt and from stipends for service in the territorial government.

10. The Pandolfini did have other kinsmen in the city in 1427; Felice di Benedetto, a *lanaiuolo* (assets: 723 florins); Jacopo di Donato (assets:727 fl.); Matteo di Pagolo, a cloth shearer (assets:166 fl.) Pandolfo di Jacopo (assets: 270 fl.); ser Carlo di Francesco, a notary (assets: 10 fl.); Catasto, 67, fols. 278r, 387r;

77; fol. 334r; 80, fol. 308r. But these poor cousins would not have provided either financial or political support for Carlo and Giannozzo.

11. Catasto, 927, fols. 306r–309r. Carlo also identified his two illegitimate sons: Vittorio (aged fifty); and Lorenzo (aged sixteen).

12. S. Salvini, *Catalogo cronologico dei canonici della chiesa metropolitana fiorentina* (Florence, 1782), p. 49.

13. R. Pesman Cooper, "The Florentine Ruling Group under the *governo popolare* 1494–1512," *Studies in Medieval and Renaissance History*, 7 (1984–85): 162.

14. Giannozzo had died by 1469. The *catasto* reports of his two sons, Priore and Pierfilippo, are in Catasto, 928, fols. 292r, 300r–301r.

15. ASF, Legazioni e Commissarie, 15, fols. 125r–128r, 6 October 1464.

16. Vespasiano da Bisticci, *Renaissance Princes*, pp. 255–56.

17. ASF, Notarile antecosimiano (hereafter NA), 14198, fols. 396r–397v.

18. R. Bizzocchi, *Chiesa e potere nella Toscana del Quattrocento* (Bologna, 1987), pp. 37–53. Bizzocchi notes that by 1514, one-half of the *pievi* in the diocese of Florence were controlled by lineages; ibid., p. 49.

19. Bizzocchi, "Chiesa e aristocrazia nella Firenze del Quattrocento," *Archivio storico italiano* 142 (1984): 211–14.

20. See the dispute over the display of the Cavalcanti coat of arms in the *pieve* of S. Piero de Pitiano; NA, 11087, unpaginated, 15 October 1448.

21. NA, 6205, unpaginated, 6 November 1459; Bizzocchi, "Chiesa e aristocrazia," p. 264; Salvini, *Catalogo cronologico*, p. 47.

22. In 1454, the Florentine Signoria wrote to a curial official, requesting that he petition Pope Nicholas V to allow Niccolò, the then fifteen-year-old student, to hold a benefice *cum cura animarum*; ASF, Missive, 40, fol. 97r, 11 December 1454. In 1459, Niccolò held the *pieve* of S. Vita de Ancisa, diocese of Fiesole, and later became a cathedral canon before his promotion to Pistoia; NA, 9170, fol. 276v, 18 December 1459; Bizzocchi, "Chiesa e aristocrazia," p. 219.

23. NA, 6213, fol. 115r (December 1473); 6219, fol. 67r (1481); 6227, fol. 627' (1493).

24. *Lettere di una gentildonna fiorentina*, ed. C. Guasti (Florence, 1877), pp. 337–38, 29 December 1464.

25. A tale from the canonization process of Archbishop Antoninus describes a dispute between Jacopo di Leonardo Mannelli and Niccolò Pandolfini over a vacant Florentine canonry (1461), a quarrel so contentious that young Jacopo was troubled by his father's mental state: "in tali causa anxium nimis et solicitum, multisque curis et vexationibus ac sumptibus perturbatum." Jacopo eventually obtained the benefice; Bizzocchi, *Chiesa e potere*, pp. 101–2.

26. Bizzocchi, "Chiesa e aristocrazia," pp. 191–281.

27. NA, 1108, unpaginated, 16 May 1448. This transfer was opposed by the occupant of the benefice, Piovano Arlotto; F. W. Kent and A. Lillie, "The Piovano Arlotto: New Documents," *Florence and Italy, Renaissance Studies in Honor of Nicolai Rubinstein,* ed. P. Denley and C. Elam (London, 1988), pp. 363–64.

28. NA, 14200, fols. 245r–246v, 3 January 1475/76.

29. ASF, Carte Strozziane, 3rd ser., 122, fols. 105r–110r, 7 January 1491/92.

30. The resolution of this dispute was not described in the notarial protocol; NA, 13504, fols. 10r, 15r–16v, 17r–18v, 19v–23r, 26r–26v.

31. Catasto, 194, fols. 304r–306v. The papal bull conferring the priory of S. Martino on Alberti estimated the benefice's annual gross revenue at 160 florins; G. Mancini, *Vita di Leon Battista Alberti,* 2nd ed. (Rome, 1967), p. 89.

32. Archivio arcivescovile di Firenze, Visita pastorale 1514, fol. 23r.

33. On this common practice, see Bizzocchi, "Chiesa e aristocrazia," pp. 213–14.

34. Examples of rental contracts of rural churches: Verde, *Studio fiorentino,* 3: 313; NA, 7943, fols. 57v–59v (1428); 9170, fols. 4v (1450); 31r, 47r (1452); 276v (1459); 10084, fol. 216r (1472).

35. A. Parronchi, "Otto piccoli documenti per la biografia dell'Alberti," *Rinascimento,* ser. 2, 12 (1972): 229–35. On Parenti, see M. Phillips, *The Memoir of Marco Parenti, A Life in Medici Florence* (Princeton, 1987).

36. The formal process is described in NA, 14198, fols. 396r–404r.

37. Ibid., fol. 408r.

38. Ibid., fols. 405r–406v.

39. The intimate relations between these "institutions" is the major theme of Bizzocchi, *Chiesa e potere.*

40. The Pandolfini's petition stipulated that the patronage rights would begin with Alberti's successor; NA, 14198, fol. 399r.

41. Mancini, *Vita,* pp. 408–10.

42. Ibid., p. 451.

43. Ibid., p. 495.

44. Carlo's *catasto* report of 1469 contained this statement: "Sono debitore di messer Battista Alberti di ducati 500 di camera," Catasto, 927, fol. 308v.

45. G. Mancini, "Il testamento di L. B. Alberti," *Archivio storico italiano* 72, part 2 (1914): 20–52.

46. NA, 10084, fols. 316r–316v.

47. Archivio arcivescovile di Firenze, Visita pastorale, 1514, fol. 23r. S. Martino had been united with the nearby church of S. Michele a Gangalandi: "et huiusmodi due ecclesie spectant ad liberam collationem reverendissimi domini

archiepiscopi florentini." The *pieve*'s incumbent was Messer Filippo di Simone Tornabuoni.

48. R. Neu Watkins, trans. and ed., *The Family in Renaissance Florence* (Columbia, SC, 1969), p. 3.

CHAPTER TEN

1. A. Crabb has written the most recent biography of Alessandra Strozzi: *The Strozzi of Florence: Widowhood and Family Solidarity in the Renaissance* (Ann Arbor, 2000).

2. *Selected Letters of Alessandra Strozzi*, trans. and ed. H. Gregory (Berkeley, Los Angeles, and London, 1997), p. 35.

3. A. Strozzi, *Lettere di una gentildonna fiorentina ai figliuoli esuli*, ed. C. Guasti (Florence, 1877), pp. 438, 525–26, letters dated 5 July and 19 December 1465.

4. *Selected Letters*, p. 33.

5. Strozzi, *Lettere di una gentildonna*, pp. 79–80.

6. Ibid., p. 160.

7. *Selected Letters*, pp. 125, 127.

8. Ibid., pp. 29, 31.

9. Mark Phillips, *The Memoir of Marco Parenti* (Princeton, 1987), pp. 45–46.

10. *Selected Letters*, p. 61.

11. Ibid., pp. 195–201.

12. Ibid., pp. 43, 45.

13. Ibid., p. 59.

14. Ibid., pp. 79–83.

15. Ibid., p. 83.

16. That this disease was bubonic plague has recently been challenged; S. Cohn, "The Black Death: End of a Paradigm," *American Historical Review* 107 (2002): 703–38.

17. Strozzi, *Lettere di una gentildonna*, pp. 37, 48, 53, 55–56, 82, 91–92.

18. Ibid., p. 82.

19. Ibid., pp. 56–57.

20. *Selected Letters*, pp. 73–74.

21. Strozzi, *Lettere di una gentildonna*, pp. 105–6.

22. *Selected Letters*, p. 165.

23. Ibid., p. 111. The woman in Filippo's house was a slave girl, Marina, who was both his housekeeper and his mistress.

24. Ibid., pp. 149–51.

25. Ibid., p. 155.

26. Ibid., p. 163.

27. Ibid., p. 175. On Alessandra's role in arranging marriages for her sons, see Crabb, *The Strozzi of Florence*, chap. 8.

28. *Selected Letters*, pp. 177, 185.

29. Ibid., p. 159.

30. Crabb, *Strozzi*, p. 198.

31. Ibid., pp. 199–204.

32. *Selected Letters*, pp. 29–31.

33. Strozzi, *Lettere di una gentildonna*, p. 89.

34. Ibid., p. 360.

35. Ibid., p. 339.

36. Ibid., p. 281.

37. Ibid., p. 104.

38. Ibid., pp. 118, 474–75.

39. Ibid., p. 568.

40. Phillips, *Marco Parenti*, p. 227.

41. Strozzi, *Lettere di una gentildonna*, p. 256.

42. Ibid., p. 257.

43. The mercantile activities of Alessandra's sons are described in Crabb, *Strozzi*, chaps. 4, 5.

44. Strozzi, *Lettere di una gentildonna*, p. 342, 3 January 1465. On the reverberations of this bankruptcy, ibid., pp. 336, 345, 351–52, 358, 421.

45. G. Brucker, "Florentine Voices from the *Catasto, 1427–1480*," *I Tatti Studies, Essays in the Renaissance* 5 (1993): 25.

46. V. da Bisticci, *Renaissance Princes, Popes and Prelates. The Vespasiano Memoirs*, trans. W. George and E. Waters (New York, 1963), p. 218.

47. *Selected Letters*, p. 17.

48. Ibid., p. 18.

49. Ibid., p. 123.

50. Ibid., p. 173.

51. Ibid., pp. 215–21.

52. F. W. Kent, "Più superba de quella de Lorenzo: Courtly and Family Interest in the Building of Filippo Strozzi's Palace," *Renaissance Quarterly* 30 (1977): 311–23.

53. The career of Filippo the Younger is described in M. Bullard, *Filippo Strozzi and the Medici* (Cambridge, 1980).

INDEX

Indexer: Roberta Engleman

Cartographer: Bill Nelson

Text: 10/15 Janson

Display: Janson

Compositor, printer, and binder: Sheridan Books, Inc.